How to Coach Individuals, Teams, and Organizations to Master Transformational Change

How to Coach Individuals, Teams, and Organizations to Master Transformational Change

Surfing Tsunamis

Stephen K. Hacker

First published in 2012 by
Business Expert Press, LLC
222 East 46th Street, New York, NY 10017
www.businessexpertpress.com

ISBN-13: 978-1-60649-377-9 (paperback)

ISBN-13: 978-1-60649-378-6 (e-book)

DOI 10.4128/9781606493786

A publication in the Business Expert Press Human Resource
Management and Organizational Behavior collection

Collection ISSN: 1946-5637 (print)
Collection ISSN: 1946-5645 (electronic)

Cover design by Jonathan Pennell
Interior design by Exeter Premedia Services Private Ltd.,
Chennai, India

First edition: 2012

10 9 8 7 6 5 4 3 2 1

Printed in the United States of America.

To Marla, Jessica, and Mark for providing a basketful
of transformational and loving experiences.

Abstract

Surfing Tsunamis gives organizational leaders, coaches, and other change agents a field-tested holistic approach for coaching and integrating transformation efforts across all levels of any organization that seeks to thrive in a radically changing world. Through transformational coaching, people learn to unleash and align the largely untapped spirit—the creative energy—in themselves, other individuals, teams, and organizations, thereby eradicating persistent performance barriers and instilling a culture where work becomes an act of co-creating a future in which everyone wins.

This is the first book to present the science and art of transformational coaching across all domains—self, others, teams, and organizations— a pragmatic yet powerful practice that has already led scores of organizations, their leaders, and their employees to achieve breakthrough results. The comprehensive approach sits at the crossroads of several leadership and management disciplines—individual and organizational development, transformational leadership, change management, organization effectiveness, employee engagement, and the growing interest in spirit in the workplace. So, be prepared to go deep and wide in this journey to embrace transformational coaching.

Keywords

leadership, coaching, transformation, performance, strategy, teams

Contents

Acknowledgments

Much appreciation goes to Tammy Zinsmeister who has joined with me in generating and delivering transformational coaching capacity throughout the world. I have observed her skill in melding transformation methodologies and the awakening of the individual spirit many times. She is a true master in creating space for individuals, relationships, teams, and organizations to experience breakthrough. Also, she and Walt Roberts helped bring distinction to several concepts and terms, and through enriching conversations they aided in hammering through modeling.

My friends and partners of Transformation Systems International have been a source of continued inspiration. I treasure each person; collectively I cherish the purposeful work we perform together within the setting of joy. What a blessing to be able to work within such a community.

Bernadette Steele, my editor, deserves many, many thanks. What a gift! Prodding for clarity of thought, consistency of approach, and the addition of personal experiences. Bernadette demonstrated the coaching expertise outlined in this book. I especially appreciate the application of her considerable business and organizational knowledge. She was more than equipped to ask the critical questions of this work.

Business Expert Press has been remarkable to work with. As with the previous work in which Marvin Washington, Marla Hacker, and I collaborated (Successful Organizational Transformation), the process was straightforward and skillfully guided by caring individuals. Thank you.

I want to recognize major contributors to the Transformation Body of Knowledge (TBoK)...Tammy Zinsmeister, Marla Hacker, Marta Wilson, Scott Sink, John Web, Altyn Clark, Sharon Conti, Cindy Schilling, Stephanie Holmes, Ray Butler, Marvin Washington, Eileen Van Aken, Gary Coleman, Ed Warnock, Mark Maggiora, Judith Aftergut, John Blakinger, Walt Roberts, Leslie Smid, Marsha Willard, Jim Lussier, Marius Buiting, Priscilla Cuddy, Paul Krueger, Anne Murray Allen, and Al Siebert.

Finally, I stand in appreciation of spirits from around the world, in so many places, doing the needed work of transforming the way we relate and organize. One of my greatest joys is to see the devotion of remarkable leaders doing the hardlifting to create anew. Traits observed and lessons learned are gathered from the many leaders I've had the privilege to work with over the years. Seeing leaders in action over time has added my knowledge and been inspiring. I am grateful for the wisdom they have gifted, in particular Doug Beigel, Larry Norvell, 'Coach' Kereteletswe, Eric Molale, Priscilla Cuddy, Craig Eshelman, Fariborz Pakseresht, Ikwa Bagopi, Bertrand Jouslin de Noray, Jim Lussier, Ken Johnson, Segakweng Tsiane, Tom Masgaller, Marta Wilson, Jim Stephens, Paul Borawski, Bob Dryden, Nancy Stueber, and Janet Raddatz.

CHAPTER 1

The Impact of Radical Change on You, Your Organization, and Your World

When I began my undergraduate studies in mechanical engineering at Tulane University in New Orleans, I used a slide rule for making calculations. Only other baby boomers and perhaps their parents are likely to have seen an actual slide rule, much less operated one. Today my children would view it with the same disdain that we accorded the washboard, or the butter churner, or the horse and carriage—an almost charming, antiquated technology. The controversy raging at the time was the utility of the newer plastic, resin-based slide rules, which most of the students used, relative to the older model with a wooden body, favored by most of the professors. This was the kind of incremental improvement that characterized our sense of technological change in the mid-1970s. Much discussion ensued in and out of the classroom about the relative durability of the two bodies and the notches on the rule, about the coefficient of thermal expansion of plastic versus wood and the implications for accuracy of the scale at different temperatures.

And it does all seem quaint in retrospect. In the second semester of my freshman year, the first handheld electronic calculators appeared on the market. I bought a five-function calculator—it added, subtracted, multiplied, divided, and determined percentages—for $150, a small fortune for a college student. And before the end of the school term, Hewlett-Packard had introduced a next-generation programmable handheld calculator.

Science and math mid-term and final exams were typically four hours long, much of that time spent operating the slide rule and estimating the solution to a given problem. (For those of you who have never used a slide rule, the best it could deliver for all that effort was an *approximate* value or solution to a calculation.) By comparison, punching the numbers into a calculator and performing the appropriate mathematical operation could produce an exact solution to an equation in seconds. I finished the exams early and left while my Stone-Age peers continued to fiddle with the best equipment slide rule manufacturers could offer.

It was my first experience with the digital divide and the thrill of having so much computational power at my fingertips. A slide rule swinging from a belt soon became a rare sight on campus. Our professors devoted the newly available classroom and testing time to take us deeper into the material, expose us to a broader range of applications, provide more hands-on lab time—in short, cram a lot more learning into a semester than was previously possible now that the most time-consuming (and least value-added) aspect of mathematical computation had been reduced to a nearly negligible effort. Today there is no doubt in my mind that the engineering education my class received as a result was far richer and more extensive than that of classes that graduated just three or four years before us. By the time I landed my first engineering job, the calculator had become a fixture in the work place.

I mention the electronic calculator here only because I am able to get my head around the transformative impact it had on my education. I adapted to the technology and dare say I mastered it. In contrast, I can't begin to comprehend all the ways the succession of developmental leaps in telecommunications, personal computers, semiconductors, and the Internet have affected my life and work over the last couple of decades. These have been more rapid, massive, complex, interdependent, and pervasive changes than anything I'd experienced before. Others of my generation and I struggle to just stay competent in a relatively narrow domain of a new world of technological wonders that continues to expand every more rapidly. But our experience is not unique.

For those of us alive today in the developed and developing worlds, the collective effects of the human body (population and labor) and the human mind (technology and culture) have transformed our world as never before. We are experiencing transformative change so rapid and pervasive that each successive generation is growing up in a markedly different world than the prior generation did, one that is also changing at an ever more rapid rate.

Transformational Tsunamis: Acceleration and Convergence

Over the span of its history, the human race has produced a host of notable technological advancements—the discovery of fire, the development of cooking, language, the printing press—that shifted the paradigms of the time and radically altered the course of human development on biological, social, political, and economic levels. However, studies of the rates of technological change present convincing evidence of rapid acceleration during the last half-century relative to historical rates, with rates of change now approaching the exponential.[1] The pattern is apparent across numerous areas: strength of materials, travel speed, computational power, communications technology, communications efficiency and content, miniaturization, and others. Technical leaps in one area have spurred changes in other areas. Such rapid technological change across many fronts propagates large-scale social as well as environmental and economic change, with a transformative effect on daily life and work.

I visualize the exponential curve in Figure 1.1 as a composite of all these changes and their impacts on the lives of anyone alive at the time. The three dotted-line segments shown in the figure depict the slope of the curve, that is, the rate of change, at the corresponding point in time. As we move to the right through time, the slope of the curve steepens, indicating that the rate of change accelerates. Let's assume for the sake of this discussion that at Point A my parents were about 30 years old, at Point B I was 30 years of age, and at Point C (in the future) my children will be about 30. As the dotted segment for Point B shows, the slope of the exponential curve is steeper at B than at A, indicating that I was experiencing a far greater rate of change at 30 than my parents had at the same stage of their life. However, my children at 30 will experience their world transforming at an even more dramatic rate than I did. This unrelenting revolutionary, not evolutionary, change will continue, thus

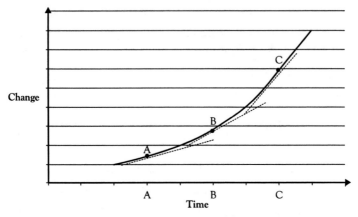

Figure 1.1. Exponential change experienced by successive generations.

escalating the pressure on their generation's individual and collective abilities to integrate this change in their work and lives. Technological advancement and the social and economic tsunamis it generates would strongly suggest that the species itself must make a huge leap in how it integrates change.

An Interconnected World

Humans have been coping with change and adapting for as long as we've walked the planet, assisted in large part by the great engine of rational thinking. As an indicator of our apparent adaptive abilities, population growth has not taken a real holiday since the plague of Black Death in the mid-fourteenth century. The number of humans on the planet, estimated to be 300 million in 1000 A.D., grew to 3 billion in 1960 and 6 billion at the beginning of this millennium, with a global population of 9 billion projected for 2040. Yet this very success contains the seeds of catastrophe.

For some 12,000 years of human history, we'd been able to produce enough food to support the population growth. However, by the end of the eighteenth century, as Thomas Robert Malthus noted in his *Essay on the Principle of Population*, the population growth had outstripped that of growth in agricultural production, an imbalance that set the stage in 1943 for worldwide food shortages—a Malthusian correction. The green revolution in agricultural technology and practices during the second half of the twentieth century greatly accelerated food production, and we were able to support a doubling of the world's population. However, in the new millennium population growth has once again outstripped our ability to produce enough food. In 2007 global carryover food stocks dropped to just 61 days of global consumption, the second lowest ever recorded.[2] Perhaps another paradigm shift in agricultural technology is just around the corner. Yet this is hardly the only challenge associated with the current and projected number of humans on the planet consuming resources and generating waste.

In fact, technology advancements, population growth, and their combined social, economic, and environmental impacts have created towering challenges that confront us as a species because we are interconnected to one another and everything else on the planet in ways we've only just begun to understand, and in new ways few would have imagined just a couple generations ago. Actions or events in one country, or in one industry, or even one company can ripple out to converge with other events or actions to generate a tsunami of change that ultimately impacts millions of beings. Even seemingly small individual actions, such as consumer decisions, when taken by millions of people have compounded effects over time and across space, with unanticipated consequences. Local action does create global change.

For example, you might drive a car that consumes gasoline and, among other factors, contributes to a huge demand for petroleum, giving the industry that produces it enormous influence in the corridors of government. Over a number of years, a U.S. federal regulatory agency that oversees the industry develops a complacent culture that influences employee attitudes and behavior. Despite a period of record-high profitability, a British petroleum company and its business partners drilling in the Gulf of Mexico make a series of questionable decisions to save time and costs. Then, over the course of a few days, the confluence of greed, less-than-perfect technology, lax oversight, and natural forces culminate in a disaster like none other the country or the earth has experienced. And it will take years to tally the toll on the environment, the economy, and individual lives and livelihoods in the region.

Finger pointing, name calling, intransigent political positions, or inflammatory rhetoric cannot eliminate the fact that, ultimately, our individual choices, as trivial or unconscious as they might seem, help to create a reality in which such disasters can—and do—occur. This raises the specter of other potential mind-blowing changes on a planetary scale.

In his book, *Hot, Flat and Crowded*, Thomas Friedman writes:

> We can no longer expect to enjoy peace and security, economic growth, and human rights if we continue to ignore the key problems of the Energy-Climate Era: energy supply and demand, petrodictatorship, climate change, energy poverty, and biodiversity loss.[3]

If we pay attention, we can learn how each one of us contributes to fouling the air and the water, depleting what we've been accustomed to view as limitless resources, just by the simple acts of daily living we in the developed world take for granted—driving a car, consuming food from far-off places, heating and cooling our homes, throwing out what we no longer use or want.

If you had been a factory manager in Michigan, rather than a fisherman on the Gulf Coast, you'd have already learned a lot about disruptive change caused by forces seemingly beyond your control. Automotive technology advanced and consumer tastes changed—in part because growing concern about fossil fuel and all its costs motivated many people to buy smaller cars. One day your factory closes, your suppliers go bankrupt, and jobs evaporate across an entire region. The implications get very personal, very fast if it is your business or your job that disappears, your home that goes into foreclosure, your retirement fund that evaporates (although you're still not sure whom to blame for that). Life as you once knew it is over.

If you live in Los Angeles and down-sized from a Pontiac to a Toyota hybrid, you drive a car with a smaller carbon footprint, doing what you can to curtail global warming and dependence on fossil fuels. But did you also take into account other wide-ranging consequences of your decision when combined with similar choices by many other auto buyers like yourself—such as a massive dislocation of U.S. auto industry jobs? Former autoworkers, forced by declines in personal income, shifted their shopping from Penney's to Wal-Mart, which now imports an enormous volume of cheaper goods from China rather than from U.S. manufacturers. As it turns out, what is good for Wal-Mart and its customers has been bad for millions of other U.S. workers and their families who have seen manufacturing jobs in their industries disappear overseas. Yet this has been good for the millions in China who can now aspire to a standard of living that begins to approximate ours.

What a complex web of interdependency. Our purchasing and life-style decisions (not all of which are voluntary) have ramifications that we might never imagine nor intend because there are so many more of us and we are now connected in ways unique in human history. This is the convergence of tsunamis of technological, economic, environmental, and social change. We are the villains as well as the victims in this larger drama, should we choose to view it from this mindset. The boundary between my best interests and yours is rapidly dissolving.

The patterns and passages we've been conditioned to think of as the "normal" cycle of life and family likewise have been altered by social and economic tsunamis. New twists and complexities add unprecedented pressure to our closest relationships, personal finances, and even our very notion of family. You and your siblings, for example, might be struggling to find affordable assisted living arrangements for your elderly parents, who, thanks to developments in medical science, are living longer but not necessarily more robustly. In the wake of the public sector cutbacks for elementary education tied to massive revenue shortfalls during the worldwide economic recession, perhaps your youngest child—a recent college graduate who cannot find a teaching job despite the enormous investment you made in her education—has moved back home. Or the marriage of your eldest child has dissolved under financial and job pressures, and your grandkids will be shuttled between both their parents for who knows how long. This wasn't your parents' vision of their golden years, or your daughter's vision of launching her career of service, or your vision of a stable home environment for your grandchildren. Evolution has not conditioned us as individuals or as a society to deal with the present, *this* present, simply because changes of this nature, frequency, and complexity have never occurred before.

The Implications in the Workplace

John Kotter, in his book, *A Sense of Urgency*, speaks to the impact of exponential change on business:

> With episodic change, there is one big issue, such as making and integrating the largest acquisition in a firm's history. With continuous change, some combination of acquisitions, new strategies, big IT projects, reorganizations, and the like comes at you in an almost ceaseless flow.... These two different kinds of change will continue to challenge us, but in a world where the rate of change appears to be going up and up, we are experiencing a more global shift from episodic to continuous [change], with huge implications for the issues of urgency and performance.[4]

A transformative change—in technology, markets, or economies—shifts or alters the value exchange between the product or service provider and its customers, revolutionizing what the customer needs, is willing to pay, and expects in return. In short, it changes the rules of the game. This applies equally to the public and the private sector. A major social, political, or economic shift can significantly alter the type, level, and/or cost of services a public agency must provide its constituents. Private sector businesses can face a burning platform that requires they find a way to provide higher value-added services or discover new market niches. Inherent in such tsunamis of change are creative opportunities to develop and deliver a new service or product that better meets customers' new needs and expectations. For individuals and organizations with no vision for how to capitalize on the new reality, or with no capability to transform themselves and what they do, radical change can be a destructive force. Sooner or later they lose their effectiveness and ultimately their ability to secure the resources they need to operate.

John Naisbitt writes in his book, *Mindset!*:

> The future is a collection of possibilities, directions, events, twists and turns, advances, and surprises. As time passes, everything finds its place and together all pieces form a new picture of the world.

In a projection of the future, we have to anticipate where the pieces will go, and the better we understand the connections, the more accurate the picture will be.[5]

When I was growing up, I used to change the oil in our family car, a '54 Chevy with enough room under the hood and around the engine to get at everything necessary to perform routine maintenance. Over what now seems a relatively short period of time, technology advances and the quest for greater fuel efficiency drove Japanese and European auto makers to build more and more horsepower into smaller and smaller engines mounted on a more compact chassis, a transformative trend that U.S. carmakers came to rather belatedly. People like me, who weren't mechanics and didn't have access to special equipment, found it increasingly difficult to change the oil in these compact engines, or even to slide underneath these smaller cars and find the oil filter. Spotting an opportunity, some visionary entrepreneurs conceived of a specialized facility that offered car owners the convenience of driving into a location and having someone else quickly change the oil and other fluids on the spot at a very reasonable cost. Enterprises such as Oilcan Henry sprouted up, giving birth to the drive-in oil-change business. Demand grew rapidly as car owners found more value-added things to do with their time. The concept expanded to include other related services that the auto owner or the mechanic at the local service station used to perform. Franchisers like Jiffy Lube and major retailers like Sears and Wal-Mart—who know a good opportunity when they see it—now dominate the drive-in auto service industry. Other franchisers have peeled off specialized repair services for transmissions and brakes, "filling" stations are now largely the domain of the petroleum companies and convenience stores, and the traditional neighborhood service station has all but disappeared. Survival in this new landscape was not a matter of more advertising or shaving costs but rather the ability to envision an attractive new value proposition with an existing or new customer base.

The experience of work itself is undergoing transformation. Consider the example of business travel. The advent of online booking for airlines, hotels, and rental cars transformed travel planning, allowing the frequent business traveler to directly interact with the service provider's reservation system without a human intermediary, which revolutionized the search process and greatly expanded the number of available choices for the traveler. New online businesses appeared, including aggregator sites such as hotel.com and Travelocity.com, as did other service innovations such as check-in kiosks at airports and in hotel lobbies, further removing business travelers from the need for a human interface and freeing them from some of the long queues and frustrations associated with travel. The downside for the traveler was a lower level of service and the loss of interpersonal relationships that accompanied human-to-human transactions. The experience of business travel became somewhat more isolating for those of us who do it frequently.

For some, the transformation in telecommunications and mass information exchange has eliminated the need to travel at all. Here on the West Coast where I live, many people working as traders or financial analysts go to work on East Coast rather than Pacific Coast time. They are working on Wall Street virtually rather than physically, transcending what used to be the barriers of space and time.

Simply adapting to changes in the workplace is essentially a reactive process. Something changes out there, you accept it—although you may not like it—and so you make a change internally, learning to integrate this new "reality" about work and what it means for how you go through your day or your week. You seek out some additional information, learn a new concept or skill, talk to someone to get the benefit of their experience, and look to the results to tell you if the changes you made are effective in producing the result you or your employer wants.

This type of integration takes some time and effort, and it's largely gotten us as far was we've come today. But it will hardly be effective for dealing with accelerating rates of change on multiple fronts. Younger workers are entering the workforce with greater expertise in some areas than long-tenured or senior employees have. Experience counts for less today because it is experience with a world and a workplace that no longer exist. Expectations and requirements for success as an employee or an organization have been up-ended.

Just as we begin to understand the implications of the latest tsunami of change that washes over us, another giant wave is forming. We feel increasingly frustrated in our inability—as individuals and as leaders—to anticipate the consequences, to shape the outcomes, to control our own destinies and those of our organizations. To attempt to cope using our "old" adaptive abilities is to risk disengagement and burnout.

One interview among the hundreds I've conducted over the years in scores of for-profit, not-for-profit, and public sector organizations stands out as a perfect illustration of this problem. When I asked a mid-level manager how he viewed his work, he said, "Work is not my life." I'd heard that comment before, but then, to my astonishment, he went a step further and said, "In fact, work is *not* life." Then what is it, I wondered? Some halfway zone, some Purgatory that you tolerate by deadening yourself for eight hours a day? I had only to look in his eyes to see that he sincerely felt that way. Something was missing—a light, a spark, the part of himself that he'd left behind when he came to work that morning, or perhaps had cut himself off from months or even years ago. What's more, I've interviewed any number of people who, regardless of their position or the type of organization, exhibited that same lack of spirit and energy, who conveyed by their posture, if not their words, a similar sense of disengagement from their work and themselves. In its least threatening form, this is the world of Scott Adams' comic strip, *Dilbert*, characters seemingly trapped in a meaningless world, responding defensively to the nonsense in the workplace. People surrender to circumstances, to the tsunamis of change, and the light goes out in their eyes. I think of them as "zombies in the workplace."

Sadly, many people today separate their work from what they consider to be their "real" life, the times when they feel most alive, energized, creative, and connected. And there are those as well who never feel this way anytime, or about anything. Both instances take a toll on the individuals, on their families and relationships, and certainly on their coworkers. All hands are *not* on deck, just when the enterprise most needs their best efforts and ideas.

There are implications for society as well. As I look across my country, the United States, I can see what happens when people become so overwhelmed by wave after wave of massive change that they shut down as a defense mechanism, and close themselves to new understanding or alternative views or willingness to even engage in constructive dialogue. They too become zombies, tuning in only to those messages and seeking only those experiences that reinforce their anger or fear or a sense of being a victim to larger forces. Even rational discourse becomes impossible as people retreat into camps that demonize those in other camps with different perspectives and experience, be they neighbors, coworkers, or just holders of different political or religious views.

Transformational tsunamis in the environment call for transformation on both an individual and a collective level. We must deeply understand ourselves, our organizations, and the connections among us and then consciously align our individual and collective energies toward creating the future we desire. Individual and collective decisions must be made from a place of greater wisdom, one that transcends intellectual and physical action in its power to create positive change for the benefit of all, in even the most complex or difficult of circumstances.

We can transform ourselves, our organizations, and our societies, but it will require that we be more aware, working and living with greater purpose and meaning, and bringing all of our energy to our jobs *and* our families *and* our communities. We need all hands on deck, fully awake, fully engaged, fully alive.

The Exponential Solution: Transformational Coaching

Personal and group transformation are concerned with expanding consciousness, first individually and then collectively, in order to tap the creative potential of spirit, thus allowing people to be more powerful in accomplishing their purpose in life. The goal is not to learn how to adjust to a rapidly changing world, an approach that would continue to limit us to two-dimensional choices—good vs. bad, better vs. worse—in response to what the world delivers to our door. Rather, we seek to discover meaning and chart a course for purposeful living. We become an active force in shaping a new reality, a new future, from among unlimited choices, both as an individual and together with others with whom we share a purpose and vision.

Transformation and steps for nurturing it and making it sustainable will be defined in more detail in later chapters. Transformation begins as a personal process, and even transformation of groups and organizations must be built upon the growing ability of each member to find the answers to a number of significant questions: Why am I here (purpose)? Where am I going (vision)? How will I know I'm making progress (measurement system)? What are my chosen boundaries (values)? What is informing my view of reality (mindsets)? How can I focus on creating a powerful future? These questions have their corollaries at the group level as well, for teams, organizations, and society as a whole.

Such transformation on a broad scale is a massive yet urgent undertaking. To harness the external forces of exponential change, to learn to surf tsunamis rather than remain at their mercy, we need a method to enact individual and collective transformation at a rate that is likewise exponential. Fortunately, transformation as a process of growth can be guided and aided by someone who has already embarked on the process personally and gained access to a deeper source of wisdom, who can relate to others on the level of spirit rather than ego. This is the role, indeed the calling, of the transformational coach: to first help oneself and then coach others to awaken to this essential aspect of our nature, the power of creation that is already hard-wired inside our being. By learning to coach for transformation in the domains of self, others, teams, organizations, and even society, the coach can awaken many individuals, who in turn are empowered to draw on their own deepening well of wisdom to provide similar assistance to others throughout their organizations and communities. Individual and collective transformation propagates at an exponential rate, leading to breakthroughs in personal effectiveness and group performance—not just once but again and again.

Awakening yourself and others to who you really are as humans is a formidable challenge, especially when people, after repeated pounding by the tsunamis of personal, social, economic, and technologic change, are treading water in an ocean of anxiety about what the future might hold. The process for making this jump in consciousness is neither physical nor mental. It can't be attained by *telling* someone his or her purpose in life— that is more the realm of demagogues and cult leaders and dictators. The transformational coach uses a structured process of inquiry to assist people and groups on a journey of understanding, with the goal of increasing their awareness about who they are (individually and collectively), what their purpose is, and what gifts they have to give their organizations and communities.

Robert Hargrove eloquently defines the role of the coach in his book, *Masterful Coaching*:

> Masterful coaching involves helping people transform themselves; impacting visions and values; helping others reshape their way of being and thinking; supporting others to achieve higher levels of performance while allowing them to bring out the best in themselves and those around them; expanding people's capacity to take effective action; making it possible for people to succeed in areas where they are most stuck or ineffective.[6]

You would not be of much value as a coach in this process if you had not embarked on a similar journey of understanding and experienced transformation within your own life.

Hargrove also writes:

> The key to becoming a masterful coach lies in having a dream, aspiration, and the bone-deep commitment to make a difference in the lives of individuals, groups, or entire organizations. It is that commitment that is the alchemical chamber in which great coaches are born. It is that commitment that unlocks your wisdom, intuition, and insight when mere technique fails.[7]

Transformational coaches who understand who they are and the challenges they face in continuing to broaden their own consciousness, who are building an expansive philosophy of engagement with the world, have valuable lessons to teach others. The coach has to be able to see the struggle within another person without having personality transference (that is, must be able to avoid seeing everything that is happening within that individual as a reflection of what has happened to the coach). Instead, the coach practices deep listening in order to understand the other person's particular journey, while at the same time drawing on the wealth of wisdom gained through his or her own personal experience.

A transformation coach, external or internal to an organization, can help trigger the spirit and passion of individual employees, who then join together with others to spark life into their teams and the organization as a whole, with significant and rapid results. During the last two decades, I have witnessed this principle in action at the scores of organizations where I've coached leadership teams and individuals. Let me provide one example of what I mean: an ongoing project with the government of the Republic of Botswana in southern Africa.

As a country, Botswana is that rare African success story: a robust democracy with a parliamentary system and an extremely responsible government virtually free of corruption, blessed with caring and engaged leaders who are well educated, well trained, and committed to building the strength of the country and being responsible in their own actions.

Botswana shares a border with four other countries, including Zimbabwe to the east and South Africa to the south. The meltdown of Zimbabwe, which is a tragic case in itself, transformed the border situation, placing Botswana's Immigration Department—part of the Ministry of Labor and Home Affairs—under extreme pressure to maintain control of its borders and immigration as a whole. The department suffered from high customer dissatisfaction, with incidents of rudeness as well as an isolated case of corruption by an immigration official in the northern part of the country. As a result, it languished at the bottom of the effectiveness surveys conducted periodically by the Ministry.

The permanent secretary of Labor and Home Affairs, Ms. Segakweng Tsiane, is herself a transformational coach. She invited my organization to help bring about a rapid breakthrough in performance across the Department of Immigration. The department had workable descriptions of vision, mission, and values, as well as a structure with clear delineation of the functions it provided to the citizens of the country and to immigrating parties. Department employees knew what was expected of them in their jobs but were overwhelmed and demoralized by high levels of illegal immigration along all parts of the very long border. In contrast to other departments within the ministry, they felt unable to do their jobs with the care, concern, or timeliness that their customers rightfully expected. A breakdown in spirit had infected both officers and frontline employees, the agents who were the department's public face.

No charismatic leader giving morale-boosting speeches on the importance of immigration and border control could have repaired the disconnection to work that employees were experiencing. Instead, the core of the solution lay in having transformational coaches—from outside the organization at first, and later internal—help employees explore why they are part of the organization, how their job fits—or doesn't fit—with who they are as an individual and what their purpose is in life. The goal: Give employees the opportunity to attain a new level of consciousness about themselves, and then build a deeper awareness for the teams they worked in or supported and for the customers they served—in short, to transform their relationship to their work.

Less than four months after implementing the coaching project, people were finding their source of passion and its connection to the work they do, and no longer feeling like victims of the daily problems on the border or the problems brought to them by members of the public seeking citizenship or some other service. Key measures were already flagging a noticeable improvement in performance: shorter queues at border control stations and passport offices, quicker turnaround times for work visas and passport applications, a flood of testimonials from customers, and widespread observations from department officers that service to customers was being delivered in a much different, better way. The breakthrough in performance clearly came from engaging employees at a very personal level with what they saw as their service to other human beings.

Although initially fueled by outside intervention and the momentum that created, the rapid turnaround in performance has been sustained by training leaders throughout the department to be skilled transformational coaches. They are able to have the deeper conversations with employees that lead to increased personal awareness and consciousness. Increasing numbers of employees have been able to bring their spirit to work, infusing their work with purpose and meaning and drawing on the creative energy of spirit to generate remarkable results for themselves, their teams, and their customers.

Other organizations and their leaders who have leveraged transformational coaching have experienced and sustained similar successes. In a number of cases, transformation has also hinged upon making needed changes to key organizational systems and processes. As the chapter on coaching organizations discusses, a transformational coach can be extremely helpful as well in providing an integrated framework for these parallel efforts.

If you have a desire to consciously create your future, and the intention to help others in your organization or community do the same, it is my privilege to share with you the information, approaches, tools, and wisdom gained from personal and collective experience in transformational coaching.

This book takes you first to the domain of personal transformation, "Coaching Self," to lay a solid foundation for your coaching by coaching *you* toward greater awareness, discovery of your purpose, and an increasing ability to draw on the creative energy of spirit in all aspects of your life. This part of your journey will also help you to determine if coaching is aligned with your life purpose. The book then goes on to present a number of ideas, processes, tools, and examples for coaching another person toward expanded consciousness and a greater ability to achieve his purpose, and then coaching a group or team of self-actualizing individuals, and finally an entire organization, to find their true purpose and operate from the creative energy of spirit. The coaching model applied in each of these four domains will be essential to you in your practice, and tools and aids will be helpful as well. We have applied the model and all the tools/aids successfully and with a wide range of individuals, groups, and organizations in the private, not-for-profit, and public sectors. However, the tools/aids will pale in comparison to the wisdom that you access on your own journey toward transformation and can bring forth to help others on theirs. The book closes with a brief exploration of shepherding societal transformation. This draws on the skill sets of transformational coaching in the first four domains as well as deeper wisdom about social change to enable leaders to guide individual and collective energies toward a desired social vision, be it at the local level (community) or for broader societal structures.

You can expect the experience of reading this book to mirror, in some ways, the transformation process itself—and you may find that challenging. You are beginning a lifelong journey that will go on well beyond the last pages of this book. I'll point you in a direction, open a door, and *you* will decide how much work you do and what you learn, which will ultimately determine the value you take away from the experience.

Many of the ideas presented early on are by nature very expansive—you could spend a lifetime studying them. And you may want to supplement what you learn here with other texts that treat the particular subject in much greater depth. To help you apply these concepts, to reflect on experiences, or to integrate new ideas through practice, the book also presents some very focused material in the form of tools and exercises for plumbing the nature and depth of your own beliefs and experiences in ways that will lead to insight and growth as well as a course of action for you to take.

My hope is that you jump right in to begin your own course of self-discovery, and open all the windows to wisdom and opportunity you encounter along the way.

CHAPTER 2

A Roadmap
for Transformation

In the last chapter I referred to the complex, macro changes occurring all around us as *transformational* changes, which in turn call for personal, organizational, and societal *transformation*. This is not simply a euphemism for "big." Let's stake out the boundaries of what is meant here by the nature of transformative change, since this is the most profound and potentially challenging territory of change, individually as well as collectively, and the type of change with which most people, coaches, and organizations have the least experience. And let's do this by contrasting transformation with two other types of change more common to individuals and groups, standardization and continuous improvement.

Magnitude of Change

Standardization, the least complex type of managed change, is concerned with reducing variation in the results of an activity or process. We modify the behavior of a system—be it a human, a work process, or an organization—so that it can reliably replicate an outcome, that is, produce the same or very similar results time and time again—in a word, consistency. At an elemental level, we are "fixing" something to make it work within an acceptable range, or prevent something that could interfere with normal functioning. For example, you have two, maybe three uncomfortable visits to the dentist and decide you need to adopt better dental hygiene. You begin brushing your teeth three times a day every day, rather than just sporadically, and within six months your dentist reads your x-rays and remarks that you are free of tooth decay. A standardized hygienic procedure is producing the desired result.

Standardization in road signage saves countless lives each minute of the day. International standards for manufacturing and quality control help assure some minimum acceptable levels of safety, durability, functionality, and performance no matter where a product is built. Good or generally accepted principles and procedures similarly assure the consistent practice of accounting, medicine, engineering, and a host of other highly skilled professions. Predictability across all aspects of their operations—quality, appearance, service, cost, you name it—has enabled fast food chains to transcend cultural and national boundaries to become ubiquitous fixtures around the globe. Controlling variation is nearly always the first step in improving any system. It also enables you to better understand how other parts of the system or process are affecting results. It also consumes the majority of our time, collectively and individually.

Incremental or *continuous improvement* strives to embed a steady stream of changes within a system, continually raising the bar for performance in order to improve one's advantage over competitors and/or to meet growing or unmet customer expectations. An individual who adopts a conscientious program of exercise, regularly modified to build on earlier improvements, can gain strength, speed, endurance, and general good health, along with a host of other physiological, emotional, and mental benefits. Small changes produce incremental improvement in results, and over time, a steady stream of this can yield impressive cumulative gains in performance. On a broader scale, the hallmark of the auto industry has been to introduce new features or more options and higher performance with each successive model year, and to do so through improvements and innovation in design, technology, materials, production, and the economics of building and operating a car.

This type of change requires a more sophisticated approach than standardization:

- A well-defined and replicable improvement process
- Careful documentation of the existing system and flows
- Collecting and interpreting data in order to understand how a system functions and how it responds to changes in the process, equipment, or participants' behavior

- A search for root causes of problems; experimentation with changes in the system
- A method of implementing changes on a broader scale and monitoring the results

The systematic quest for quality through incremental improvement, built upon the modified Shewhart cycle of Plan-Do-Study-Act, was launched in the middle of the 20th century. Organizations have since made continuous improvement a byword of management, and have deployed such methodologies as Lean, Six Sigma, Systems Thinking, and Supply Chain Rationalization to many of the key business processes that enable them to gain increasing cost effectiveness, productivity, quality, and performance. On an individual level, mastering the skills of incremental improvement is essential for raising the quality of our work, our relationships, and life in general.

Transformation marks a radical change in an individual, organization, or other system, occurring on such a deep level that the system's elements are altered in some fundamental way, making a large shift in its effectiveness or performance in a particular area. A force of nature such as an earthquake or tsunami can wreak devastating changes for those unprepared or unfortunate enough to be within its path. We would judge them to be destructive for man and manmade systems, according to our value systems, even though these could be seen alternatively as part of a planetary system of creation and renewal. In this book, transformation is considered a phenomenon to be employed toward a greater good, rather than as a force intended to victimize.

Let's formally define transformation as follows:

Transformation is the marked change in the nature or function of a system that creates discontinuous, step-function improvement in sought-after result areas.

Discontinuous, step-function improvement is not the extrapolation of steady improvement we expect from incremental changes but rather a leap away from the improvement curve, a break from old patterns that is possible because the nature of the system itself has changed. Producing faster, strong horses through breeding, nutrition, and training still limited the gains that could be made in transport speed because we were working within the system of the horse. It took the invention of the automobile—an entirely new system—to produce a step-function improvement in transport speed, range, and power.

Sought-after result areas denote a purposeful aspect to transformation, a vision, if you will, about some future state radically "better" than the current state. "Better for whom?" you might ask. Ideally, for everyone, which is why transformation must be guided by wisdom rather than self-interest. On an individual level, expansion in consciousness impacts the core of the person, greatly modifying or shifting base beliefs and outlooks, giving access to the wisdom and creative energy of spirit, which can now drive new behaviors. Greater wisdom, greater energy, and behavior aligned with a higher purpose create a step-function improvement in those areas where we desire it—and need it—the most.

As with the other two types of managed change, we know transformation has occurred by observing the results. A curmudgeon may burst into the office on Monday morning proclaiming his transformation at a weekend workshop on relationships. Is he transformed? Has his behavior changed? Do people respond to him differently as a result? Only observation over time will reveal whether he is making true friendships at last, and whether his social attractiveness has so improved that people seek him out, invite him to parties, interact with him at gatherings, and converse with him in hallways.

Figure 2.1 illustrates the differences among the three types of change—standardization, incremental, and transformative—in terms of results over time. Each of these types of change is valuable and necessary to ensure progress, whether within the individual, a relationship, a team, an organization, or society. Standardization is necessary for systematizing and replicating an incremental or transformative change in order to sustain its impact. Incremental improvement prevents transformative gains from being eroded by ongoing changes in the environment (markets, competitors, inputs, etc.).

Transformation science incorporates standardization and incremental improvement for an integrated approach whereby (1) greater consciousness and a clear purpose generate a new idea or radically different process

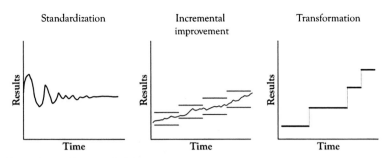

Figure 2.1. Types of change.

that promises breakthrough performance; (2) changes are systematized and embedded into daily practice; (3) support systems are aligned with the needs and goals of the new system; and (4) results are closely monitored, and processes fine-tuned as needed. In this way, transformational change becomes sustainable. Of course, this calls for a great deal of personal and organizational commitment.

A study of successful organizations points to around 80% of their efforts being devoted to standardization—finding what work methods or procedures produce the desired result and then training employees in these standard operating procedures so they are able to achieve this target performance again and again.[1] McDonald's Hamburger University and the U.S. Army are great examples of organizations that do this well. About 15% of the organization's efforts should focus on one form or another of continuous (incremental) improvement. Typically these efforts are extended across multiple organizational levels to involve management as well as nonmanagement employees, and often-multifunctional teams—for example, in the Kaizen continuous improvement process everyone plays a role. Finally, at least 5% of an organization's change focus should be on transformational change. Most transformational efforts they observed in the organizations studied were concentrated primarily in the higher levels of the organization; might not be done in any methodical or systematic way; and were focused on responding to a particular challenge—a "burning platform," for example—rather than building a systemic capability for radical change. For both the public and private sectors, transformational change is still largely in the pioneering stage, on the leading edge of organizational development and performance improvement initiatives.

Science is just beginning to discover the "physiology" of change as it affects an individual human. Brain imaging and brain wave analysis technologies have made it possible to locate what parts of the brain "light up" when the person is given a particular challenge. In standardization work, the mind is tasked with finding deviations. Incremental improvement calls on the primary brain function of problem solving. While Tibetan monks meditate in order to raise their consciousness, the cornerstone of transformation, specific parts of their brains synchronize with much higher electrical frequencies than those found in the brains of people not adept at meditation.[2] While there is still much more to be understood about the interplay between the brain and different types of change, at this juncture we can say that change is physiologically taxing in all of its forms, and shifting focus from one type of change to another is not an easy task for individuals. Emotionally, all types of change involve, to a greater or lesser degree, modifying our behavior, which means moving outside the zone of the familiar to the unfamiliar, which requires effort and can trigger fear.[3] This is precisely where a transformational coach can be of great help to others: Recognizing what type of change is called for, helping them to see the benefits of the change, and then easing the individual or group into a "mode" appropriate for the challenge at hand.

As Figure 2.1 suggests, the nature and scope of transformational change that we seek here shares a characteristic with incremental improvement: It is not a "one-shot" deal that happens just once, or all at once. It is not a lightning strike and suddenly boom, you've arrived—nor is it "enlightenment" in the mystical sense of the word, the moment in which all is revealed. Rather, transformation occurs over repeated cycles of redefinition and renewal—think of them as growth curves—that extend over the lifetime of an individual, team, or organization—or may never end in the case of a community or broader society—an ongoing journey toward ever-greater consciousness, wisdom, and effectiveness.

The Personal Phenomenon of Transformation

The definition of transformation introduced a few pages ago is largely an objective perspective on what has occurred—how the phenomenon appears to an observer, to the transformational coach, or even to the individual or group reflecting after the fact upon the result of their work thus far. The process has a subjective aspect as well, the personal experience of transformation, which takes place within the body–mind–spirit construct of human existence, individually and collectively.

Body–Mind–Spirit: The Three Forces of You in the World

Senses Wide Open: The Body

First, there is the Source. You may understand it as the life force, as the Divine, or even as quantum energy. Whatever concept you feel most comfortable with or drawn to, it is from this Source that the physical realm, the universe, composed of matter and energy, is created or manifested, and then operates under a set of physical principles and laws that we are still attempting to understand. The process of making something out of seemingly nothing, in the physical sense, is referred to as creation, and creative energy is the transformative power that fuels this process.

The life force, transmuted into matter, has countless forms, and our main concern here will be with a physical entity we shall refer to as you, and others of your kind, which currently number nearly 7 billion members of the human species. We are from the Source—the River of Life, the force behind intelligent design, children of God, or however you prefer to think of it.

The aspect of you that is most noticeable to other members of your species is your *body*, a brilliant mechanism that engages directly with the world of matter. For our purposes, the body includes the brain. The body is equipped with sensing systems—sight, hearing, taste, touch, and smell—that can access certain types of information from the physical world. Instincts and genetics are two important physical systems that govern how your body responds to stimuli from the physical world—in essence, the experiences of our ancestors encoded in our bodies that direct many of our functions and behaviors at both the macro and the micro (cellular) levels.

During its development from infant to adult, the body accumulates experiences, that is, interactions with the material world. Through the process of learning from these experiences, it develops a large set of "conditioned responses," patterns of behavior that are then activated and reactivated in response to similar stimuli or situations. Other "living things" with physical forms, such as microorganisms, plants, animals, operate, albeit to varying degrees, within this spectrum of existence.

Through physical actions—touch, voice, movement—the body is your vehicle for acting in the material world. By *doing*, you can modify, destroy, and create aspects of your world—for example, moving from hot sun into cool shade, consuming a piece of fruit, conceiving a child. In the process, you might also change aspects of yourself—for example, get a sunburn, be ill from overeating, experience a strong paternal instinct to protect and care for a child. But when the body is the sole or primary *driver* of your actions, then your actions are largely in reaction to forces and impulses that act upon you, and what you can do in response is contained within a relatively narrow set of options possible within the physical systems of instinctual, genetic, and conditioned responses. You see an apple on the ground and your stomach growls in response. You know instinctively that eating the apple will allay your feeling of hunger. However, a number of prior experiences has taught you to first inspect the apple to assure it has no rotted flesh and is free of worms, and thus unlikely to produce a really bad taste or uncomfortable stomachache. Meanwhile, the world and other life forms in it respond according to physical laws and their biological imperatives. You pick up the apple and notice too late a winged insect beneath the apple. What follows almost immediately is a sharp, burning sensation that radiates from your fingertip to your wrist. Voila! Your reality, built upon the accumulation of your (and your ancestors') prior interactions with the world, expands somewhat to encompass this new personal experience.

Acting from the body alone, and especially without the mechanical advantages of technology or the combined labors of other humans, a lone human is rather limited in his impact on the world, as is his perception of reality—his "life." He can leverage his own action, and thus increase his impact, by joining forces with others, which requires some social instinct to negotiate this. Or he might be fortunate enough to have access to a device—one conceived, designed, and constructed by someone operating at a higher level—that activates mechanical or electrical systems far beyond his understanding.

Tyranny of Thought: The Mind

But, of course, you and other humans also possess a *mind*, which can't be detected by the five senses but which the human race nonetheless rightfully considers to be even more powerful than the body for navigating the world and modifying it to individual and advantage. The mind has produced some very large ideas—society, modes of government, the economy, technology—that have set the course of human history.

Although the mind may have biochemical and bioenergetic (physical) aspects linked to or operating within the body, much about it is still unknown. Mind is an abstraction, the realm of emotions and thoughts. Emotions are "felt" or sensed by the mind and the body, and thoughts express themselves as an inner voice usually through a learned language.

You were born into mystery. What might a smile or a frown from Mother signify? What causes pain, and how can it be stopped? How do you get more of what tastes or feels good, and less of what doesn't? A base level of effectiveness in the world—survival—depended on your seeking the meaning of life experiences in order to dispel the mysteries and uncertainties.

As a child, your curiosity about a new world was fed by your senses in a highly charged input mode, which channeled huge amounts of data to an impressionable young brain. You self-initiated interactions to hunt for responses that would further explain how the world operated. Your brain organized the sensory data into information, and then searched for patterns that might provide meaning and predictability. When it saw connections, it ascribed meanings of cause and effect. You learned. These were further assembled into more complex arrangements of beliefs and paradigms, a sort of software that could be recalled as needed. Eventually your brain "hardened" these beliefs and paradigms into robust neural networks that became hardwired responses, no longer simply possible or situational explanations but now base programming—operating systems, if you will—lodged in the hard drive of your subconscious, automatically "booting up" with the right triggers and without any examination of

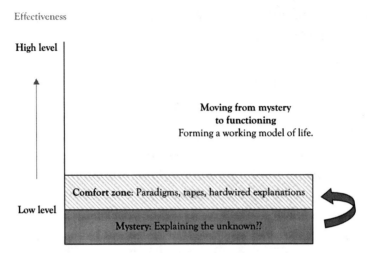

Figure 2.2. From mystery to comfort zone.

the present validity of the assumptions embedded in their structure. You moved from mystery to certainty, from hypothesis to confidence—the comfort zone shown in Figure 2.2.

As a whole, these systems, taken together with the body, "create" your sense of self, of a unique identity separate from all the rest of the material world. This becomes your inner reality, an awesome web of filters that rapidly catalogs your new experiences into some familiar framework of meaning constructed from past (and especially early) experiences. The mind is a miracle of speed and efficiency in a large number of situations, self-reinforcing, and self-perpetuating, affording a much wider and richer range of options for responding to the external world without having to "think" much about it.

But not everything that has found its way into your base programming is valid or necessarily helpful, particularly once you are an adult. (This is why early child development is such a fertile ground for exploring how worldviews are constructed.) You've achieved some level of effectiveness in the world, but seem unable to move any further. Some—perhaps many—of the assumptions, the cause-and-effect relationships, that underlie this programming led to behavior that produced results counter to what you consciously desired. Confused and disappointed, you sometimes repeated the unproductive behaviors, hoping for a different outcome. At any point you could reflect and choose to rewire the connections, just as you can learn a new language that, with enough practice, becomes second nature. But without questioning why you think as you do, repeated reactions to similar situations fortify existing beliefs, and you see it as simply the way the world works. You rebuff challenges to your belief system, even when they are offered as just another view. You don't entertain different ways of seeing the world because in the comfort zone, your beliefs are inseparable from your identity—different beliefs threaten the very existence of your ego. Instead of realizing the deeper spiritual being you were born to be, you become a narrow collection of beliefs about the way it is. You are unconscious.

David Bohm in his book, *Thought as a System*, speaks to the dangers of not questioning your thinking, of remaining unconscious of your thoughts:

[Thought] produces tremendous effects inwardly in each person. Yet the general tacit assumption in thought is that it's just telling you the way things are and that [it] is not doing anything—that "you" are inside there, deciding what to do with the information. But I want to say that you don't decide what to do with the information. The information takes over. *It* runs *you*. Thought runs you. Thought, however, gives the false information that you are running it, that you are the one who controls thought, whereas actually thought is the one with controls each one of us. Until thought is understood—better yet, more than understood, *perceived*—it will actually control us; but it will create the impression that it is our servant, that it is just doing what we want it to do.[4]

Thought has a "mind of its own." Thought is not pure, without bias and fabrication. The comfort zone from which thoughts arise is the realm of mindsets, complex constructs that drive intricate behavior patterns. As Bohm puts it:

When you are thinking something, you have the feeling that the thoughts do nothing except inform you the way things are and then you choose to so something and you do it.... But actually, the way you think determines the way you're going to do things.

Then you don't notice a result comes back, or you don't see it as a result of what you've done, or even less, do you see it as a result of how you were thinking.[5]

Mindsets that you hold over a long period of time can eventually create the overarching structure of your entire life. A conscious individual can see the mind at work and understands that the mind moves to such constructs. An individual seeks to become conscious by uncovering the prevailing faults in their thoughts and choosing a different way to view a given situation. As we'll discuss in much more detail later in this book, some mindsets are far less productive than others.

Thought patterns and mindsets play out in our minute-to-minute experience of life. For an individual who is unconscious of how his mind functions, this can be disconcerting and uncomfortable. Let's say you're walking along a residential street on a late spring morning, under a blue sky, in the warm air, the trees just beginning to leaf out. You're feeling good. Unexpectedly, you spot an apple on the ground, and your stomach growls. It's been several hours since breakfast. You assess the apple's appearance to the degree you can without touching it first—nudge it a little with your foot to get a full 360° view. It looks like a McIntosh, your favorite, and conforms to your personal standards of an attractive apple aesthetic. You spot an empty trashcan a few feet away at the end of a driveway. You look at your watch: 9 a.m., Tuesday. You begin to speculate on the apple's history. You wonder, *Could it have fallen out of the can when the Waste Management guy emptied it into his truck earlier that morning?* Now a woman is approaching from the other direction. *What would she think if I picked up the apple: that I'm homeless, or can't afford to buy an apple?* The memory of your granddad's apple tree in the yard flashes across your mind. A wave of nostalgia washes over you. *Haven't called granddad in a while. "Waste not, want not," he always says. All those stories about his childhood during the Great Depression.* You feel disgust. *What kind of person would throw out a perfectly good piece of fruit?* You look up at the house at the end of the driveway—you notice it is bigger than yours and has better landscaping. *Obviously people who don't understand the value of a dollar, as Granddad would say. I'm taking it. He'll get a kick out of this. I'll call him as soon as I get home.* You enjoy the virtuous feeling washing over you.

Dump that load of guilt about not talking to him for so long. Suddenly the lady passerby stoops down, picks up the apple, drops it in one of those reusable cloth shopping bags, and continues on her way. Rage rises like a geyser. *My apple! How dare you.* You resume your walking. Your anger subsides. *Granddad was right: You gotta grab for all you can get.* You look up at the sky. *Man, what a crappy day.*

This sums up about three minutes in the lifetime of a thinking but not very self-aware person. Judgments, contradictions, conflicting desires, and rational *and* irrational conclusions. Does he remember when an apple on the ground was just an apple on the ground? Apparently not.

If the mind, when confronted with such a seemingly minor situation, can whiplash you back and forth through a range of largely irrelevant thoughts, memories, and emotions, how can you count on it to navigate a course through a really serious situation, when you're hit with a tsunami of changes that present entirely new situations—your customers are fleeing in droves to an aggressive new competitor with a radical new business model, or your wife lost her job, or a family member has been diagnosed with a serious health problem. Here the stakes are even higher and the wellbeing of others may be involved, and you have no experience and perhaps few skills to draw upon.

The colliding tsunamis of disruptive technological, environmental, economic, and social change are the results of collective and cumulative actions driven, for the most part, by mind and body. The unforeseen consequences and their implications for the planet are evidence of the limitations of human mental and physical activity and their surrogate, technology. And although we in the West have been prone to believe that technology will create a better world—indeed, it may be an essential tool to this end—when deployed in narrow, self-serving interests such as power and profit, it can be as destructive as it is beneficial.

What's more, as a collection of industries and nation states—each with its self-interest as its primary goal, and collective thinking patterns riddled with faults—we can't all agree on solutions to the problems we face together, or in cases such as global warming, that a problem even exists. Our limited models cannot assure a solution won't have substantial negative impacts down the line. The potential solutions that are envisioned are cast within the limited context of trade-offs, costs versus benefits, a zero-sum game where some will sadly suffer while others will gladly gain, thus assuring the absence of a collective will toward personal and large-scale action.

The Power to Create: Spirit

This brings us to the third aspect of you, spirit, the part of you that is gifted from the Creator, still embedded in the Source, and connected in mysterious ways to other human spirits. In his book *Care of the Soul*, Thomas Moore defines the spirit as the outward manifestation of the life force within you, a powerful, profound transformative energy directed through your mind and body and into the world through conscious purpose. Spirit is the impulse to create: making something anew, thinking anew, seeing anew—indeed, being anew. This "breath of life" is a divine aspect of our nature, residing within each of us and manifesting our thoughts and passions in material form through the creative process.

Because it is rooted in the Source, spirit taps into a great intelligence, a pool of *wisdom* that transcends individual and collective human experience. Throughout our history we have been tapping into this deep pool, some individuals more than others. It is the source of great inspiration in any field of human endeavor. Here resides the answer to one of the most perplexing questions of human existence: What is the purpose of *my* life? What am I to use my spirit to achieve in the world? And because this wisdom transcends the individual, it can inform us about what is the best course of action to take in the world, the one in the best interests of *everybody*.

Some access spirit through intuition, others through trauma, sudden or chronic, when the ego, through pain, injury, frustration, or despair is profoundly "shocked" into recognition of its own smallness and powerlessness. Others actively seek it through desire, a deep-seated longing to feel this connection with a greater, wiser power, inspired perhaps by a master whose teachings and example opened a window into the possibilities of a new and better life for anyone willing to seek it. In reality, spirit can be accessed by any human who undertakes a process of personal transformation. As a matter of course, relatively few people live day-to-day consciously connected to spirit.

If you are largely unconscious of your spirit and your purpose in life, you are in a zombie state of unconsciousness and ineffectiveness. You experience reality through the body and are thus limited to reacting to the world around you. Major changes in the systems around you—work, the economy, family—or within your personal systems—say a significant health problem—feel like onslaughts, like destructive tsunamis. Your senses take in copious amounts of data, much of which the body perceives to be tons of noise or even threats. Your mind, in turn, reacts in conditioned and usually fruitless ways, activating unrestrained emotions and unproductive mindsets that give rise to ingrained patterns of behavior that are ineffective at best, damaging at worst, in the new situation. You are often frazzled and discouraged. Your spirit, which first entered the world as curious, joyful, and full of delight, becomes so masked by the mind that it sours. The body-mind uses spirit as its instrument, and your current beliefs, or mindsets, about you in the world direct the generative power of spirit toward *preserving* this very constrained (and distorted) perception of reality.

The bridge from this current state to a better life is a journey toward greater wisdom. Through successive cycles of the transformation process, you become increasingly conscious, aware of how and why your mind and body function as they currently do, and are better able to see the results of your behavior in terms of your effectiveness as a human being, a family member, an employee, a citizen of the world. You open yourself to the greater wisdom and power of the Source, and are rewarded with an understanding of your true purpose in life and a vision of how to express that in the world. Your spirit, then grounded in awareness of your purpose and increasingly adept at tapping even greater reserves of creative energy, brings the body and mind into alignment with your purpose, reveals other options for behavior, and becomes a generative force for a greater personal and collective good, the captain of your journey through life. With growing awareness of body, mind, and spirit, you can better assess how effective your behaviors and actions really are in achieving your purpose and vision; you learn from your experience and grow in wisdom, ready for the next cycle in your transformation.

Spirit, informed by purpose, is now the driving force in your life, the interpreter of your current reality and architect of your future. The noise recedes, allowing clearer perceptions of cause, effect, and opportunities. Feverish activity gives way to calm, purposeful action. Through successive transformation cycles, you learn to stay awake to spirit, to keep from losing the best of yourself in that zombie state of unconsciousness and ineffectiveness.

Let's take a closer look at this journey toward wisdom and effectiveness.

The Wisdom Journey

Becoming more effective as an individual—that is, producing better results for yourself and others—is not simply about changing your actions in the world, although this is certainly an essential aspect of transformation. The actions needed to transform results are often straightforward and simple in nature. We have access to abundant knowledge—books, seminars, role models, case studies—of what actions to take to yield better results in nearly every life or work situation. Yet how is it that an action doesn't produce the desired result? Or that two people can engage in the very same action, can do identical things in identical situations, and produce very different results? The same questions hold for organizations.

For example, training and advice about how to relate to others usually focus on actions related to better listening, creating openness in body language so others feel welcome, managing agreements, getting clear with your words, and acting responsively to the needs of others. Training videos depict the differences between rude or isolative behavior and the recommended behaviors for positive engagement. The excellent content and signposts found in such training material are often already known cognitively by the trainees, but the material provides a shared experience among a group, an entertaining moment of individual and collective awareness. If not carefully positioned, it can also create a false sense that the answers to human relationship are simple. I participate in an interesting listening exercise and I am now the master of listening—a nice idea but untrue.

Our actions are always linked to the intention or purpose behind them, and the results in the outer world always reflect our inner world. If I believe that people are difficult, I will encounter (or at least perceive) difficult reactions no matter what my actions toward others. A cramped spirit, directed by a self-serving purpose, will generate a far different result than an expansive spirit in service of a greater purpose. Actions are sourced from the well of spirit. The more conscious we are of *who* we really are, and *what* we are intended to accomplish while we are in the world, the deeper the well, the greater the power, that influences and drives our actions.

Similarly, on the physical level, if I envision a breakthrough in my personal health, the easy answer is to learn more about health. I discover that I should diet, increase gym time, and cease smoking. The actions required are not complicated in themselves—put better food into my body, get my body moving more, and don't put cigarettes in my mouth. I set out on this course of clear action, and a few weeks into it my enthusiasm wanes, I find reasons to not follow through, I feel guilty as a result, and—yes, I am soon eating and smoking more rather than less to suppress the guilt, which only worsens my sense of failure. My program for better health has led to poorer health. Why does the execution of my new knowledge and the seemingly simple tasks it calls for so often end in failure? Unconsciously, could I be more vested in failure than success, because failure is part of a mindset about the person I've been conditioned to believe I am?

Organizations rush to adopt the latest management fad and roll out all the "right" steps in a well-constructed implementation plan. A few months later, the first wave of enthusiasm wanes, the initial good results begin to peter out, and the initiative no longer shows up on the executive committee's monthly agenda. With enough repeats of this, employees begin to cynically greet any new initiative as the "flavor of the month."

Attempts to enact deep change by focusing on just the surface behaviors (those which can be readily seen) rely upon the discipline of self as the sole driver of results. Discipline is a marvelous attribute to begin a course of action, but without deeper work it has a very limited life span, as we just saw in the example of a program toward better health, which produces frustration that leads to failure. With enough false starts powered solely by discipline, self-loathing creeps into our self-image or our identity as a group.

The ability to transform is as much about the context in which action occurs as it is about the action itself. It is a *wisdom journey* that entails a great deal of exploration long before the person, the team, or the organization strikes out in a new direction.

Transformation begins not by first taking actions but rather in the commitment to develop and expand consciousness, to shift spirit, to cast vision, and to choose productive mindsets. Behaviors then flow from a much larger container of consciousness. Transformation requires a deep individual inquiry, or collective inquiry in the case of groups, a swim in the deep end of the pool. If you prefer to float on the surface, thinking it is safe, controlled, and known, then you are a sitting duck for every tsunami that crosses your path.

The overview of the Wisdom Journey that follows speaks primarily to individual transformation, and we'll return to it again in the chapters on self, team, and organizational transformation. To be able to coach others on their wisdom journey, you must first embark on one of your own.

Developing and Expanding Consciousness

As shown in Figure 2.3, your wisdom journey begins with a deep dive into developing and expanding consciousness, a dive that you'll make time and again as you explore the mysteries of who you are, what you know and how you know it, how you relate to the world, and the kinds of impact you make—and want to have—by living your life and doing your work. Let's take a moment here to define consciousness, since the work of expanding it will be the key to your transformation and is likely to entail some of the most demanding and profound work you or any human can take on:

Individual consciousness is the state of being aware of self and one's individual experience of the world beyond the physical or mental processes. Consciousness consists of reflections upon one's thoughts, emotions, will, and the essence of self, of one's personal identity.

To develop and expand your consciousness is to increase your ability to reflect and see self from an observer-self position, that is, more objectively. You open the door to understanding your inner reality, which has been the primary architecture of your outer reality.

Developing & expanding consciousness	← →	Defining spirit	← →	Casting vision	← →	Choosing productive mindsets	← →	Living in the experience
Delve into transformational spheres: *being, knowing, relating, generating*		• Understand life purpose • Realize your calling		• Identify what spirit will create • Sense for revelation		• Source from spirit • Assess results & effectiveness		• Be in the moment • Act purposely toward vision

Figure 2.3. Wisdom journey.

For years the scientific community has pursued a reductionist and scientific method to explain self-awareness, a subjective phenomenon, but this usually devolves into a conversation about the mind. Although our understanding of the mind and of basic biology are greatly expanding at this point, we have far to go to really learn the links between the physical brain, with its untold numbers of neuronal interactions, and what gives rise to consciousness. For any reader who wants to explore the concept further, I recommend the text *Conversations on Consciousness*, in which author Susan Blackmore interviews 20 of the leading scientists and philosophers working in this area.[6]

Consciousness can also be experienced on a collective basis:

Collective consciousness is the awareness of the "we-being," the awareness of us, being reflective of itself and its collective experience of the world, primarily in the created culture.

Both types of consciousness enable us to move beyond our instinctual, or animalistic, nature of reaction—simply springing into response. Steve McIntosh explores this in his book, *Integral Consciousness and the Future of Evolution*:

Why does this self-consciousness in humans make such an evolutionary difference? It's because with self-awareness comes the ability to take hold of the evolutionary process itself. Through self-reflection, humans have the unique ability to see themselves in perspective within the scale of evolution, and this creates both the desire and the ability to improve their condition relative to the state of their animal cousins.

And for generation after generation, humans have generally continued to improve their conditions.[7]

Consciousness is the gateway to improvement, to purposeful change in direction, to "creation" of a better reality. With greater self-awareness, we can increase our effectiveness and our impact in the world.

McIntosh also talks about collective consciousness:

> Consciousness is contained and upheld not only by its biological host but also by the culture in which it participates. Our bodies "hold up" our consciousness from the outside and our culture holds up our consciousness from the inside.... The development of consciousness and the development of culture are mutually dependent, and thus their interactive co-evolution is best understood when considered together as a whole.[8]

There is power in numbers. Individuals with self-awareness can have an even greater impact on the world when they come together with other conscious individuals to co-create, to bring forth into physical reality an idea held within the collective consciousness. To share a purpose that resonates with our purpose as individuals expands our creative potential. The chapters on coaching teams and organizations will build further on this idea.

As part of the Wisdom Journey, the work required to develop and expand consciousness occurs in four fertile areas: *being, knowing, relating*, and *generating*. Known as the Four Spheres of Transformation, these realms of human existence offer rich territory for better understanding yourself and the underlying influences and forces at play in your current life, particularly those that have shaped a reality that may be unfulfilling, difficult, and perhaps even painful. Together the Four Spheres provide a platform, an ongoing practice of reflection and questioning that serves up important insights for the other parts of the Wisdom Journey. Much of the next chapter will be devoted in more detail to this work within.

Defining the Spirit

Expanding your awareness opens a door to who you are beyond your mind and body. You are able to define the spirit, which means realizing what your life purpose is, why you are here. That realization leads to an understanding of what you have been called, either by your higher power or yourself, to make happen with your presence here, your vocation, and your voice and work in the world.

History serves up many examples of people, working alone or with others, who felt a strong calling to follow their purpose, and who achieved something admirable or even astonishing and of great value to the world through their courage and dedication to this purpose despite all the odds against them. Members of Greenpeace didn't place their small rubber boat between whaling ships and their prey because the pay is good—they did it because they felt called to fight for the planet, expanding awareness around the world about harmful practices and global threats.

Purpose is not necessarily fixed: it may change over time as you grow and, particularly, as you become more effective in the world. Perhaps one of the most celebrated cases of *redefining* one's spirit was Mother Teresa. Her original religious calling as a member of the Loreto order of Roman Catholic nuns, which led to her becoming Head Mistress of the school at which she taught in India, shifted at the age of 39—what she termed her "second calling"—and she left the safety and comfort of the school to serve the poorest of the poor in the dirty, dangerous streets of Calcutta. Her selfless actions, tireless work, and unstinting dedication to her new calling drew the praise of millions from all faiths, and inspired countless people to discover and live from spirit in their own lives.

Nonetheless, she was criticized for not tackling the cause of the poor's suffering, the Indian custom, or tradition, of discarding the no-name class. And here is where it becomes clear that Mother Teresa had a profound understanding that the call of spirit comes from *within*; it can't be ascribed to us by another human, an organization, or society. The calling she felt and followed was to serve the human dignity of the weakest of society, of the dying, of the most vulnerable, by showing them the face of Christ as she saw it. In her own words: "I will never tire of repeating this: What the poor need the most is not pity but love. They need to feel respect for their human dignity, which is neither less nor different from the dignity of any other human being."[9] This is not the same as working at the political or cultural level to change the values of the society in the hopes of eradicating a major cause of extreme poverty. That is surely a noble purpose, but it was not *her* purpose as she understood it. The awareness she brought to the plight of the poor might awaken others to find they had a calling, directed by a greater wisdom, to advocate for social and political change that would benefit the poor; as for her, she was very clear about her calling—to be on the streets, demonstrating love to the poor day in and day out, which she did with a zeal that attracted others who had a passion to do the same. She built the Society of the Missionaries of Charity, not to lobby governments for new legislation but to feed and nurse and teach the poor, wherever they existed around the globe.

The call of spirit is noble, is sacred, whatever form it takes.

Casting Vision

In the context of the Wisdom Journey, vision reveals what the spirit will *create*, what it will build or make happen in concrete terms, in order to manifest your purpose in the world. Vision is the translation of purpose into a particular new reality. Many individuals might share the same purpose, but each might have a different vision for how they themselves will express that purpose. For example, a group of like-minded people share a purpose to protect the planet. One might do so by conducting scientific research; another lobbies to have protective legislation passed; a third does community outreach with schools and civic associations; a fourth writes about the issues and the efforts of the other three; and a fifth organizes and manages lean administrative operations than enable the other three to do their work with minimal overhead costs. And so five or a dozen or hundreds join together in an organization with this shared purpose, and each member has a distinct vision for what he will create to fulfill this shared calling to protect the planet. This is how the best of organizations form and flourish and, especially, stay the course despite the challenges.

As with defining the spirit (your purpose), seeing the form in which your spirit will express your purpose also comes from listening within, tapping into a deeper wisdom, rather than through any process of deductive reasoning. You don't craft a vision like you might an annual plan. Nor do you just borrow one from the group or organization you might be affiliated with. It has its roots in your spirit, your purpose for being here, and it reveals itself to you. You access it from the wisdom deep within you by being quiet, listening to the spirit, and sensing or receiving the knowledge about what you are called to actually make happen, to create in the world. Thus we call it "casting a vision." This vision will become more concrete over time as you learn from experience (yours and others), continuing your work in the Four Spheres of Transformation and growing in your awareness. Moving forward to fulfill your vision will require some sort of planning, which draws on a person's or group's rational thinking in a process very familiar to organizations and individuals—except with the difference that now the spirit directs the logic and reasoning (thinking).

Choosing Productive Mindsets

Remember the discussion on body–mind–spirit earlier in this chapter, the notion that mind could "sour" the spirit? If we live unconsciously, through body and mind alone, our experiences shape our view of how the world works, and these mindsets, these templates of beliefs, are the operating system through which spirit expresses itself in our life. You may not have consciously discovered your true purpose in life, but unconsciously your mindsets have filled in the blanks. You might absorb, develop, or otherwise acquire them, and once embedded, they color your perceptions of reality and drive your actions in response to your perceptions.

Some mindsets are less productive than others in terms of generating actions that lead to positive results. If you operate from a victim mindset, for example, you believe you are at the mercy of others, unable to effect changes yourself, which gives rise to a large load of resentments, frustration, and anger. Because a mindset mediates between the spirit and the external world, it directs the power of spirit into actions compatible with that mindset, actions that it already knows from your experience will produce results that reinforce, and strengthen that particular mindset. If you believe you are a victim, even if such a belief has never been in your awareness, you will act as a victim and receive, in turn, results that you can interpret to be a confirmation of your "victimhood." Actions do not change unless the mindset operating behind them changes. And with growing consciousness and awareness, you will have the power to discard one mindset for a more productive one—with some effort and commitment, of course.

Your work within to define the spirit and cast a vision has revealed who you are and what you are really here to create in the world. Now comes the work of (1) discovering what mindsets currently operate in your life; (2) assessing whether they support or work at cross-purposes to the achievement of your vision; and if the latter, (3) beginning to adopt and nurture more productive mindsets aligned with your purpose and vision. If you hold one or more unproductive mindsets, these have, in essence, hijacked the creative energy of spirit, causing you to act and to draw results to you that will preserve the reality within the mindset. Your purpose remains a distant longing.

Replacing an unproductive mindset with one better attuned to your purpose involves more than just changing the language you use. Despite the very intimate connection between mindset and action, changing an action alone cannot change the mindset behind it. This takes deep and fearless work, exposing the mindset to the bright light of reflection, understanding how it has affected your life up to now, and making a strong commitment to change. Only then will your actions support your choice to dismantle one mindset and adopt one more likely to make you more effective in fulfilling your purpose and achieving your vision.

In Chapter 3, you'll delve deeply into examining what types of mindsets might be currently active in your life, where each is sourced (what experiences created it, from whom did you learn it), and how well it has worked for you thus far in your life and work. You'll learn some of the alternative mindsets available to you, in particular those associated with more effective leadership, relationships, and becoming a positive, creative force in the world. As importantly, you'll see that taking accountability for what happens in your life—owning the results, even those you don't like—is absolutely essential for changing those results.

Living in the Experience

You have a sense of your purpose and a vision of what you are to create, and seen how more productive mindsets would help you to act in accordance with your purpose and achieve your vision. Now you let this new understanding inform how you live each day. At this stage in your Wisdom Journey, you put into action what you have learned thus far and then experience what effect it has on your life, work, relationships, and your ability to achieve your vision. You live in the experience of doing your work by living in the moment with a new clarity and openness to whatever happens.

Eckhart Tolle, in his book, *The Power of Now*, conveys a wealth of wisdom about learning how to live in the moment, unswayed by fears or experiences from the past, and with no undue expectation of outcomes or the future.[10] You stay aware, fully present, allowing your purpose and vision to direct spirit toward action, rather than defaulting to old conditioning and thinking—you act "on purpose." Your full presence enables you to more clearly experience the results of your actions, and to consciously change your actions if necessary. You reflect on new experiences with a clarity and openness to what you can learn, returning to the Four Spheres of Transformation to glean new wisdom from your experience. You grow in consciousness, and continue a new cycle of your Wisdom Journey, further refining your understanding of purpose and vision— including what the spirit is *not* asking you to do—and increasing your ability to act in greater alignment with them. This is deep learning. You are also better able to contemplate external changes from within the framework of your purpose and vision, seeing what choices may now be available to you for acting purposely toward your vision.

This journey never ends. It becomes richer and richer—perhaps not necessarily easier but more fulfilling, more satisfying—as you experience yourself becoming more effective in terms of your life calling.

Bringing Spirit into the Workplace

The great work invention to come out of the First World War was skill separation (Taylorism, or Scientific Management). Time and motion studies broke work into smaller and smaller parts, and what a person was good at in terms of a fairly narrow skill set was the basis for "matching" them to the work task that required that skill set. Thanks to Henry Ford and the U.S. Army, what the person brought to work was primarily dexterity and certain physical attributes, and a few mental attributes for machining and the like, which determined what they did and where they did it. The system was increasingly refined to the point where work became highly specialized and compartmentalized, quite different and separate from other parts of life, drawing upon only a small portion of the "whole" person.

This differed dramatically from the experience of work during our agrarian age, where most adults were either out in the field with cattle or crops or supporting the farm by keeping the homestead going. Life was not fragmented. It would have been bizarre for someone to go to his father and tell him that family was taking time away from his vocation as a farmer, or distracting him from his spiritual journey, or that he wanted to pursue more recreation in order to feel more fulfilled. Life was—and still is—but one thing: It is life.

Ian Mitroff and Elizabeth Denton write in *A Spiritual Audit of Corporate America*:

> People do not want to compartmentalize or fragment their lives. The search for meaning, purpose, wholeness, and integration is a constant, never-ending task. It is also a constant, never-ending struggle. To confine this search to one day a week or after hours violates people's basic sense of integrity, of being whole persons. In short, the soul is not something one leaves at home. People want to have their souls acknowledged wherever they go, precisely because their souls accompany them everywhere. They especially want to be acknowledged as whole persons in the workplace, where they spend the majority of their waking time.[11]

> People have much more to offer their organization than the organization is currently contracting for—namely, their creative spirits. Likewise a job filled with meaning and purpose can nourish the whole person and thus support all the dimensions of one's existence.

Mitroff and Denton's work was the first comprehensive study to look at spirit in the workplace. The overall finding was that corporations acknowledged the value of spirit and wanted it to be active in the workplace. It is not something foreign to them. *Espirit de corps*, which means work spirit or team spirit, is recognized as a very desirable characteristic of organizational culture. Even more significantly, the formation of organizations such as United Way, Ford Motors, Hewlett-Packard, Dell, Nike—and even these United States—is a testimony to the power of spirit and vision when a person or a few people come together with a passion to create something special. This is the lure of the iconic entrepreneurial startup, the freedom to pursue a dream that has deep personal meaning.

Indeed, a group of people who have come together in order to have something happen, to create something that did not previously exist—be it for profit, not for profit, or governmental—have created an entity with a mission and a spirit of its own.

Most often, however, as such a group grows in size and complexity, it begins to take its cues from organizational theory, cloaking itself in structures and more mechanistic approaches that, in turn, rob it of the very thing that fueled its early success, the spirit and passion of individuals wanting to co-create something meaningful. Its workers gradually begin to see it only as a place of employment. Fortunately, early organizational models based on kingdom, church, or military have been giving way to more enlightened models, including those based on a premise of greater worker empowerment. But the bizarre notion of work as separate from life has only taken greater hold, particularly as more and more families have both adults in the workforce; organizations increase the pressure on their employees for ever greater productivity; and the proliferation of technologies keeps us connected to work nearly all the time, from anywhere.

We have entered a new and even more complex age, with its convergence of massive tsunamis of change, in which organizations must be transformed to generate unprecedented levels of creativity and stewardship of resources. This requires the involvement of highly conscious employees who can bring forth their passion and creative spirit in pursuit of a shared vision.

John Stuart Mill wrote more than two centuries ago in his *Essay on Liberty:* "A state which dwarfs its people, so that they may be more docile instruments in its hand, even for the most beneficial reasons, will find that with small men no great things can be accomplished."[12] Just as it is true for democracies, the individual is the base of the power in an organization, the source of creativity and innovation. While it is not uncommon for organizations to pay lip service to this concept, there are few organizations that actually live the principle of investing in their people. Rather, many organizations have somehow come to view the health of the organization as resting in the hands of leadership, generally defined as a strong charismatic individual. We can see this in the huge gap between the highest and lowest levels of pay in companies, where executive compensation levels have reached the ridiculous.

Some organizations appreciate the importance of individual spirit in organizational success. Intel, for instance, offers a sabbatical in order to help the individual reawaken the spirit. Some organizations give employees time off from work in order to help charities or engage in community activities. As laudable as these actions may be, they are but baby steps toward bringing spirit into the workplace. I don't think organizations yet know how to fully celebrate the individual without feeling coerced to accommodate their employees in a way that organizations were never contracted to do.

Being highly competitive, inventive entities, some organizations are beginning to figure out how to "harness" spirit, but not necessarily by helping individuals becoming awakened and conscious. By absorbing or incorporating other activities of living into the workplace, work comes to be the primary experience people are having, and—not incidentally—the primary source of personal identity. On a visit to Google or other admired companies such as Nike, you'll find a cafeteria that serves three meals a day—all free, in the case of Google—snack bars, on-staff masseuse, recreation room, nap room, bring-your-pet-to-work policies, and a host of other "perks" designed to enable the employee to spend *more* time in the workplace. Certainly all these are not bad in themselves, and they play a role in reducing employee stress. But beyond the fun and the camaraderie, impressionable employees who are not self-aware or conscious enough to understand their own purpose in life can learn to stake their identity to that of the company. What happens to the person whose sole identity is Nike when he is separated from the organization because of downsizing, or relocation overseas, or whatever the reason? Who is he without the organization? Especially in a number of high-tech companies with a very young workforce, unseasoned people who have not yet learned who they are as individuals, nor developed their own viewpoints, can quickly give their spirit and passion entirely to the business and become just one more cog in the machine—albeit a very high functioning cog in a very savvy, very successful, greatly admired machine. Companies need to be attuned to the risks here. Employees whose attachment to their employer fills a void of having too little sense of themselves as individuals do not have access to the phenomenal power of individual spirit; they draft off the energy of others.

The mission of an organization in no way represents the entire life purpose of its employees. Just as it is not directly responsible for employees' physical fitness or academic achievement (even though both can ultimately affect the employee's performance as well as the cost of doing business), employers are not responsible for their employees' spiritual enlightenment—it is the individual's responsibility to work toward a high level of consciousness about who she is, why she is here on earth, and where she is going in life. However, neither should the employer encourage an unhealthy identification with the company, that is, one that is not rooted in the individual's sense of personal purpose and vision. Far better that the organization acknowledge the "wholeness" of each individual, recognizing that the "nonwork" aspects of a person do affect his or her participation in the workplace and are to be not just accommodated but actually celebrated. Said another way, the individual, who for so many years has been told to separate work life from the rest of life, is invited and encouraged to bring her total spirit to bear on the challenges of the workplace. In short, the whole person is invited to show up at work, not just the "work face." Then the person will be an even a brighter source of creation in the workplace.

CHAPTER 3

Coaching Self: A Personal Journey

Your quest to help others, teams, organizations, and society to transform begins with your personal transformational journey. This journey will hinge upon your ability to coach yourself through a process that will rarely be easy and at times may be downright uncomfortable. Through practice, the emerging coach in you must learn to step forward, especially when you are feeling most challenged, and remind you of the value of this process, to push you further into inquiry when you resist finding the truth, reinforce your successes, and find the learning opportunities in your disappointments or frustrations. This coach in you will grow in strength, and when you begin to see a longed-for breakthrough in an area you've been working to improve, you will learn to deeply trust this coach.

Coaching others to transform their work or other aspects of their lives is inextricably linked to the quality of your self-coaching effectiveness. Learn to coach yourself well and you have a foundation for your calling to coach others. Fail to embark upon a serious and dedicated journey to awaken yourself to spirit and a greater wisdom, and your coaching efforts would better be served by directly handing a coaching text to those you wish to serve.

The Dalai Lama speaks directly to beginning with self:

> When our focus is on others, on our wish to free them from their misery—this is compassion. However, only once we have acknowledged our own state of suffering and developed the wish to free ourselves from it can we have a truly meaningful wish to free others from their misery.[1]

The coaching of self is enough work for a lifetime … or three. To believe that one could emerge from a few weeks or months at a mountaintop retreat as an all-wise guru is unrealistic. When you take on your first coaching relationship, you will still be a work in progress. The same will still be true for your twentieth or fiftieth coaching relationship. The relationships themselves will aid your personal growth, provided you engage in them openly on the level of spirit. Your ongoing struggles with self will aid in keeping your approach to coaching others fresh and relevant. The insights you gain as your own journey progresses will serve others.

The general roadmap for each cycle of your personal transformation journey, shown in Figure 3.1, will follow the course of the Wisdom Journey discussed in detail in chapter 2. This chapter will loosely follow the general forward progression shown in Figure 3.1. Although the figure, and therefore the chapter, implies a sequence of "steps," in reality the process is not linear. At any point you may find yourself revisiting or cycling back to an earlier step, but now with added clarity. The insights you gain at any point in this journey can ripple both backward and forward to affect other elements in the process. At any point it can be exciting but also daunting and overwhelming, which is why structured coaching is invaluable.

The 3Es Transformational Coaching methodology, adapted to self-coaching, provides you with just such a structure to approach this important work within. The self-coaching approach involves three stages, each of which we'll discuss in greater detail later in this chapter:

1. *Explore* your current mindsets and cause-and-effect relationships; analyze your current effectiveness in terms of past results and the thinking behind them.
2. *Enroll* yourself into more productive mindsets, new ways of thinking informed by purpose and vision.

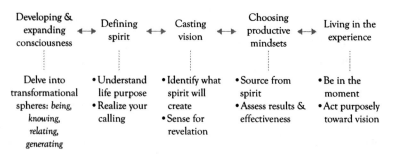

Figure 3.1. Wisdom journey.

3. *Encourage* a journey of continuous personal growth in consciousness and increasing effectiveness.

The methodology reflects the process by which people learn and eventually master new skills and behaviors. It anticipates the barriers and resistance that the human ego marshals against any change it perceives as a threat. It addresses the natural tendencies to regress to old behaviors, as well as the temptation to rest on one's laurels and plateau after a success.

As you apply the self-coaching model to your own transformation journey, you lay down the foundation for coaching others. The approach becomes ingrained. Although the dynamics of coaching individuals and groups will be quite different than what you experience in self-coaching, the coaching structure will closely mirror what you have practiced with yourself.

Throughout this chapter (and those that follow), the "voice" on the page that asks you questions and nudges you forward may initially seem to be mine. Be open to considering this voice, the questions, the counsel, and the cautions as emanating from your internal coach, who takes them in as models that might later be incorporated into or modified for your coaching practice with others.

In this chapter, you'll also receive some tools to facilitate the important inner work that propels you along your journey. These are synergistic and thus very effective with the structured approach to self-coaching, but I caution that they are no substitute for coaching. You may also discover other tools and coaching aids you find helpful, for example, in gaining greater self-awareness. By all means experiment, but anchor these tools in the solid base process for transformational coaching offered here.

Developing and Expanding Consciousness: The Four Transformational Spheres

We might sum up the transformation of self, as represented by the Wisdom Journey in Figure 3.1, as a process of staying awake to life itself (remaining present in the moment), observation, study, reflection, internalization, and ultimately new mindsets that lead to new actions and improved effectiveness. The spheres of *Being, Knowing, Relating,* and

Generating provide the grist for the mill of transformation. Each sphere is a deep well of learning. Together they form a center core for your wisdom journey, one to which you will repeatedly return with questions and new experiences during your journey, and reemerge with fresh insights that open new possibilities for viewing the world and new alternatives for engaging with it. The exciting aspect of the transformational spheres is the seemingly inexhaustible opportunity for personal growth.

The four spheres will become territory for new, deepening knowledge about self that you draw into your moment-to-moment existence, an expanding platform for viewing your reality, your choices, and the results of your actions. As you navigate these fertile realms, you grow in awareness and wisdom that fuels your transformation even as it prepares you to guide others in their transformational journey. As life and coaching bring new experiences to you, you will find yourself returning again and again to the four spheres. The work to be done is continuous.

The discussions below about each sphere will acquaint you with both the substance and the process for exploration, including some self-coaching questions to get you started. But don't stop there. An abundance of material about each sphere is readily accessible in the form of literature, communities of inquiries, and sacred practices.

Also, you might find a powerful approach for investigating these spheres in the context of your current faith and religious practices. I am disturbed by the outright rejection of several thousand years' worth of wisdom simply because some religious institutions have lost their way, delivering dogma rooted in self-preservation of the institution. Seeking meaning in life and deep understanding of self are not solely a twenty-first century undertaking. Faith-based spiritual development can lead to profound learnings and transformative change. The dismissal of ancient religious texts and practices is shortsighted at best. Draw from the wisdom of the past while charting a forward-looking course for your life. The quest of Being, Knowing, Relating, and Generating is rich with wisdom from the past as well as present.

As you saw in Figure 2.2 in chapter 2, the spirit of the unconscious individual is hostage to embedded mental models and paradigms of unexamined beliefs that make up an individual's comfort zone. These are very shallow roots in the face of today's tsunamis of change. Work within the four spheres roots your spirit in a greater spiritual source found in the eternal, be it a deity of your faith or the culmination of the wisdom that preceded your birth and now flows from other sentient beings. The life-creating spirit in you thirsts for the wisdom that resides in the deep wells of Being, Knowing, Relating, and Generating.

Being

Coming into consciousness of your life purpose is the foundation stone of your transformation journey. Transformation in this sphere is powerful—it changes you at a core level, opens the door to your understanding of *purpose*, and awakens your creative being. The spirit, the animating force that flows through your body, is directed into the world through conscious purpose.

Your purpose in life is point zero on the yellow brick road. From here you stretch out as a creative source into the world. Without a strong sense of purpose, you stand vulnerable to the world and its tsunamis, your life twisting and turning at the whim of invisible forces you feel helpless to control. Living a purely reactive life is not very pleasant.

In the context of transformation, we define being as follows:

> **Being**: *The pure, unchanging, formless ground of existence from which individual and collective creations are manifest; the essence of you.*

Being encompasses your essence, the core of who you are, the distilled reason for your existence. When rooted in this "ground of existence," you have a solid stance from which to address the significant changes that increasingly complicate life. Without a strong sense of being, your responses are driven by preservation—survival—animalistic in nature, moving toward pleasure and away from pain, or instinctual or conditioned reactions rather than spirit-driven creativity.

One of my favorite quotes on the topic of purpose is from Viktor Frankl's *Man's Search for Meaning*:

> Ultimately man should not ask what the meaning of his life is, but rather he must recognize that it is he who is asked.... Each man is

questioned by life, and he can answer to life by answering for his own life, to life he can only respond by being responsible.[2]

Frankl is saying, first of all, that man must answer to life with his understanding of his purpose. Imagine sitting at the edge of an open field or by a lake in the dead of a clear night. You look up at the stars, and you are, at once, overtaken with a strong sense of connection with the universe. Whatever your faith or belief system, you suddenly cry out to a divine intelligence or creator, "Why am I here? For what purpose do I exist?" And to your surprise a clear and potent answer comes forth, "Great question. You go first." You are asked to start the conversation, to formulate an answer to your life's purpose, your reason for being, however imperfect that first expression of purpose might be. "Why am I here?" is the beginning of perhaps the most important conversation of your life—a conversation with life itself. And the way to find the answer to this life-sized question about your purpose is to simply begin by writing down your first thoughts on this.

The next aspect of Frankl's quote is the idea that you alone answer for your own life. As a sentient being, it is for *you* to discover the reason for your existence, your calling—your answer is a personal response. In the cult world of Jim Jones and Marshall Applewhite (who led mass suicides at Jonestown and Heaven's Gate, respectively), the leader or group, through coercive psychological mechanisms, imposes a "purpose for living" on other individuals. Be cautious of anyone who provides you with a ready-made answer to your life's purpose. By all means take counsel— you might clarify your own thinking by sharing thoughts with those who know you or may be wrestling with the same question of their own purpose—but you must personally answer the question of your life's meaning.

The third facet of Frankl's quote concerns your response once your purpose is clear to you. Being responsible to your calling is to live life according to this discovered purpose, to make choices that are aligned with this purpose. The variety of individual purposes we see expressed is astounding: from serving others in specific ways to consumption, to experiencing life itself, to serving a deity. We might personally see a particular purpose as inherently good and noble, or evil and narcissistic; regardless, a life purpose moves an individual forward. Whatever the purpose, the "responsible" response is to live according to this life calling.

The Purpose Statement

Practically speaking, the place we should begin is to develop a life purpose statement, to do our best to answer the big question, "Why am I here?" But instead we join organizations or teams that have a mission (purpose) statement and then work to see our fit with that group. How odd, having unconscious individuals join together under the umbrella of an organizational mission. An enterprise populated with people who have no clear sense of their own purpose is like an engine outfitted with a governor that limits its power and speed.

Later in this chapter, you will be asked to draft a statement of purpose as part of a Life Plan. My advice to you is to start on this now while you are immersed here in the sphere of Being. Reflect on what you believe your purpose in life to be. Capture your purpose in a written statement. This might be the first time you have done such an exercise; if so, then this is Purpose Statement version 1.0. If you have done this before, write your purpose again. Check it for truthfulness and exactness in describing your reason for being. Wear this purpose for a time, testing if it suits you and best expresses your life's calling. Make corrections and take it to the next version. Put it down, come back to it again and again, revise, or redraft, making it more specific.

As you rework this statement over time, you'll likely see the excess verbiage disappear and each remaining word grow in meaning. The statement gains clarity and approaches a deeper truth. Where at first, with your mother figuratively peering over your shoulder, you wrote intent on producing a noble statement that would make her proud, your statement now rings clear with your voice and your truth. A statement of purpose expressed at its deepest level represents who you know yourself to be, and to have always been. You will revisit this statement periodically to reexamine and refine it as life proceeds and you grow in consciousness and effectiveness.

Being–Doing–Having

We differentiate *being* from the states of *doing* and *having*. You first determine who you are (*being*), your purpose on earth, and then move forward in life making decisions and taking actions (*doing*) in accord with that purpose. As a result of this *doing*, you accumulate things (*having*)—house(s), cars, money, awards, recognition, titles, clothes, electronics and so on. However, individuals often confuse the order of *being-doing-having*. You might think that your *doing* has resulted in your *having* many things, and that these things—house, car, money, etc.—represent your *being*, the essence of who you are. This presents a serious dilemma: If the house, wealth, and job are taken away, then who are you? By definition in this scenario, nobody. But you are *not* your house, your wealth, or your job. Nor is the corollary true: You are not your unemployed status, your broken marriage, or your heart condition. These may be the outcomes of who you are *being*, but they are not you.

If you believe in a creator of the universe, do you know this entity as the Supreme *Haver* or the Supreme *Doer*, instead of the Supreme *Being*? Are you a human *haver* or a human *doer*, rather than a human *being*?

It is an ultimately painful experience to live life believing who you are is what you own, particularly since having typically leads to the need for more having. Many highly successful people, after acquiring great personal wealth, discover the futility of allowing "things" to define the self. Developing clarity of purpose maintains your perspective about the proper order of the flow of life, from *being* to *doing* to *having*.

Many of the world's religions, as well as their rituals and practices, convey a common message about the power of love and the pure presence of being. Do you have a sense of a pure state of being, the ground of existence from which all of life arises? Can you sit still and quiet your mind enough to feel another deeper presence? Or do you think you are solely your thoughts and emotions in the moment (quite the opposite of the quiet state I just described above)? If you sit quietly and still sufficiently long and you have a determined will to understand the sacredness held within life itself, you discover that what you are at your essence is simply awareness. You are just one of the many that are actually one—a life-transforming experience in its own.

Your capacity to access this deep ground of being, from which all of life is manifest, creates a field of freedom for others to step into new possibilities. In fact, to effectively coach others in transformation, you will call upon this capacity time and again.

Knowing

We are living organisms connecting to a world body in profound and mysterious ways. We get messages constantly from sources our ears can't hear and our eyes can't see. Our bodies and minds both receive and censor these messages. Our perception—the meaning we attribute to the information coming into our human form, equipped as it is with limited reception—further adds clarity or distortion. And yet most of us accept what we know as an accurate reflection of our world, how it operates, and how we operate within it. How do you know what you know? What has your mind's eye let in or kept out because it does or doesn't conform to some idea you hold? What information does your body sense or reject because it "knows" it will produce a particular emotion?

In his classic book, *Crack in the Cosmic Egg*, Joseph C. Pearce summed up the impact of this filtering of life through what we already know: "Our world to view is determined by our world view." We will see a world that conforms to what we think we already know to be true about the world. As we reflect on this conundrum, we come to realize that what we "know" about the world, about life, is unlikely to be the unbiased, unvarnished truth. If our experience of the world, of our reality, stems in part from a set of incomplete or faulty perceptions, we might rightfully feel some urgency around closely examining what we do know, as well as how we came to know it.

There is a third important aspect of this sphere: what you *don't* know. We operate on a ground of varying hardness, bedrock in some areas perhaps, quicksand in others. To understand that you lack information or knowledge in certain areas is to acknowledge your state of partial knowing, and this opens the door to more learning.

In the context of the transformational spheres, we define knowing as follows:

> **Knowing**: *One's knowledge and wisdom as accessed through the full range of human senses and experience, derived from the exploration of life's mysteries.*

Life is full of mystery. Our natural thirst for understanding drives our exploration of the world in which we find ourselves. A primary quest is knowledge and wisdom about ourselves as individuals. Many before us have sought answers through the sciences and theology. Some of these answers have proven strong in the face of time, and others have been discounted as we explore more deeply. The odds are great that we will not know everything before we depart from life. So consider your time on this earth as a continuation of mankind's long exploration. Be open to what others have learned even as you examine their truths from the vantage point of your experiences, and strive to learn more.

We seek in transformation to access this deep well of knowing. And we begin to do so by reflecting on "What do I know?," "How did I come to know that?," and "What is unknown?"

What we know can be heavily influenced by how we are taught to think. Daniel Pink speaks to this in his book, *A Whole New Mind*:

> But the contrast in how our cerebral hemispheres operate does yield a powerful metaphor for how individuals and organizations navigate their lives. Some people seem more comfortable with logical, sequential, computer-like reasoning. They tend to become lawyers, accountants, and engineers. Other people are more comfortable with holistic, intuitive, and nonlinear reasoning. They tend to become inventors, entertainers, and counselors. And these individual inclinations go on to shape families, institutions, and societies.
>
> Call the first approach *L-Directed Thinking*. It is a form of thinking and an attitude to life that is characteristic of the left hemisphere of the brain—sequential, literal, functional, textual, and analytic. Ascendant in the Information Age, exemplified by computer programmers, prized by hardheaded organizations, and emphasized in schools, this approach is directed *by* left-brain attributes, *toward* left-brain results. Call the other approach *R-Directed Thinking*. It is a form of thinking and an attitude to life that is characteristic of the right hemisphere of the brain—simultaneous, metaphorical, aesthetic, contextual, and synthetic. Underemphasized in the Information Age, exemplified by creators, and caregivers, shortchanged by organizations, and neglected in schools, this approach is directed *by* right-brain attributes, *toward* right-brain results.[3]

A prolonged reductionist approach has provided society benefits, from the exploration of physical and life sciences to the building of large and focused organizations and optimized functions of societal subsystems. But the price has been an undervaluing of the knowledge of the whole and sources of learning from a more holistic thinking. Many thought leaders, using different terms but making similar observations, see a broad movement from the Information Age to the Conceptual Age, where holistic, intuitive thinking finally receives its due.

How does this relate to you and your work in the sphere of knowing? Your knowledge-gathering approach could be a result of personal inclination and/or conformance to a societal bias, and it might inherently limit the information you take in and how you process it (how you learn from it). For some, the societal bias has led them to reject other means of taking in information from the world—for example, closing down or never developing their intuitive capabilities.

Don't let this apparent uncertainty about what you know and how you learned it mire you in apathy and inaction, wherein you decide, "Why try at all?" Such a fatalistic stance as this walls you off from any meaningful learning and growth. If an action produces an unfavorable outcome, delve into the knowledge that informed your action and be open to reexamining it and how you came by that knowledge. Is it so-called wisdom conveyed by a parent? A personal learning from an earlier experience? Perhaps a lack of sufficient knowledge to make a better-informed decision? This is a rich source for investigation and growth.

I strongly encourage you as a budding transformational coach of self and others to also tend to the things you don't already know. Explore the large body of wisdom and learning in philosophy, psychology, spirituality, and organizational development. Bring into your sphere of knowledge the frameworks and mental maps that can assist you in understanding individual and collective development. Draw from it to guide your personal transformation and your work in guiding the transformation of others.

Relating

Life presents each one of us with countless material elements, people, situations, and ideas, which we could ideally view in an unattached, nonjudgmental way: They are what they are, existing today or in the past, and have no hold over us when we encounter something similar in the future. But we *do* impose a meaning to these things; we interpret them and adopt a point of view that, if unexamined, can harden into a firm fact against which we define all similar encounters or experiences going forward. Our way of relating to one aspect of life—or indeed, all aspects of life—becomes grounded in concrete, immovable and immutable, casting a long shadow over how we respond to what life brings our way in the future.

For instance, ask yourself what meaning you attach to money. Do you see it primarily as a tool to facilitate the exchange of goods, as it was designed to do? Or does money represent power, or security, or perhaps the evils of consumption? Is it the yardstick by which you assess the inherent worth of yourself and others? Your answer reveals how you *relate* to money. To dig more deeply into the reason you choose to see money as you do opens a door to greater self-knowledge, expanding your consciousness about what drives the decisions you make, the actions you take, and the results you produce in this aspect of your life. Most importantly, it frees you to change your relationship to money in order to generate more desirable results.

Note that a desirable result in the case of money doesn't necessarily mean *more* of it. Depending on your particular purpose for being, better results might mean ceasing to worry about your finances; having greater appreciation of your job because it enables you to provide well for your family; diverting energy toward more satisfying nonmonetary pursuits; opening to the full humanity and value of other people; or contributing money to philanthropic causes. Exploring how you relate to money gives you the freedom to realign this relationship with your purpose, a true leverage point for transformation.

The third sphere of transformation is formally defined as follows:

> **Relating**: *The quality or disposition of thoughts, beliefs, and emotions that inform the choices of one's connection to self, others, and all aspects of life.*

Insights flow in abundance when you cultivate deeper consciousness of how you relate to "all" in life. You develop a better understanding of why you have chosen to view each of these relationships as you have. You can see your point of view as a choice you made in the past, a stance you might want to reevaluate if it seems to be a barrier to having the life you desire. Transformation often springs from making alternative choices in how to relate to something or someone.

Explore how you relate to another aspect of life: How do you see your body? As a temple, perhaps, the carrier of your mind and spirit, or a vehicle that restricts your life experiences, your opportunities, your relationships? If you are overweight compared to accepted medical standards, what meaning do you attach to this statistical fact? If medical norms are not relevant to you, do you have weight concerns that arise from comparison to an ideal planted through advertising, cultural icons, or peer pressure? Whether or not your weight conforms to some societal ideal, do you relate to it as a blessing or a curse; as the reason you have or haven't moved ahead socially or in the office; as a projection of wealth and power? In any case, your weight is weighed down (pardon the pun) with a lot of meaning. Uncover the meaning you imposed on your weight, and your body more generally, and you create the leverage point for transformation.

Let's say I ask a person, whom I'll call Bob, why he wears eyeglasses. Bob answers, "I have to." This simple response speaks volumes about how he relates to the glasses, most notably, it implies that some external force has imposed the requirement on him, and he thus he has no choice but to wear them—Bob is victim to something outside himself, powerless. I respond that other people I know don't seem to "have to" wear glasses. After a lively though somewhat confusing conversation, we eventually get to crux of the matter: Bob desires to see more clearly. He visited the optometrist for a diagnosis, accepted the prescription, purchased the glasses, and has since put them on of his own volition every day. No victim here. The glasses are the manifestation of his will to have better sight. So why did Bob develop a victim stance in his relationship to this piece of hardware? If he is willing to explore this further, Bob can learn something important about why he relates to his glasses this way, and whether such a victim stance might color the way he relates to other parts of his life.

How do you relate to possessions, to accomplishments and failures, your personal history, key relationships, nature? It might be more complex to discover how you relate in some areas than in others, but do not be deterred.

How do you see the connection you ultimately have to everything in the world, be it good or bad, right or wrong, desirable or unpleasant? Do you relate to the world from a causal stance, in which you see you play a role in creating outcomes, or perhaps from a victim stance that takes no responsibility for past or future outcomes? In the first case, your will is applied to creating change, and in the second case your will is withheld, thereby preventing change. You are connected to every occurrence on the planet by means of applying or withholding your energy.

As you explore how and why you relate to the myriad aspects of your life, do so without judgment. For example, you may strongly endorse an organized religion and are a vocal defender of a set of beliefs and the institution. On the other hand, you might have a visceral hatred of organized religion and aggressively attack others' beliefs and the institution. Avoid seeing either case as right or wrong, desirable or undesirable, and instead keep probing to find the reasons you choose to hold the set of beliefs that you do. To see your answers as good or bad will generate resistance from the start.

As you work in the sphere of relating, pay close attention to emotional triggers in a situation, those knee-jerk reactions that seem to come out of nowhere. When the emotions suddenly and unexpectedly flare, you can be certain that your relationship to the incident or person is not neutral but rather loaded with meaning that bears close examination. Dive in to understand what is behind your reaction.

Generating

Let's start with the definition of generating, the fourth sphere of transformation:

> **Generating:** *Manifesting from spirit; bringing forth visions, mental models, and actions that give rise to new possibilities and transformation.*

The evidence that a transformation has occurred in an individual or an organization rests in the nature of the results the individual or organization produces—the impact of their actions in the world as compared with the outcomes they had consciously intended. What you generate from your spirit in an external sense is the measure of the degree of your personal transformation within.

Spiritual Amperage

Manifesting from spirit, from the definition at the start of this section, means to direct spiritual energy toward creating some new aspect of a desired future state. Here, the amount of energy that one can channel toward the objective is a factor in producing the outcome.

Let me use the analogy of electrical current to discuss the magnitude of spiritual energy available to an individual or collective. An ampere is the unit of measure of electrical current. If we think of the amount of spiritual energy available in terms of "spiritual amps," we could hypothetically relate different states of awareness/consciousness to the amount of spiritual amperage each made available for creating something in the world. The more spiritual amps, the bigger the change.

If you were unconscious to the spirit within you, living solely out of the mind/body alone, you would have little energy available to you to change your life and actively create a better future (the Zombie state in Figure 3.2).

When you awaken to self, to the power within you as an individual human being, you gain access to creative energy that was unavailable to

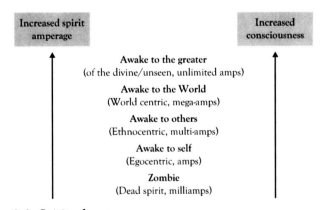

Figure 3.2. Spiritual amperage.

you before. Simply being conscious about a purpose for your life, for instance, improves your choices, enabling you to better select from potential actions to best support this purpose.

You access even more spiritual amperage when you awaken to your connection with others and choose to serve them. Their energies are combined with yours to generate a joint or common outcome.

As Figure 3.2 suggests, each successive state of consciousness connects you to a more vast pool of creative energy and to wisdom about where and how to direct it for an even greater good.

Staying Awake to the World

To be a generative force in the world requires that you stay awake to who you are *being*, to your purpose. But remaining fully present, fully awake to the world can be difficult. Life brings love and pain, successes and failures, satisfactions and disappointments. To deaden the impact of the unwanted experiences, many individuals resort to escape mechanisms: drugs and alcohol, sexual affairs, high-risk behaviors, isolation, even excessive sleep—the list goes on and on. There is no shortage of ways to fall asleep to the world around us. The technology explosion in entertainment media, for instance, makes "zoning out" seductive, easy, and socially acceptable.

Marie Winn, author of the 1977 book *The Plug-In Drug*, raised the alarm about television's addictive influence on kids. She called attention to the passive mental state TV watching induces in children, removing them from living a real life with real-life connections. When she first penned the text, she could have hardly imagined total hours of mind-numbing usage by today's children—and adults.

A more recent large-scale, national media usage study conducted by the Kaiser Family Foundation found that with the advancement of new 24/7 technology for delivering media content, the average child aged 8–18 spent more than 7.5 hours per day in 2009 using media for entertainment purposes (not school-related activities), up 20% from just five years prior.[4]

Although the amount of time spent watching regularly scheduled TV actually declined by 25 minutes per day between 2004 and 2009, the new delivery devices such as TV-Internet, cell phones, and iPods increased overall TV consumption from 3 hours and 51 minutes to 4 hours and 29 minutes per day. When non-TV entertainment options are considered— music and videos on computers, MP3 players, iPods, and cell phones— electronic entertainment consumes a full 7.5 hours daily, 29% of which is spent multitasking (engaged with more than one entertainment source). Youth are spending more time in the virtual entertainment bubble than ever before. According to the study, the heavier the usage, the poorer the grades earned in school.

How has this passive consumption of entertainment influenced the adults of today? How has it influenced you? Do you find yourself sometimes wanting to "veg out"—to vegetate, to go unconscious? If so, what is your drug of choice?

The generative person has learned to "stay awake" rather than "fall asleep" in tough times. She sees opportunity for learning in the unwanted and uncomfortable experiences of life as well as in the "glory times." She builds her generative capacity in small steps, repeated again and again.

Building Your Generative Capacity

You gain proficiency in generating—manifesting what you truly desire— as you bring your expanding consciousness about *being, knowing,* and *relating* into the present moment. The more you pay attention to what is happening moment to moment and the effect it is having on you—that is, being fully aware—the more clearly you see the choices you have for acting, including choices that have never been apparent to you before, and for assessing what action is most likely to generate the outcome you desire in the situation, the outcome most aligned with your purpose in life and the vision you have for what you want to create (more about vision later).

You also build your generative muscle by evaluating through reflection what you have created in the past. Your results over time are the evidence of your "true will" at work, even if you claim to have wanted different outcomes. Investigating, honestly and courageously, the gap between what we think or say we desire and what we actually draw to us affords powerful insights that can be leveraged for transformational change.

A man we'll call Tom has worked for a series of three male bosses over a period of 12 years. He believes that none of these men ever appreciated his work or understood what he was capable of contributing to the company. They gave him lukewarm performance reviews, pay raises that were always a tad below average, and, as he saw it, kept him off any kind of promotional track. Periodically he feels resentment and asks himself, "Why do I get such lousy bosses? Why isn't my career going anywhere?" He complains to his wife and fantasizes about leaving the company, although he's never acted on this.

One day he buys and begins to read a book on personal transformation. He's highly skeptical of the notion that these relationships he has with his bosses, his record of little career growth, are all outcomes he has created. It takes a little time for him to conditionally accept this notion—what does he have to lose?—and he feels ready to ask the question, "What do *I* get out of these relationships with unappreciative bosses?" He begins to pay more attention to his interactions with them, to how he feels, and what he thinks in the course of a day at work. He sees that he doesn't apply much effort or creativity to his work activities, that he has a sense of "coasting," satisfied to meet what he assumes are his boss's low expectations of him. He follows that deeper and has an insight that surprises him: He doesn't really expect himself to succeed, no matter how hard he tries (although he's never put this to the test at work). As a matter of fact, the last time he really tried hard at anything was learning to play baseball as a kid. His older brother was a terrific player, a natural, and no matter how hard Tom practiced, his dad took every opportunity to point out how much better his brother was. Tom truly felt he was doing his very best to learn to bat, field the ball, and run the bases, but his father diminished his accomplishments, always holding up his brother's feats as the standard Tom had to meet to gain his father's approval.

At some point in his early teens, Tom decided it was futile to try and please his father, but instead of learning to play baseball for his own pleasure and sense of gradually improving his skills, he quit entirely. He started pulling back in other areas of his life as well, assuming he'd never be any good at what he attempted, or if he was, there would be no one who would acknowledge it. This spared him the work of stretching himself physically or mentally. It was a short leap for Tom to see that he had created in his adult work life a situation where, by his own choice, he performed at a level that continuously fell short of bosses' goals and expectations. Brighter or harder working colleagues passed him by. It all served to reinforce the familiar if uncomfortable belief that he was a failure. Despite what Tom told his wife and himself about wanting a better job, deserving higher pay, the situation he had created delivered just the opposite outcomes. And only he had the power to change it by exploring his purpose in life, his beliefs about success, his relationship with his father, and wherever else these inquiries led.

What are you generating in your life? What results did you *not* desire? Look for patterns, for repeated disappointments, frustrations, and unwanted outcomes. What choices did you make that are responsible for creating these undesirable results? How might these results be serving you, even though you pronounce them as unwanted? Where has your unconscious motivations sabotaged your pronounced desires? This is difficult work. Guard against any tendency to move to self-judgment and self-doubt. You are fallible, but the beauty in possessing a spirit and free will is the ability to transform. Return to a conscious understanding of your purpose and check to see that your actions are in accordance. We so easily get off track; a deep investigation of the results we are generating puts us quickly back on track.

What results in your life please you, and why? Do they bring long-term joy? How do the "positive" outcomes relate to your purpose in life? These demonstrate your ability to generate desirable outcomes through application of your creative spirit—build strength and confidence from this. Sharpen your skills in clarifying the means and outcomes that flow from your conscious will. When you are clear about what you want to generate while living in a purposeful manner, you'll be surprised how apparently unrelated forces align with your creative efforts. Be open to serendipity, those happy yet seemingly accidental discoveries or occurrences that work to bring us what we want.

The same is true when acting as a team. What results are you generating together? Why and how did the team generate these results (both wanted and unwanted)? As a team are you predisposed to claim positive results as manifestations of the team's collective will, and view unwanted results as the fault of someone or something else? What could be learned if the team paused for a moment and looked to these results as coming from "us"?

A Personal Experience in the Four Spheres

Engagement with the Four Spheres of Transformation is an iterative process. You will have an experience that you later reflect upon in the context of one or more spheres. You are rewarded with a new insight that broadens your self-awareness and expands your consciousness. You take that forward into a similar situation, and a better way of handling it occurs to you in the moment—and you *do* handle it more effectively, with better results! The value of the Four Spheres as deep wells of wisdom becomes more evident, and so you try it again in the future with another experience in your life. Soon it becomes a self-reinforcing process, a virtuous cycle. Your interest in and understanding of *what* happens to you and *why* grows, and you become evermore present for subsequent experiences. Regardless of the immediate outcome, you value experiences for their ability to teach you something important about yourself and how you relate to the world. And gradually, or sometimes suddenly, the outcomes you generate are undeniably more positive—your life is changing for the better.

I am a big supporter of United Way. From the beginning of my more than 17 years with Procter & Gamble, I became involved as a volunteer with the United Way organization and other community agencies that P&G heavily supported. When I became plant manager of P&G's Kansas City Folgers Plant, I became even more deeply involved as a leader in the community and as a volunteer to help companies in the area strengthen their internal appeals for contributions to the United Way and to connect their workforce to the needs of the community. I found it all very satisfying.

My last assignment with P&G was as the paper plant manager of a large mill complex in rural Wyoming County in Northeastern Pennsylvania, where we manufactured Pampers, Luvs, Bounty, Charmin', and many other well-known brands of household products. With more than 3,000 employees, the facility was by far the largest employer in the county. As was typical each year, I headed up the plant's annual United Way campaign. I called together the 300-plus leaders of the complex, who were

COACHING SELF: A PERSONAL JOURNEY   69

responsible for cascading the campaign down to the individual teams and departments, to view a short professionally made film about United Way's history, the needs it served, and how, with a strong message threaded throughout the film that we are one community. Just as I had in previous years, once the film ended I stood up and began to talk about why we should all support this largely poor rural community with its many basic subsistence needs, and why I through we should connect more closely with this community. I stopped suddenly as an insight flooded my mind, reverberated through my spirit, the closest thing to an epiphany I'd ever experienced. Although only a few moments transpired from the audience's perspective, I felt time stop.

It dawned on me with great force that a year ago when I'd given the speech, I had thought about the community as "those people out there." Then just months after that, my wife and I adopted from another rural Pennsylvania community a 2-1/2 year old girl, Jessica, whom we had not known before the adoption. A year prior, she was one of "those people" out in the community. But now she was my daughter, for whom I'd readily give my life, bonded with me in a way I could not have imagined earlier, inseparable from what I now thought of as our family. At that moment in the speech, I understood at a visceral level that any child "out there" in the community could become a beloved member of my family. (This did in fact become true again in another year's time, when my wife and adopted another child, one-year-old Mark, from within the community.)

Adopting a very young child came with an inexplicable regret that I hadn't been there for Jessica the first years of her life to protect her and nurture her.[5] Yet in another flash of insight that flowed to me during the speech, I realized that the local United Way and its affiliated agencies in the community had made it their mission for years to serve these children and their families. They'd been there for Jessica and her community before I came into her life. Their work suddenly took on an even larger and more personal dimension for me; gratitude filled my heart.

I finished the speech rather quickly and sat down, finding it difficult to speak any longer in the wake of these insights. We went on to have a very successful campaign that year, but something significant had changed for me.

In all my prior United Way campaigns and community volunteer activities, I saw the value of the work, knew the mechanics of what needed to be done, and felt called to be a leader in these efforts—it was who I was "being." But now my purpose, my spirit had shifted from leadership to *compassion*, to truly being one with this community, experiencing a degree of connectedness entirely new to me.

My epiphany also brought a profound shift in the other spheres of transformation.

I had *known* the needs of the community, how to do fundraising, the functions of the United Way organization—all of which enabled me to be of service, primarily through raising money, which the agencies desperately needed. I knew there was a difference between me and the people who benefited from this fund raising—indeed, between me and everyone else in the world. After this epiphany, I knew what it meant to have a profound connection with the world around me. I knew that people who were once strangers could become family; that I was capable of caring deeply about people even if they weren't blood relatives. The boundary between stranger and family, between the rest of the world and me, had disappeared. The truth for me now was that we are all connected in a non-self-serving manner.

Before, I *related* to the people in the community as having missed the advantages I had. I was fortunate to be born into a middle-income family to parents who put me on a path of study and work, leading me to get an engineering and business education, which in turn opened the door to joining a very reputable organization that further nurtured me. Few in this community had those advantages or had seized those opportunities, but I could help them along the road to success, or help alleviate their pain and suffering. How I related was based on my giving and them receiving, an essentially detached position for me. After my epiphany, the basis of my relating was transformed into a relationship of oneness. I'm not *here* and they are not *there*, but we all are truly together as one, what is termed the "we-being." I didn't reproach myself for not having had this deeper sense of connection in my past volunteer work, yet I clearly understood that I would now be able to contribute in a different way that held even greater meaning for me.

With respect to *generating*, before, my spirit was generating funds/ monies and support for good services to the community. Nothing wrong with that! But now I strongly sensed that my purpose was to generate a stronger bond between the people who worked in the community and those who lived there, a type of unification that extended well beyond meeting physical needs and having sympathy for the less fortunate.

I have remained involved with United Way and continue to be a big champion of the entire effort and model. But the tenor of my involvement is much different than it was in those days as a hard-working fundraiser and volunteer. I see my role in the world differently, not as one of supporting other individuals but as bringing into communion all my sons and daughters, mothers and fathers, and brothers and sisters across the world. It had a profound effect on me and my life path, and my experiences and outcomes have since confirmed the rightness of this new role for me. Do I occasionally slip back into the old "transactional" relationships with the world around me? Of course I do. But by stopping, taking a moment to reflect, to meditate, to pray, I find that I can move back into this greater calling, emerging stronger and hopefully more effective in what I can create in the world.

Life Plan 1.0: Purpose, Vision, and Action Plans

The sphere of generating encompasses your ability to generate new visions of what you want to create and envision new ways of how to make it all happen. So the important consideration for you, now that you've had some practice writing your purpose statement, is specifically what are you going to generate? Where are you going to direct your creative energy? What concrete changes do you want to make in your life in order to live a life of purpose? To answer these questions, you'll draft your first version of a Life Plan. Your Life Plan will be a roadmap of the creations you consciously choose to generate. This is not about overly scripting every move for the rest of your lifetime but rather setting a direction for moving forward toward goals and objectives that match your understanding of your overall purpose for being in the world. Not having a Life Plan doesn't mean your life will be pointless; but having a Life Plan helps point you toward a place where fulfillment resides, and with increasing accuracy as you refine and update it to reflect your experience with it.

The Life Plan Document, which is in Appendix 3.1, includes the following elements:

- Personal assessment of current satisfaction in eight areas in the Wheel of Life: spiritual, family/relationships, body, finance, intellectual, fun/recreation/play, vocation, and community
- Life purpose, as well as core values and operating principles that set the boundaries for actions and behaviors
- Life narratives of how you came to be you—your past story—and who you are becoming—your future story
- A 3- to 5-year vision of your desired future
- One-year action plans for each of eight life areas in the Wheel of Life Personal Assessment, including current state, desired state, milestones, and planned actions
- Conditions for success, in terms of what you need to change in order to remove current barriers and facilitate success (mindsets, motivation, commitment, support, perceived risks)

Writing your Life Plan 1.0 on paper or typing out the words on your laptop is the first essential step in manifesting the future you desire. It is not enough (although it might be a good start) to prop your feet up on your desk and plot in your head some grand arc to your life. But your first real act of generation is to give it physical form as written words. Don't underestimate the power of seeing your Life Plan made "visible" in words.

The life planning process is easy to walk through, but it should be far from a mechanical or superficial exercise. The questions asked in the Life Plan Document are spirit provoking, and the process of inquiry can take you deep into the transformational spheres to find the answers that are authentic for you.

That said, often the first version on paper might seem superficial to you, or sprinkled with clichés as your "top of mind" thoughts spill out first—initial attempts at a Life Plan commonly tend to be wordy. But rewriting as you search for a more meaningful way of articulating a purpose or a vision is to conduct a conversation with your spirit. Its voice gets louder and clearer as you pare away the noise of unnecessary verbiage; as with poetry, unproductive words not only take up room but also lessen the energy of the plan.

As your consciousness grows and you gain greater awareness, you will revise the plan, perhaps many times. Free yourself from any pressure to "get it right" on the first pass. Learn to be comfortable with *not knowing* where the process of writing and revising your Life Plan might be headed. Ego will become more open to what spirit is trying to say. I have seen individuals who were very hesitant about writing a Life Plan, as though putting into writing their answers to such profound questions—why they're here, where they're going, what they most value—were to etch them in stone. Far from it.

Create your Life Plan 1.0 now. Revisit the discussions about defining spirit/purpose (chapter 2—Wisdom Journey, and this chapter—Being) and casting vision (chapter 2—Wisdom Journey) to help you with these portions of the Life Plan. Your purpose, vision, and action plans will serve important roles later in this chapter as you move further into your wisdom journey to assess your current effectiveness, analyzing the mindsets that operated to produce current results; and enroll in more productive mindsets and behaviors that can lead to breakthrough results in key life areas.

Often the first version of the Life Plan will tend to be overly ambitious. After you have outlined your action plans and goals in each area of life, sit back and take a look at the whole. Do the plans taken together seem overwhelming to you? Where is there synergy between the life categories? How might you leverage or merge actions in several areas? Be smart and take manageable first steps. You can ramp up your efforts when you develop more proficiency for formulating and executing plans. Transformation is truly not about working harder, but about targeting opportunities where the alignment with your purpose is strong and you find your spirit soars.

Share your Life Plan with someone else. Ask the individual to listen to your understanding of yourself at this point as it is reflected in the Life Plan. Feedback is not necessary, only a strong listener who will ask clarifying questions.

Once your Life Plan has taken form, you have a practical framework for daily choosing actions that align with your purpose, vision, and values; without such alignment, transformation does not occur. Furthermore, daily experiences and their outcomes will test your purpose and sharpen your understanding of how well it captures your sense of who you are. Provided you stay aware of what is happening in the moment, you can reflect on it for what it can teach. Are you living your purpose? Do you experience fulfillment when you find yourself on purpose? Likewise, the visions you hold, the creations you are bringing about, are being checked for their sticking power. Does the vision statement truly reflect all of what you feel called to create? Is the vision a wish list of items or real, purpose-driven images?

And so Life Plan 1.0 becomes Life Plan 2.0, and eventually 3.0. You grow to appreciate how this iterative process continues to refine and clarify your path forward, allowing you to focus your energies where most needed. You begin to see the Life Plan as a living document that accompanies you through every cycle of your wisdom journey.

Explore Mindsets: Analysis of Current Effectiveness

My wife informed me one day during my son Mark's last year of elementary school that he would do a project for the school's science fair. She said that he had a project in mind already, and what a wonderful father–son experience this could be. I readily bought into the vision of laboring in the workshop with Mark for the purpose of bonding and creating memories.

When the time came to build a working model of the idea Mark had conceived, we went into the shop and brought out the wood working tools. Within a matter of minutes, Mark was disheartened and his enthusiasm depressed. He left the shop and went directly to my wife and announced, "Working with Dad is a drag."

I sat down on a stool in the workshop and pondered how I'd generated an outcome so entirely different from what I'd intended. I thought I was clear in undertaking a fun project with my son that would lead to a deeper connection between us. I could have blamed the undesirable outcome on Mark or on the school for giving him such an assignment. But I'd had quite a bit of practice over the years examining my effectiveness and owning the results, and knew my own thinking had most likely dragged me "off purpose" and led to the dismal results we'd just experienced.

By probing further, I saw that somewhere between the announcement of the project and the moment we entered the shop, my original objective of co-creating something together had been sidetracked by the desire to win the blue ribbon for the best science project—my competitive impulses at work, not Mark's. Also entangled in my thinking was the notion that there are "right" ways and "wrong" ways of doing things, which I proceeded to show Mark instead of guiding him through the steps so that he could learn by doing it himself. My purpose may have been clear—teaching, creating, and bonding—but my base programming, that hardwired comfort zone of automatic responses to a situation, directed my actions, which then produced a far different outcome than I'd envisioned. To improve the outcome, *change* had to begin with me.

I committed to act more consciously, in ways that would keep me "on purpose." Retrieving Mark, I suggested we start over. And we did, this time with me holding in my consciousness the objective of co-creating and enjoying the spirit of the father–son relationship. This second go-round met with a much more satisfactory result.

Whether it's the next couple of years, as laid out in your Life Plan, or a specific situation like the science fair project above, knowing your purpose, having a clear vision of what you want to create, and developing a plan of action for achieving it still doesn't guarantee getting the results you desire. These are essential elements; without them you are merely casting around in the darkness of wishful thinking that your life will change somehow. But as the graphic of the Wisdom Journey (Figure 3.1) suggests, the mindsets with which you carry out your actions are a mighty influence on the results your actions generate.

Mindsets are part of your hardwired responses, the base programming you developed to respond to the world. As mentioned in chapter 2, at the time you first "configured" these paradigms and modes of response—in early childhood, for the most part—they enabled you to function more effectively in the world than if you had remained in the depths of mystery. They have brought you to where you are today, shaped and colored your past experiences, and generated outcomes, some of which have pleased you, some of which have not. If the idea of personal transformation appeals to you, then you already have some sense of wanting or needing significant improvement in one or more areas of your life.

For example, the Wheel of Life Personal Assessment you undertook as part of your Life Plan 1.0 may have identified one or more areas where your satisfaction is relatively low (the current state). If you went on to designate where you want that satisfaction level to be in five years (the future state), then you can see the gaps between where you are and where you desire to be. These are clues that performance-limiting mindsets, ineffective base programming, are working at cross-purposes with your conscious will, leading to disappointing outcomes.

At this point in your Wisdom Journey, coach yourself to explore the mindsets that have created the world, the life you see. Given that our base assumptions are connected to so much of what we think and how we act, to unearth these programs is to position yourself for radical change. As you'll see later, radical change is inextricably linked to unwrapping these mental models, replacing them with better thinking, and then practicing new behaviors that emanate from this new thinking. However, the place to begin is an *analysis of your current effectiveness* in order to understand what thinking, what mindsets drove you to create the results you see in your life—the good, the bad, and the ugly. Analysis drills holes into the Comfort Zone, exposing the wiring implanted in the past so that it can be examined for how well it serves you today (see Figure 3.3).

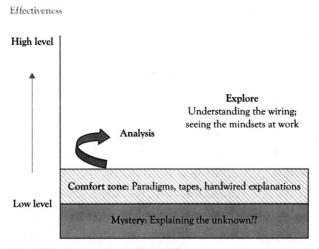

Figure 3.3. Effectiveness growth - explore.

In this analysis, *effectiveness* is in the context of your life purpose, the spirit you have been called to be. You have at least an initial sense of your purpose from the work you have done on your purpose statement in the Life Plan. This provides an immediate focal point. You don't need to learn to be highly effective in everything; the goal of transformation is to become highly effective in expressing your particular purpose, your reason for being here. Similarly, your transformational coaching with a team or an organization will focus on efforts within those areas encompassed by the team's charter, or the organization's mission.

The subjects of your analysis are the *past results* you have created in your life, the outcomes generated by your thinking, and the actions that arose from it. Getting full value out of this analysis rests on your willingness to own these results. To refuse any responsibility for helping produce an outcome, and thus reject that your thinking and actions played any role in the results, is a performance-limiting mindset that stands firmly in the way of your growth. This is not to deny that other individuals may have been a party to these results; it is to acknowledge that you can change your own behavior, you can be more effective in similar circumstances going forward. A change in your behavior will ripple out to affect others, so do not discount your potential impact in any situation you face.

The objective of your analysis is a deeper understanding of the cause-and-effect relationships currently at work in your life. Explore what types of thinking, beliefs, and assumptions—the way you see the world and its workings—have led to what types of outcomes. Once these become visible to you, brought finally into the light of your consciousness, you'll see radical improvement opportunities that were hidden from you before. Sufi wisdom records, "Opportunity is in the wind," it surrounds you if you know how to see it. Your eyes will open to different ways of thinking, which in turn reveal new options for action.

You might begin by observing the results you have created to date in those areas in your Wheel of Life Assessment that you see as most important for fulfilling your purpose but where large gaps between current and future state are evident. How did you arrive at this point? Perhaps you started off with a conscious target, resolved to accomplish something specific, but as you moved forward, conflicting objectives came into play, you got off track, off purpose. What automatic responses were triggered, and what thinking, beliefs, or assumptions were behind them?

Because these belief systems are hardwired, part of your base programming, you currently think them to be true. But are they? It's time to extract from the deep well of *Knowing*, to ask, "How did I come to believe what I now assume to be correct?," "How did I come to know that what I believe is real, certain?," "How did I learn this particular automatic response to this particular situation?," "Why do I believe the world works a certain way?"

As Figure 3.3 illustrates, we do not like mystery and therefore rush to supply meaning so we can move on. In the process, we build upon both legitimate and false truths to create our comfort zone of beliefs and assumptions. The problem now is in discerning a deeper truth, and that involves suspending our belief systems, bringing into question why we do what we do.

In his autobiography, *The Story of My Experiments with Truth*, Mohandas Gandhi outlined his efforts to uncover the truth in such subjects as nonviolence and celibacy. Gandhi devoted himself to questioning why he and others rushed to violence as the automatic response for combating violence. Were there alternatives? Was it possible that in fact a more successful response might be the antithesis of returning violence for violence? He worked to understand in himself this automatic response to violence, and with the insights he gained, he offered and advocated a different world response, that of nonviolence.

Questioning what we believe is not a step backwards, but actually a process of evaluating foundation beliefs for how well they have served us as we strive to live a life full of purpose. Where necessary to be more effective in that purpose, we readjust or remove key belief blocks that have proven by their results to be barriers to our calling. We open up our spirits to be the creative force we were born to be, and the mind begins to become subordinate to the spirit.

High Performance and Performance-Limiting Mindsets

Mindsets operate as a lens that directly influences how we see ourselves, others, problems, opportunities, and the world. How we see influences the action we take, which impacts our performance and the results that we produce; these are the determinants of our effectiveness in one or more aspects of life. Some mindsets distort what we see, and lock us into a kind of syndrome where we keep experiencing the same things and responding the same way, only to receive the same unhappy outcomes. Other mindsets free us to see things and opportunities more clearly, to reveal that which may have been hidden from us before about ourselves and our relationship to life, and enable us to create generous, positive, even profound outcomes for the benefit of ourselves and others. It is a responsibility of a transformational coach to understand his own mindset(s) and shift from a mindset that is nonproductive to one that is associated with a high degree of effectiveness (performance). Otherwise the coach's performance-limiting mindsets become entangled with the performance-limiting mindsets of the individual or team he is coaching, and he risks all becoming mired in a self-reinforcing negative pattern that leads nowhere good. Self-observation and inquiry are the coach's essential tools for delving into habitual mindsets behind any negative patterns currently active in his life.

Mindsets are sourced from spirit; they are anchored in even bigger beliefs derived from *Being, Knowing, Relating,* and *Generating.* Many belief systems and mindsets are archetypal in that they are common to a great many people. The particular set of circumstances that led to their adoption as truth is perhaps unique to each individual, but the mental models themselves can be characterized in a general way, which is invaluable in identifying whether any may be active in an individual's life.

In our research, we've identified ten archetypal mindsets that impact effectiveness in work and the world.

These include five sets of what can be viewed as pairs of polar opposites; one mindset is consistently associated with poor or *nonproductive* results, and the other mindset with *high performance* that manifests as very productive results. The pairs are shown in Figure 3.4 and defined below. Consider these ten mindsets as you analyze your effectiveness and establish what mindsets and mental stances are behind the results you experience. Others may apply as well, but these are good starting points for beginning to recognize the kinds of beliefs and assumptions that may be behind the patterns that characterize your approaches to life.

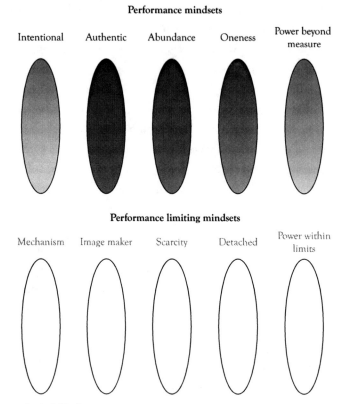

Figure 3.4. Mindsets.

Intention Versus Mechanism

- *Intention:* Sees will as a powerful force; has causal relationship to outcomes
- *Mechanism:* Views self as victim; excuse making and blaming

An intention mindset seeks to find the connection between personal will and the world. Willfulness is the driver for creation. The easiest way to see your intentions, both conscious and unconscious, is to examine past results. Your achievements point to your willfulness to achieve something you desire: It's your name on the diploma, the bank account, the auto title, and, by inference, the bumper sticker that says, "My Son is an Honor Student." You claim these accomplishments in part or whole, as you do many others. Congratulations, well done. Your successes are testimonials of perseverance and triumph over barriers.

Now what about the disappointing results to date? Whose name do we find on the divorce decree, the employment termination notice, the delinquent bank loan, and the school's letter about your child's discipline problem? Do you attribute the undesirable results to circumstances, other people, bad luck, or other mechanisms beyond your control? To deny any personal responsibility for the unwanted outcomes might stave off unwelcome blame, disappointment, guilt, and emotional hurt attached to these outcomes, but denial of your role robs you of the valuable lessons such experiences contain.

Intentional mindset leverages causal relationships. Holding an intentional mindset begins with viewing will as a powerful force of choice. And the lessons to be learned from generating the good, the bad, and the ugly *all* lead to a better understanding and appreciation of our wills. On the other hand, a mechanistic mindset is victim-based thinking; it is a cheap, temporal relief to remove yourself from the results you don't like. Once you choose a victim stance, you will constantly fulfill that expectation. You will remain a victim until you choose anther mindset. This is not to imply that what has happened to you in life is necessarily right, just, or deserved. But seeing the connection to all events opens the door to different choices and perspectives in the future, so that the unwanted doesn't occur again.

Authentic Versus Image Making

- *Authentic:* Identity derives from a strong sense of being
- *Image Making:* Distorts reality to fit the image of self; fear of looking bad

Living authentically is being grounded in a strong sense of your being, the essence of you, the core of who you really are. From work in the transformational sphere of Being, you discern the difference between being, doing, and having. What you do and what you have are not the source of meaning in your life, they don't tell the story of the real you. Finding identity in your enduring reason for being, your calling, is tough, but it is the foundation on which you are building the transformed you.

To project an image of oneself based on a work title, a social position, wealth, physical appearance, accomplishments, etc. is to uphold a false identity that does not represent your fundamental nature. These are but the outgrowth of what you do, or have, or wished you had.

An image-making mindset is cumbersome and energy sapping. Having to remember what image you are projecting is difficult as you change venues, from work to family to friends to strangers. But upholding an inauthentic image to *yourself* is the most taxing of all, a seven-day-a-week job of distorting reality to fit the image you have of self.

Rather, be both the God-inspired creature and the failed human you are. Take a moment to laugh at your fallibilities. It is true that you are a magnificent, benevolent creator one minute, and a buffoon the next. Isn't this a funny life, an interesting experience for the spirit?

Abundance Versus Scarcity

- *Abundance:* Sees possibilities in all situations; having everything one needs
- *Image Scarcity:* Sees limitations in all situations; never having enough

Do you see the possibilities in all situations, or do you focus on what is missing? Living in abundance speaks to the belief that you have all that is needed; what is wanted is present. By adopting this viewpoint, you look for ways to bring forth the creation sought.

Living in scarcity involves never having enough. Something is always wanted. Creativity drops as the waiting begins. "If only I had…" is the rally cry. And when that something is delivered, then something else is missing. Conflict arises with others who you believe have what you need. Since there is a limited amount, an insufficient amount for all to have, you fight to get your share.

Were you in an arid land, for instance, your scarcity mindset would likely focus on the absence of water. Given the soil's retarded ability to absorb water, when it does rain the runoff quickly collects into temporal fast-flowing rivers, producing life-threatening flash floods that kill a certain number of people each year. Still locked in your scarcity mindset, you see the situation now as one of too little water most of the time and too much water some of the time—undesirable situations in both cases about which you can do nothing.

If you were to adopt an abundance mindset instead, you could reframe the situation to see new possibilities. You might see that the problem with those occasions of too much water is that it is distributed in an undesirable pattern, which benefits only a few people. You envision the building of many micro dams that would catch the floodwaters without inundating large swathes of land. These catchments would not only control flooding but also provide a water source for nearby crops. And you see further that inexpensive and very efficient drip lines for irrigation, because they deliver water right to the base of each plant at a rate it can absorb, would make it possible to deliver water to even more crops. As a result, many farmers benefit over a longer period of time. This is the power of abundance thinking.

Oneness Versus Detached

- *Oneness:* Understands that all life is connected
- *Detached:* Sees little connection between self and the rest of the world

Oneness is tied to the understanding that all life is connected. Martin Luther King noted the connection of all and the error toward detachment:

Social psychologists tell us that we cannot truly be persons unless we interact with other persons. All life is interrelated, and all men are interdependent. And yet we continue to travel a road paved with the slippery cement of inordinate selfishness.[6]

Connected to each other, yes, and connected to something bigger. You form both separate and collective consciousnesses. This "both" may be confusing, and the default position might be to identify with the consciousness represented by a tangible body. But this would lead to a mistaken mindset. Albert Einstein said:

A human being is part of the whole called by us universe, a part limited in time and space. We experience ourselves, our thoughts, and feelings as something separate from the rest. A kind of optical delusion of consciousness. This delusion is a kind of prison for us, restricting us to our personal desires and to affection for a few persons nearest to us. Our task must be to free ourselves from the prison by widening our circle of compassion to embrace all living creatures and the whole of nature in its beauty. The true value of a human being is determined primarily by the measure and the sense in which they have obtained liberation from the self. We shall require a substantially new manner of thinking if humanity is to survive.[7]

Albert Einstein might be impressed with more recent evidence of what is called the quantum Zeno effect. Simply stated (as if anything concerning quantum physics can be simple), when an unstable particle is observed, its decaying pattern alters. In other words, the measuring of the particle causes a change in decaying behavior. Some cognitive scientists have used this finding to speculate about profound notions concerning the means by which conscious will effects change. You may indeed will the cosmos into being at a particle level.

On the other end of the spectrum, a detached mindset sees little connection with the world beyond the obvious physical contact. When you hold such a mindset, removing people or matter from your world disposes of their influence. You terminate someone from the office—they are gone. Send a computer into the landfill—it's gone. Draw a boundary around a township, county, or country and suddenly problems beyond that boundary have less impact on or concern for you. Draw enough boundaries around yourself, and you are isolated—others can't touch you.

Power Beyond Measure Versus Power Within Limits

- *Power Beyond Measure:* Having all the power you need; an unlimited supply of power is available
- *Power Within Limits:* Having too little power; power is granted from somewhere else

If you bemoan the lack of power to effect change, then you hold the mindset of power within limits. There is never quite enough power to get the job done; you await the next level in the pyramid structure to grant you the needed authority. You see power as bequeathed, granted by some other power.

Although positional power is a force, history tells us it is far from the only source. Revolutions are by nature the upsetting of the power structure, and there have been many revolutions in our past. Human history points to many great leaders who arose without the blessing of the power structure. Before they gathered followers, they believed they had the power to achieve what many thought impossible. The uplifting biographies of the underdogs fill the bookshelves. Do you believe you have all the power you need? With the mindset of power beyond measure, you undeniably do have all the power you require—the power to influence, the power of will, the power of connection, and the power born of tenacity. And unlimited power is available when you draw on power beyond what you can see, the power of the cosmos, of the Creator.

Your Connection to Results

Your analysis of current effectiveness is likely easily achieved when addressing your successes. Select something you are proud to have accomplished. How did you bring this accomplishment into reality? What truths do you believe guided you in this undertaking? List them down on a piece of paper.

Now, turn to something not so pleasant in your life—a failed relationship, an undiscovered passion, a dream not achieved. How did you bring about this happening? What mental models drove this result? Again, write them down. Your tendency most likely will be to assign responsibility for unwanted life occurrences to someone or something outside of you. If this is the case, then you will learn nothing from these experiences. Call on your internal coach to gently prod you through deeper inquiry until you see your connection with the results. Your internal coach tells you it is not a matter of blame or guilt, but a matter of connection. How were you involved? What did you choose to do or not do when the situation first developed? What did you see or avoid seeing early in the process?

In the case of poor or unwanted results, the mechanism (victim) mindset is often active. The mechanisms of life either conspired or just aligned to make a bad situation come about, despite your efforts. This mindset prevents growth. Or perhaps another mindset is at work: You believed that you didn't have enough power to have changed the situation then, or you moved quickly to detachment, having written off the incident and the people involved as no longer important to you. Whatever performance-limiting mindset might be at work, you distance yourself from the outcome—usually to avoid blame or hurt or disappointment—and thus keep yourself mired in an unhelpful, perhaps even destructive, pattern that dooms you to the same results in the future. It is only when you seek your connection to the outcome that you open yourself to discovering a better path—and generating better results—next time around.

Throughout your analysis, continue to return to your purpose, your reason for being, as the base against which you test your effectiveness. A result that appeared to be a failure at the time it occurred might look differently in light of what you now understand your purpose to be. Let's say that a couple years ago you tried to start up a small retail and service shop for computers and related electronics, but had no success in establishing a large enough customer base to support you and your family, and so you closed the business. Now, as you work on your Life Plan 1.0, you better define a strong calling to teach computer use as a way to empower people, and your vision is to provide in-home instruction to seniors and house-bound individuals to help them stay connected to family, agencies, businesses, and information that would otherwise be out of reach. In this context, the lack of success of your retail endeavor might be inconsequential to your true purpose and vision. It wasn't where your passion lay. Your intention in your analysis of current effectiveness is not to become better at retailing. Failures can often assist you in sharpening your purpose and shift you to a more powerful, aligned vision.

Enroll in New Mindsets: From Concept to Action

Your analysis in the Explore stage of the 3Es transformational coaching model led you to the discovery of the mental programs operating within you, some (perhaps several) of which are sources of unproductive behavior that have generated undesirable results in the past. This new understanding is an important step in the transformation process but not the end goal. The next step is Enroll in more productive mindsets, to reprogram your thinking so that new behaviors are possible. But not everyone successfully shifts gears to the Enroll stage of the process.

An Eddy of Consciousness

Some individuals trap themselves between the Explore and Enroll stages. They are content with knowing the cause of their ineffective behaviors; and they might use this knowledge to excuse or even justify their dysfunctional conduct. Self-justification is not self-understanding.

Let me give you an example. I observed a leader I was coaching respond angrily toward an individual who had just brought him the update he had requested on a customer service issue. I later questioned the leader, "Why the outburst of anger? The individual just did what you had asked of him." In an off-handed manner, he explained the reason for his flash of anger, "We're been having a problem with a manufacturing process that's been producing quality problems ever since we put it in place. I've been really frustrated over that." He then acknowledged that the individual was neither the source of the customer service problem nor directly in charge of solving it, nor had any direct involvement with the manufacturing issue. The leader sat back as if the discussion had been brought to a satisfactory closure, content that he knew the origins of his bad behavior. He gave no indication that his behavior should have been different, or that he was committed to behaving differently in the future. He might as well have declared, "Hey, that's just me. Get used to it." Even the possibility of apologizing to the wronged individual did not occur to him as a possible response to the situation. Without further inquiry on my part as his coach, the opportunity for real change would stall, go nowhere.

Just having the understanding of what drives our behaviors is insufficient to create transformative change. You gain awareness, becoming more conscious of why you do what you do, which is a fertile place from which to make a leap. But if you return to your comfort zone, like an eddy in a river, where the water simply turns in a localized whirlpool, nothing moves forward. Insights become just excuses, which feed inaction, reinforcing this eddy of consciousness (see Figure 3.5). Your understanding must be directed toward change, otherwise no new mindsets

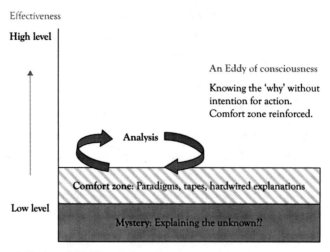

Figure 3.5. An eddy of consciousness.

emerge, no new behaviors arise, and you can count on seeing the same outcomes. Steer clear of this form of analysis paralysis, which keeps you confined to your comfort zone. Instead, break the circular flow of excuse-offering, commit to a different response to an experience or problem, and the creative energy of your spirit will flow productively toward greater effectiveness in life.

The S-Curve of Increasing Effectiveness

The Enroll stage of the 3Es transformational coaching model opens the door to decoupling from unproductive mental models and inserting new ones that will eventually give rise to new patterns of behavior, new actions by you that generate better results. I won't mislead you into thinking this is easy, particularly since the real work here occurs in the "heat" of living, as it were, while the world is in your face, with no time-outs, no retakes. What's more, you practice a "new you" with the world watching. At times it will feel like high-wire practice without a net. Perhaps you are beginning to sense why self-coaching is absolutely essential at this stage. It won't be difficult to manufacture excuses for turning back, especially if you stumble or don't get the result you thought you would. A new mindset doesn't just miraculously take hold; like any growing thing, it must be planted and nurtured and from time to time pruned until its roots are deep and its expression in the world is lush and bearing the fruits it promised.

All that said, if you understand how behavior change occurs, you'll find the process less daunting as you experience it. You'll appreciate that what you might be experiencing at the moment is a normal part of the process. And you'll take heart when you recognize the signs of real progress. The 3Es Transformational Coaching model visualizes the process of transformational change as a series of the S-shaped curve shown in Figure 3.6. (Similar curves are used to depict rates of learning over time in economic analysis, psychology, and other fields). The S-curve of increasing effectiveness notes the difficulty in beginning a new way of thinking and behaving. You must first be willing to risk making a change in one area, to move out of your comfort zone into unfamiliar territory. Progress in effectiveness is neither straightforward nor immediate. In fact, effectiveness might even drop for a time as you engage in an unfamiliar behavior, but with practice your effectiveness grows; feedback enables you to further fine-tune your "technique"; and your improvement in effectiveness attains breakthrough levels—the true measure of transformation in the area of focus. You have mastered one area and are ready to move on to the next.

Choose the first area to focus on based on your analysis of current effectiveness, an area where a change in mindset offers significant potential

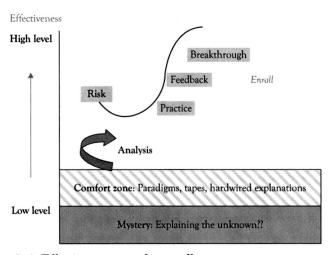

Figure 3.6. Effectiveness growth - enroll.

for improvement in results. This might be an area where your Wheel of Life Assessment in your Life Plan noted a large gap between current and future state; ideally it is also an area where you feel a high degree of energy and motivation to change.

To get a feel for how the S-Curve in Figure 3.6 might play out in the Enroll stage of self-coaching, consider the following example. You are a professional basketball player, superb at right-hand dribbling—you are simply the world's best. You *are* your right hand, and the opposition is mesmerized by your moves as you successfully charge the basket. You are riding high until an opposing team puts into place an effective defense against your right-hand dribble. Soon other teams have copied the strategy, and your attempts to move the ball down the court for a score are increasingly stymied. What would be the logical counter move for you to take, given the strong defense of you right side? Your coach naturally says, "Practice your left-hand dribble." Having little or no skill with your left hand, you protest. Maybe you claim it is unfair for the opposition to guard your right side to such a degree, a mindset that, in the very next game, proves a futile response to the situation. True, an external factor—the opposition's improvement in their defensive effectiveness— has eroded your on-the-court effectiveness; you didn't ask for this, it's not your fault, but it is the new reality you face in your work life. "You want them to drop a strategy that's working?" your coach asks. "It's not going to happen, fella. So that attitude gets you nowhere. If you want things to get better, then the ball is in your court."

You finally accept that you're the one who has to make the change, and you choose to believe that you have all the power you need to succeed. You risk left-hand dribbling. Since your skill level with your left hand is poor, you lose the ball, which unleashes some hearty taunts from the opposing team's supporters, and you experience moments of humiliation as your overall performance dips. But with enough practice and your coach's support, you start to improve. Positive feedback—including an uptick in team wins and your per-game scoring, accelerates your left-hand performance. When you reach a level of proficiency with your left hand, the game breaks open. The opposition's defense falls apart when confronted with your awesome versatility, your ability to change your offensive tactics in an instant.

Your effectiveness soars, and you eventually attain a new, higher plateau of performance. This outcome hadn't seemed all that probable when you took your first left-hand dribbles, but you continued, you stayed the course, and you look back now on the whole experience with a great deal of satisfaction.

Enrolling into new mindsets and behavioral patterns can be difficult, especially since you have had some success seeing the world a particular way. Learning to ask questions when you have been rewarded for knowing all the answers is a big adjustment. Listening when you are noted for telling others what must be done is trying. Asking for help when you are normally the first to lend a hand is tough. All are left-hand dribbling challenges.

You might fear taking a risk with change because it could temporarily reduce your effectiveness. But without the risk, there is no development. If you must, mitigate the risks by experimenting where the stakes are smaller; practice where there are fewer hazards.

Perhaps you fear looking foolish in front of others and so you hesitate to try a new behavior. Ask yourself if this might be an image-making mindset at work. People will have positive or negative thoughts about you regardless of the risks you take. So coach yourself to just move forward. It's only life; you never got a chance to rehearse for it. Losing the ball is part of the experience. If you saw it on YouTube with someone else in the starring role, you'd think it was funny. So learn to laugh at yourself.

In the end, you have what you need. It isn't about intelligence or savvy; rather it's just a matter of going out there and doing it, failing and doing it again until you succeed. A key tenet of Taekwondo, the Korean martial art, is Indomitable Spirit (Baekjul Boolgool), which speaks to maintaining inner strength regardless of winning or losing. A related saying advises, "Fall down seven times, get up eight." The enrolling process is rooted in taking the risk and having the spirit grow in the experience.

One of my favorite quotes, which forms my personal mantra, is from John Paul Jones. Considered to be the Father of the American Navy, he earned tributes in an extremely difficult time, the American Revolution. Neither from among the privileged nor from a highly honored family, he threw himself into the freedom fight with unorthodox methods. Greatly focused on winning battles, he met with several colonial captains of the weak American Navy to discuss how best to beat the British. Instead of battle strategies, the captains concentrated on the style and ornamentation of their uniforms as compared with those worn by British captains. Enraged, Jones sent a letter to Robert Morris, a friend and member of the Marine Committee that oversaw the navy. "We have had sundry meetings here for this purpose without being able to effect anything," wrote Jones, who had therefore decided to make his own suggestions about battle strategies. "I have determined," he continued, "that if I subscribe to nonsense it shall be nonsense of my own, not that of others!"[8]

There is much nonsense in this world. Knowingly subscribing to others' nonsense is a grave mistake. You can decide to go along with other people's thinking, believing they must know what they are doing, or you can strike out with your own spirit. You might be wrong; you might fall, seven times even, but getting up eight is the true testimonial to your spirit.

Encourage Continuous Growth in Consciousness and Effectiveness

Once breakthrough or transformational change has been achieved in one area, the performance flattens out, as attested by the S-curve. You have gained the bulk of the benefits in one area. Now the experiment continues in another area. Encourage yourself to stretch out and risk again. The S-shape curve is approached once again. (See Figure 3.7.)

When a pattern for transformation has been internalized, a short cut can be accessed quickly to create another steep growth curve. Take a meaningful look at the results you are creating, assess if these results are in line with purpose/vision/values, and if so celebrate your purposeful living. For the results that are not in alignment, ask questions of yourself concerning your role and mindsets in creating such results. Again, don't move to self-judgment, move to self-evaluation.

Encouragement involves reflection of past growth in effectiveness and its consciousness underpinning. What was learned? What discoveries

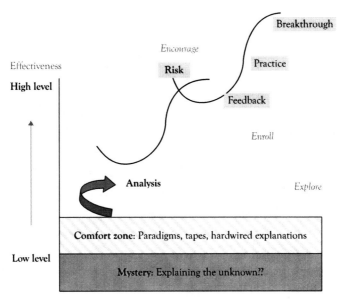

Figure 3.7. Effectiveness growth - encourage.

were made in Being, Knowing, Relating, and Generating? How did the experience inform your spirit and the flowing mindsets? How was your understanding of your calling matured?

Quiet, focused, and routine reflection is a key to continued growth. Jumping into the next day without giving thought to the previous day or becoming centered on the day ahead is choosing unconscious living. Often when things are going well or the pressures of a self-imposed busy schedule crowd our "free time," time to reflect is abandoned. Make reflection, through study, meditation, and/or prayer, a daily requisite. And then periodically, monthly as a minimum, set aside time to review your life plan and your progress. Reflect. Make adjustments to the plan as you benefit from new self-discoveries.

Also, sharing your journey with a trusted friend or partner is a powerful reflection approach. I better assess my level of clarity when I share my plan and journey, having to articulate my learning to someone else. Choose a person who is also on a purpose journey and exchange life plans. Hearing yourself outline where you are going, your vision, and your results to another can bring valuable insights.

Journaling

Keeping a journal of your learnings and insights helps paint a progressive picture of your development along the Wisdom Journey. Capturing your insights in writing generates a rich, complex internal dialog that reveals themes of understanding. Write with abandonment; don't censor your insights. It is this internal voice that will serve to strengthen your resolve for the next growth curve.

At the conclusion of each entry, I suggest capturing the "so what." What is the takeaway from the internal dialog? What does it mean for going forward? What call to action might it reveal?

Review your vision in light of your learnings. Rewrite your vision given the experience. In his book *Synchronicity: The Inner Path of Leadership,* Joseph Jaworski emphasizes the importance of capturing a clear, specific vision:

> It is through language that we create the world, because it's nothing until we describe it.... To put it another way, we do not describe the world we see, but see the world we describe.[9]

And journaling in difficult times pays extra dividends. To directly confront your fears—fear of failure, of non-acceptance, even of accomplishment itself—will hearten you during stressful times. Along these lines, Peter Marshall, the noted Presbyterian minister of the first half of the twentieth century, offers the following prayer:

> When we long for life without difficulties, remind us that oaks grow strong in contrary winds and diamonds are made under pressure.[10]

Finally, journaling pulls you back into the Life Plan document. The reflections and learnings you record in the journal stir the spirit and strengthen its voice. Return to your descriptions of your purpose, vision, values, and actions to be taken, and listen to what your spirit has to say.

Developing Insights

1. Reflect upon the mindsets that contributed to your interactions with others today. What mindsets were at work in moving you forward or backward in your relationships?
2. What productive mindset(s) do you believe you have obtained high proficiency in? What evidence do you have to support this claim?
3. What productive mindset(s) are you having the most difficulty holding? What about the countering performance-limiting mindset(s)? What inside of you holds onto the performance-limiting mindset(s), and why?

CHAPTER 4

Coaching Individuals for Transformative Change

Once in mystery of how the world works, an individual—let's call her Linda—has assigned meaning to each life experience. Positive impacts—as well as negative—carved paths that dried into permanence over time, a geography of predictable responses—her comfort zone for moving within the world. Now when similar situations present themselves, she is ready with actions that arise automatically from embedded paradigms, which have the permanence of concrete, barring any conscious attempt to change them. In other words, she is where you were before you began your personal transformation journey (although your respective comfort zones might look like different countries if viewed side by side).

As a leader, perhaps Linda has created many successes in her career, and possibly in other aspects of life as well. She has been living from her comfort zone, hardwired for a certain degree of success because past outcomes reinforced specific responses as a fruitful strategy in many work-related situations. Past success, however, is a two-edged sword for Linda. Her profession, her company, her industry, and, as a result, her job have all undergone massive change in the last several years. For her, these tsunamis have somehow rendered ineffective many of her past strategies and tactics, once so reliable for getting done what needed to be done.

She may have read a number of management texts and even tried to put new practices in place for herself, but they don't seem to stick. She continuously finds herself slipping back into what used to be tried-and-true methods and behaviors, with a noticeable lack of positive results. At this point, she is mystified. She has shared her frustration with her boss (who, coincidentally, might be you), who has seen her struggle in situations but believes she is committed to learning and growth.

In organizations this is often the situation with the people who might seek transformational coaching. They are leaders trying to lead in radically changed circumstances for which their past experience has not prepared them, and their embedded mindsets throw up roadblocks to seeing or learning new approaches. As discussed in chapter 1, this is, in fact, the situation that a great many individuals increasingly face in their work and personal lives.

Your role as a transformational coach is to awaken such individuals to a future of conscious creation, to help them build greater effectiveness within the aspects of their lives where they feel dissatisfied or greatly challenged, or where their organization looks for a much higher level of contribution than they seem currently able to deliver. As chapter 3 emphasized, your ability to effectively coach such individuals in a one-to-one context hinges upon achieving a level of competence in coaching yourself toward self-mastery. Self-mastery is the cornerstone for building meaningful relationships with other individuals. You've gained a deeper understanding and appreciation of self, moving away from the auto-response mode. Falling awake will always be a challenge, but your spirit is becoming more perceptive about the mind/body relationship and directing the way. Engaging in a coaching relationship, however, will test you in new ways even beyond the acquisition of new skills. You will be putting your spirit on the line, testing your ability to hold ego at bay and maintain self-awareness even as you guide another in awakening to spirit and expanding self-awareness. Coaching will be a growth process for you, a continuation of your wisdom journey, even as it launches others on their own journey toward transformation.

As issues arise in a coaching session, a coach must possess a sufficient degree of self-awareness to avoid getting hooked by the subject at hand. Coaching techniques are of little value if the coach is sound asleep to the self. Unfortunately, it is not unusual to see a less than fully competent coach move from effective listening to a dysfunctional working of personal psychological patterning or agendas. Living the productive mindsets within yourself allows you to assist others without such entanglement. A sufficient degree of self-awareness enables both empathetic listening and purity of engagement, that is, involvement uncontaminated by the coach's issues.

Do not confuse the reach for self-awareness and purity of engagement with the objectivity of a clinician, such as a physician or psychotherapist, who is for the most part engaged in a transactional relationship with a patient or client. Unlike medicine or clinical psychology, there are no standard diagnostic codes or accepted treatment protocols in transformational work. The source of wisdom regarding what will lead the individual to greater effectiveness and growth is accessible through spirit, not mind. To connect with another person at a spirit level, the transformational coach consciously brings forth her own authentic being and stays present to the being of the other. This is a most profound, sacred connection in which the energies of the two parties interact. Two spirits are engaged in determining the nature of life force and how to be most effective in the world. This is not to say that a physician's or psychotherapist's relation to a patient or client never develops to this degree: Certainly we value, for instance, the physician who connects with a patient at a spirit level when conveying a diagnosis of terminal illness, information that can quickly bring the patient to the precipice of a transformative experience. But clinicians are not trained to relate at this level; this intimacy of interaction is not part of the treatment model.

Mind-to-mind engagement is well suited to cases where a person requires technical advice for base skill development, a type of engagement frequent in our daily lives inside and outside work. What's called for is an intellectual response sourced from experience and subject knowledge. But guiding someone toward radical improvement in personal and professional effectiveness requires a connection at a much deeper level. It might seem counterintuitive, but it is often easier to start at this new level of being when no relationship has existed prior to the coaching relationship. Backing into a meaningful spirit-to-spirit coaching relationship can be a difficult transition from a long-standing relationship based on a mind-to-mind connection. Nonetheless, it is necessary, and it can be achieved. We deal with this in more depth later in the chapter, in the context of the challenge of a leader providing transformational coaching to a direct report.

Creation of the Transformational Coaching Relationship

Your experiences in self-coaching required that you "give birth" to a nurturing internal coach who would spur you to deeper inquiry, reflection, trying on new ways of thinking, finding the courage to embark on new ways of acting, staying the course through disappointments, and celebrating successes. Now you the whole being moves into the role of coaching another individual, who has a free will and hardwired patterns and motivational make-up largely (perhaps entirely) unknown to you—as are yours to him or her. The quality of the relationship you build together will be a determinant of the success of the coaching engagement. The nature of the relationship you will co-create might be well beyond the bounds of the person's prior experience. And in your initial coaching engagements, you too will likely find yourself in entirely new territory, with new relational challenges, not the least of which will be holding two spirit-sets simultaneously: self-awareness, which brings forth authenticity, and the oneness of spirit-to-spirit relationship with another.

Your authentic spirit should walk through the door first. Who you are and the life purpose that drives your actions should become quickly apparent to the other person. This is not to say you begin by babbling on about your life plan. But with your genuine spirit leading your mind and actions, you can begin the coaching conversation by sharing what coaching another has to do with your being, why you wish to engage with this particular person, what brought you to this action of connecting with this person.

The coaching relationship then evolves through the work you do together in the three stages of the 3Es Transformational Coaching Model for coaching individuals (discussed in later in this chapter). However, initially, the person may not feel comfortable engaging with you in an open, honest conversation about problems and areas of ineffectiveness, and it may take a bit of time, perhaps several sessions, to develop a sufficient level of trust before the individual is ready to take a risk on you. The individual's native communication comfort zone may at first inhibit certain conversations. Beyond this, social and organizational norms for communication could stand in the way, as James Flaherty notes in his book, *Coaching: Evoking Excellence in Others*:

> The forces shaping communication remain invisible to participants within a given culture or organization. Participants are unaware that they are, in fact, not speaking about certain topics and not bringing up certain ideas, or that they are inhibiting others

from speaking to them. When an outsider attempts to broach these subjects, many excuses are immediately presented to justify the continuation of the moratorium on them.... What can a coach do to ensure that freedom of expression exists in a coaching relationship, even when the dynamics described are in place? First, the coach can recognize that freedom of expression has to be constructed within an individual coaching relationship.[1]

Broadly, you focus on beginning the coaching relationship at a level that allows the trust and sharing essential to progress. Particularly in organizations, you and the individual may already have some kind of relationship; if so, demonstrate that a new beginning is under way. You are moving the relationship to a meaningful, spirit-to-spirit level. Social norms, diversity differences, and organizational culture are playing their songs and should be considered; you'll need to get past these. Yes, be cognizant of not destroying the opportunity for initial connection by leading with an aggressive spirit. But hesitation to be fully authentic at this moment will cost you time and effort in getting to real transformative coaching. How fast can you safely move to getting real spirit to spirit?

Social interactions are highly influenced by the cultural context, especially in the initial introductions. These social mores are easier to acknowledge than to extinguish. Honor the traditions of coming together, but after the customs have been observed, it is time to dive into more substantial meaning. Not until you reveal and offer your spirit can an uplifting, generative relationship be formed.

So, move the conversation toward deeper disclosure of your purpose for being, and inquire into the spirit of the other person. From your work in coaching self to discover your purpose for being, you are equipped to handle such a conversation of exploration. Move beyond the clutter of social conversation to share what holds true meaning for you in daily life and how your life's calling is directed toward this purpose; this allows the other person to see the spirit of you. If the individual momentary recoils, be patient. Learn how to transition from the ordinary to the meaningful. Importantly, do not dwell on projecting image or indulging image making by the other person; at best, this leads to a mutual appreciation of each other, and at worst, to an ego battle.

3Es Transformational Coaching for Individuals

Using the 3Es Transformational Coaching model in Figure 4.1, you'll skillfully move individuals through the stages of Explore, Enroll, and Encourage. The stages will be similar to those you employed in coaching self, in chapter 3, but now with a focus on the other person's story:

- *Explore* with the individual, in a process of co-discovery/ co-assessment, his/her consciousness level, current mindsets, and performance effectiveness.
- *Enroll* the individual into productive mindsets, new ways of thinking and being informed by purpose and vision.
- *Encourage* the individual in a journey of continuous personal growth in consciousness, effectiveness, and awareness.

As we move through each of the three stages, let's assume that the person you are coaching is a leader in an organization, perhaps someone similar to Linda, whom you met at the start of the chapter.

Explore

As a transformational coach, you seek, through general conversation about the nature of the problems and/or opportunities facing the leader,

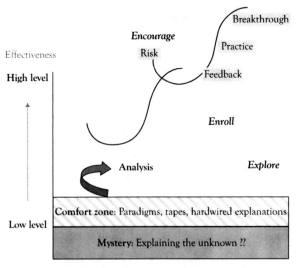

Figure 4.1. Effectiveness growth.

to determine the level of consciousness and the macro constructs used in the leader's storyline. The storyline reflects how the person makes sense out of life experience to date, the movement out of mystery and into a comfort zone of ascribed meaning, manifest as paradigms and beliefs (see Figure 4.1). Your coaching ear listens to the language the other person uses, which provides insights into thinking and degree of wakefulness: "I tried but they prevented me from accomplishing …" is disempowering language that signals a victim reality and a self-justification rather than creation focus, whereas "I tried and failed and here is what I learned about myself …" suggests an individual in a creation mode who exercises personal will and owns the outcomes.

You ascertain how the leader sees the current situation and personal responsibility for the current state—the degree of personal causality. How did the current state become what it is, both the positive and negative attributes? Encourage the person to probe deeply in order to be explicit about his or her thinking process relative to the current situation. Your goal at this point is to understand the leader's working mindsets.

Ask questions that go beyond the story's content to explore the storyline as a conscious act of personal creation. As you develop deep listening skills as a coach, you will learn to discover the purpose of others as manifested in their "creations"—the outcomes in their lives to date—a purpose that may conflict with their notions of who they see themselves as being.

As a good listener, routinely check understanding by repeating the story being told. Ask frequently if you have captured the story. This helps to clarify the leader's own understanding, bringing personal truths and beliefs into the light of consciousness. In this sense, the Explore stage is very much a process of co-discovery, of co-assessment of the leader's current effectiveness and the thinking patterns that drive actions and approach to the world. It's not enough for the coach to detect these patterns; the goal at this stage is expanding the leader's self-awareness and consciousness, allowing the leader to see his or her backside, the aspect of self that is holding back performance.

The Explore stage should reveal the spirit expression and operating mindsets of the individual. Remember, the spirit informs the mind, so the mindsets are flowing from the person's spiritual attributes—the description of their spirit. You could call these characteristics of the spirit a "spirit-set," and they inform the thinking programs known as mindsets. Through careful listening, you will discover the often deeply conditioned "spirit-set" in the story line. However, you do not move into problem solving concerning the immediate difficulties the leader faces; you avoid taking on the guise of expert and "fixer." Keep the focus on co-discovery of the individual's effectiveness and intentions. These are the underlying issues that must be brought into full awareness; current problems, regardless of how painful they might be, are just the surface symptoms.

As with the Life Plan in your own wisdom journey, the leader's clarity about purpose, vision, values, and operating principles is essential for creating a context and a direction for transformation. Through conversation, delve into the level of awareness about the person's reason for being (purpose), the specificity of what the person desires to create (vision), and the values and operating principles that set the boundaries for the manner in which this vision will be achieved. Talk through the role of these life-planning elements in producing a directional map. (Revisit the discussion of these elements in chapter 2's section on the Wisdom Journey.) Avoid simply handing over the Life Plan document as an assignment. Instead, take the time to explain how the life-planning tool aids people in better aligning their efforts and actions with the calling of spirit, to direct their creative energies toward that which holds great meaning for them. You can use your own life plan at a high level to demonstrate how it aided your focus. (The Life Plan document is in Appendix 4.1.)

Enroll

Enroll the leader in further crystallizing the purpose/vision/values in his or her Life Plan 1.0. The Life Plan helps to highlight the challenges ahead, that is, the gap between the current state and the life the leader wants to have. This provides you with an opening to enroll the leader into new ways of being and doing, to get buy-in for embarking on the "maiden" S-curve of improved effectiveness in Figure 4.1. Inquire about the leader's success in achieving difficult objectives and where the drive to persevere originated. Explain how to work from the inside out, from spirit to the mind and then to the body.

There will be areas of discontent, where results are not forthcoming. Ask why the person acts in such a way that fails to produce different results. The co-discovery probably will point to past actions that were at one time successful. In other words, the *mystery* that once existed was replaced with actions that created a *comfort zone.* And when new and different circumstances presented themselves, the person reached into these comfort zone actions and hoped for similar success. Striving for a higher level of consciousness, help the person probe the mindsets behind the actions. Uncovering the mindsets informing these actions opens the door to change.

The closed loops of current problem sets can be broken if the person can see more productive ways of approaching situations to generate different results. Use the high-performance mindsets (chapter 3) and conversations about possibilities to broaden the leader's conception of available options. For instance, if a *scarcity* mindset informs past decisions, enroll the person into considering the alternative outcomes possible with an *abundance* mindset. Maybe actions are being driven by the belief that there is only so much money, resources, recognition, energy, or rewards available. Offer the possibility that a limiting mindset may be producing the low performance outcomes. Remove these constraints in the individual's mind in order to expand possibilities; ask the "what if" question around limitless resources. Possibilities will flow. The conversation will move to ways of tapping into the limitless and away from constraints.

Through a dance of inquiry, feedback, and sometimes bold assertions, you help the leader to assess the risks/costs of *not changing*—of staying locked in current mindsets and behaviors—vis-à-vis the potential benefits of alternative approaches that better align with the individual's passion and values and bring a vision closer to reality. You help the person face the risks the might come *with change*, and to evaluate them relative to the potential gains.

Often people become so vested in a way of seeing the world, the story they tell reflects hard-and-fast assertions of "the way it is." The old seeing found within our comfort zone is more than the boundaries within which we operate; it often becomes who we think we are. Finding the best question to chip away at the hard exterior of a particular set of circumstances can be a challenge. Hopefully you will have built a sufficient foundation of trust that the person permits you to suggest other ways to view the same state of affairs. You present these as different perspectives for viewing the problems and challenges facing the leader, being careful to not push the individual to accept an alternative. You are offering suggestions in order to spur alternative thinking, which can produce breakthroughs. True transformation of the individual, of relationships, of organizations is possible when a "new seeing" emerges.

To better see this, think of your role as that of a suit salesperson. Your customer, the leader, has a problem with the types of suits he wears and wants your help. You have taken great care in the Explore stage to understand him and his needs, the circumstances in which he wants to wear a new suit, the type of suit he typically wears, and why it is no longer serviceable going forward. You are now enrolling the customer to the idea of buying a suit that will best meet his needs. You draw on your expertise, which comes from your own experience in choosing and wearing new suits (your journey of self-transformation), as well as the experience of other customers and experts in the field, to offer different "suits of ideas" for the leader to try on. You work in consultation with the customer, offering suggestions, avoiding any temptation to steer him toward a purchase that might prove be a straitjacket for him. You recognize that satisfaction with the suit will rest, at least in part, on the customer making the choice and "owning" the decision as his. His options are to buy the suit of ideas you are offering, alter the suit of ideas to better fit his needs, or to simply reject the whole idea of replacing his old suit with a new one.

Work with the leader not only on the different ways of seeing the current state but also on projecting the multiple outcomes possible. Help paint the journey ahead. What new approaches could be taken now and what openings for new, powerful results are possible? With the leader steeped in deeper insights, proceed toward enrollment of the leader to take action. Outline possible next steps. Reach some agreement to move forward, understanding that risk will certainly be part of the new practice. In fact, there is a high probability that in employing a different approach there may well be initial setbacks. You didn't learn to ride a bike the first try. The S-curve in Figure 4.1 shows a dip in early adaptation of new practices. Create realistic expectations for what experiences and challenges might come with putting new practices into action. Perseverance will shorten the learning cycles and ensure breakthrough occurs.

A great temptation, particularly for unseasoned coaches, and a major threat to a fruitful coaching relationship, would be for you to think that you know what is best for the individual. Your enrollment process then becomes one of convincing the person to follow a certain path. And sometimes, quite frankly, individuals being coached will falter on the side of asking for too much guidance rather than drawing on their own spirit to paint the way forward. Ben Zander and Rosamund Stone Zander speak of this process in their book, *The Art of Possibility*. "Enrollment is not about cajoling, tricking, bargaining, pressuring, or guilt-tripping someone into doing something your way. Enrollment is the art and practice of generating a spark of possibility in others to share."[2]

The transformational coach seeks to awaken individuals to their own possibilities, to have them begin to think in terms of increasing their engagement with life and seeing risk as an opportunity for growth in consciousness. Avoid thinking of yourself as the fount of all wisdom or the source of all answers; your role is to facilitate the individual's growth and transformational leap in large part by opening them to the source of wisdom that lies within their own being.

Encourage

Moving with the leader through the risk-taking and practice phases of new performance curves is one place where the coach's encouragement is welcome. When setbacks arise as a result of taking risks, as anticipated in the enrollment phase, hearten the leader to practice the new behaviors until a level of proficiency is reached. Support the leader when feedback comes in the form of performance/outcomes of the new behaviors (sourced from purposefulness and performance mindsets). Encourage the leader to move forward and not regress to the comfortable but unproductive ways.

Let's take an example using the same shift from a scarcity to an abundance mindset and resulting behaviors. I worked with a state manager tasked with leading a particular social service. He described the situation as one where the desired results appeared impossible given budget restraints and an existing service delivery model with state employees.

When I encouraged him to view the situation from the perspective of abundance, he noted that a great many citizens, dissatisfied with inadequate results, had expressed concerns—they saw the service as an important one. He also noted that the work of other departments overlapping the efforts of his department. So there appeared to be an abundance of energy to address the issue of having enough labor to deliver services. He envisioned a solution for increasing performance by expanding the service delivery model to include additional volunteer labor and achieving better sharing of state labor resources across department lines.

Now, involving volunteers and breaking down silos between departments are huge tasks, with lots of barriers. Simply having a good idea and implementing a solution are two different things. Understandably, this leader experienced setbacks as he moved in a new direction with the new intention of focusing resources not under his direct control. We talked about the choice of going back to the old problem set—constrained resources unable to meet demand—or continuing on the new course of learning how to gather and deploy the abundance of resources that had a high interest in addressing service performance. He moved forward. Although experiencing many falls, he did not fail. My role was to help keep *his* declared purpose, vision, and values at a conscious level and put risks in the context of *his* calling.

One of this state manager's learnings was a newfound appreciation of language. In this case, the language of scarcity is evident in expressions of limitations: "Not enough," "If there was only more," "There is only so much," "This is what there is, all I have to work with." The language of abundance seeks possibility and opens up sources: "What if there was more?," "Where is there additional energy for this in the universe?," "Who else shares my passion for this?" By looking at his language, he could spot any slippage back to the scarcity mindset. By changing the way he spoke to himself and others, he could better access the abundance mindset. The coach helps leaders to apply this access language to high performance mindsets, and likewise to recognize when his/her language is accessing a performance-limiting mindset. It can become a short script technique to consciousness and redirection. This is encouragement in action.

New mental models and new access language are in place, but they will set deep roots only with engagement and practice, and atrophy without them. Old thinking patterns will re-emerge. As coach, you want to reinforce the person's ability to fall awake (heighten awareness) in crisis, to remain effective through tsunamis of change, keeping self-awareness and creation flowing strongly rather than dropping back into the spiritually hopeless, powerless state of the zombie.

After the person has had a positive experience of breakthrough performance, it may be tempting to level off to a new comfort level after the breakthrough. Resting on past growth is a potential danger. Neither life nor spirit exists in long-term homeostasis. Spirit grows with effort or declines without it.

Persuade the individual to move toward the next growth curve. Review together this cycle's learnings and celebrate the growth, building confidence in taking on new risks. Then move to define objectives for the next transformation cycle.

For Leaders Coaching Direct Reports

We have already touched on one of the challenges of transformational coaching in an organizational setting, an entrenched culture and communication style. Where a hierarchical structure of power is greatly emphasized, a relationship in which the leader is the transformational coach for a direct report can face other obstacles as well, to which the leader-coach should be prepared to respond.

Relationship to the Hierarchy

At the crux of transformation, particularly in an organizational setting, is the courage to break from a viewpoint that authority is the measure of individual worth, and to adopt instead a view that values a person's purpose and vision. We find that the best organizations today, the most effective, value individuals who are their "own person" over the dutiful zombie. Let's say that you are a leader-coach and will be coaching your direct report, Linda, the leader we met at the beginning of the chapter. Explore Linda's perspectives on the hierarchy; after all, you are technically part of the hierarchy, and your direct report's beliefs about the hierarchy could be projected onto you. Is she respectful of the organizational structure and the work of you and other senior leaders while conscious of her alignment between individual passion and energy and the goals of the organization? Or does she believe that the organization's goals supersede her own? Is she causal in her relationship with the hierarchy, or does she view herself as a victim of its decisions and actions? Depending on the person's current mindset with regard to the organizational hierarchy, the two of you may have work to do in this area as part of laying the foundation for a meaningful coaching relationship.

In your coaching sessions with your direct report, if you encounter a lack of openness around questions such as, "Why do you choose to put your energy into this organization?" or "What inside of you keeps you going during tough times?" take these as an indication that distrust already exists. Distrust means decreased effectiveness not only in the coaching relationship but also for your team, of which Linda is a member. If you are committed to leading a highly effective team, you are compelled to press forward with her to establish a trust-based relationship. This might also be a signal to you to reflect deeply on your past relationship with this person to discover what behavior on your part might have prevented trust from developing in your working relationship with each other. From your own journey of self-transformation, you have discovered the importance of a causal mindset in generating better outcomes in relationships as well as other aspects of life.

Earlier in the chapter we discussed the importance of presenting your spirit to the other person by openly sharing your purpose in life, your reasons for wanting to coach and so forth. The spirit-to-spirit relationship you are striving to co-create with a direct report requires equity. If you ask Linda how she relates to her work as part of the team, yet you are unwilling to share your personal motivations for participating in the collective work, you are signaling a low-trust environment as well as your participation in maintaining it. Time to return to your work on self to uncover the issues at play.

In either case, building the relationship to a higher level of trust will involve risk, exposure, and time investment.[3] When the workplace has been reduced to an analytical, task-oriented, spiritless environment, the awakened individual has a choice of either working to transform the environment (risk taking, yes) or to find another setting where spirit, this newfound energy sourced from knowing one's purpose, can flourish.

Performance Evaluation Versus Transformational Coaching

If you are a leader of an organization or a team or a project, you are continuously making decisions about your staff or team members' contributions based on the outcomes. You are evaluator and sometimes performance trainer with respect to their outcomes relative to performance expectations. In this capacity, when there are performance outages, you hold one or more conversations with the individual, who we'll call Ron in this example. You take on the perspective that Ron's performance is of his making—he "owns" his performance. The two of you agree on what actions on his part are necessary to turn performance around, and what support you and the organization are prepared to provide, including transformational coaching if you believe it might help, particularly in the case where skills training and similar measures have not led to improvement. However, it is imperative that you both clearly understand that your role as performance evaluator/trainer with respect to Ron's job is separate and different from your role as transformational coach. Your coaching role does not alter your responsibility as Ron's work supervisor to establish performance criteria, evaluate his work results, and hold him accountable for meeting expectations.

Clarify that performance evaluation conversations (and any future ones) will be separate from coaching conversations—establish clear cues, a changing of gears, between the two types of conversations or meetings, as the dynamics, including your role, will be different. Regardless of the outcomes of the coaching engagement, Ron is still held to the performance requirements of the current job as long as he remains in the role; engaging in coaching will not remove the consequences of continued poor performance.

You coach your report according to the same 3Es Transformational Coaching methodology as outlined earlier in this chapter. Your focus in this role is to move Ron toward greater self-awareness and high-performance thinking so that breakthrough change can take place. Frequently increased self-awareness will result in a performance turnaround in the job. On the other hand, the individual might discover a deeper connection to another type of role, which the organization may or may not be able to accommodate. He makes the choice of how to respond to his new awareness about his purpose and its degree of alignment with the current job.

Let's say that through the transformational coaching process, Ron becomes aware of his deeper purpose and discovers less alignment with the mission of the organization. Whether or not his actual performance on the job meets the organization's requirements, the time has arrived for Ron to find the place where his energy has the most value. I have experienced this throughout my career, even early on when I worked as a team manager and confronted individual performance issues. I have often found individuals who had great potential, great life energy that was not being directed toward the work at hand—a mismatch of personal purpose and organizational mission/vision. I have been continually surprised that once this mismatch surfaced in a coaching session, the individual often made a decision to move forward and leave the organization—leave not with anger but with an understanding that there was a better match elsewhere. With discovery of purpose and vision came the understanding that lack of performance was a matter of will, and the person chose to separate voluntarily.

Evaluation and employment actions (both positive and negative consequences) do take place—role redesign, transfers, move into a different job, voluntary termination. But with a now deeper understanding of purpose and vision, the employee is an active partner, better able to evaluate the degree to which his goals align with the organization, and exercising the power to change his situation if the fit is not a good one. The organization benefits by retaining people who, in finding a strong source of personal motivation to work toward organizational goals, can more fully align their creative energies with others in the organization.

The We-Being

Connecting with other conscious beings is a gift unlike any other. When working with a person at such a level for a period of time, the we-being might emerge. The two conscious individuals within the relationship can experience a tangible flow between them, a new construct, a new creation, beyond the obvious additive nature of two separate I-beings co-existing and communicating. A third voice emerges, a collective consciousness, a collective spirit sacred in the same manner as the individual spirit of creation. This miraculous formation, generative in nature, arises from the creative energy of each individual fueling and blending with the other's. The third voice gives rise to a collective mind, and the result is the "we-being," a new entity with certain characteristics—a voice, a personality, a creative capacity, and a presence—that an outside observer can easily distinguish from those of the two individuals. This we-being produces a higher level of performance when applied to projects outside of the relationship, such as creating transformational change in a team, organization, or society. The leader remains the leader, you remain the coach, but now there is the potential energy beyond the simple combination of your efforts to create great organizational performance.

You may have experienced this in only a few significant relationships, but the prospect of forming such powerful connections with countless others exists once you have learned to relate on a spirit-to-spirit level and the nature of the work at hand calls for close coordination. The transformational coaching relationships you develop with others are fertile ground for the we-being, especially when you are coaching a leader in a broader transformational effort, say within their organization to bring forth system-wide breakthrough. You and the leader become more conscious of the we-being you are experiencing, moving to co-created transformation and enjoying the sense of flow that accompanies it. You both share access to the collective wisdom and creative energy of the we-being, and thus your role as coach transitions toward one of encouragement and consulting. Obtaining a state of we-being with another allows for heightened coaching of both self and others. Eventually transcending the coach-leader traditional role to one of shared creation holds promising rewards.

We may hesitate to participate in we-being relationships for fear of losing our I-being. The we-being does not replace the I-being. Although the loud I-being voice may be subordinate to the we-being, the state of we-being does not eliminate the I-being consciousness; rather the individual holds two consciousnesses at the same time. It is in cults and similarly unhealthy constructs where the I-being voice disappears, robbing the individual of self and soul.

The popular axiom of "there is no 'I' in team" is likewise flawed. A team then of what? Performance research certainly gives credence to the existence of individual will and skill in high-performance teams. The members master the ability to hold an "I" mindset and a "we/team" mindset simultaneously. There is an "I" in "high-performance team."

Far from being lost to self, holding I-being and we-being consciousness harmoniously generates great power. If it helps, think of a tandem bicycle, a bicycle built for two. The two riders and the bike compose a single unit, clearly visible in sight and performance. Yet each rider also has the experience of being a single rider peddling the tandem bike. Each rider is an I-being and a we-being in the same moment. Similarly, strongly connected partners in dance or team play can experience the dual flow of I-being and we-being energies that result in great performances.

The maturation of the coaching relationship is a journey in itself. As the person you coach moves into a more enduring conscious creation mode, the prospect of co-creating, of building, the "we-being" becomes a real possibility. Recognizing the growing we-being voice can mark a significant growth step in the relationship.

Now for a short quiz. What do you get when two zombies come together? Easy answer when reviewed from a consciousness stance: Zero consciousness plus zero consciousness equals zero collective consciousness, and certainly it is zero sum for any multiplier effect. So, for the third voice to arise, the participants must be able to interact with each other in a deeper manner beyond questions about the weather or zombie-like social engagements. If an individual believes that a level of consciousness intimacy poses risk to the ego, to the constructed self-image, if he is unsure who he is apart from the image he projects, the we-being cannot develop. What arises between two individuals at this level of unconsciousness is at best mind meeting mind; a relationship created from mental constructs and often devoid of spirit or soul. Each has much work to do in the realm of self-mastery. For the "we-being" to emerge, both individuals must know who they are and why they exist—they must bring their wholeness of being to the relationship.

Your journey of self-transformation has taught you to bring forth your spirit. Your developing skills as a transformational coach make you increasingly effective in drawing out the spirit of others, giving them the experience of spirit-to-spirit relationships. If and when you co-create the we-being with another, you will come to appreciate the amplification of spiritual energy for generating new realities. You'll see the possibilities for teams, groups, and organizations to extend well beyond the aggregate efforts of their members and tap the greater magnitude and spiritual amperage of the we-being to create what might otherwise have been wholly impossible.

Developing Insights

1. Obtain agreement to coach someone. Explain your desire to develop skill in transformational coaching and solicit their help in allowing you to coach them. Enter into an agreement as to the number and length of coaching sessions.
2. Following this trial with transformational coaching, ask for feedback in terms of your effectiveness from the one you coached.

APPENDIX 4.1

Life Plan
Self-Mastery Exploration

Workbook
Index

This is your life.
This is your LIFE.
This is YOUR life.
THIS is your life.
The gift of life is yours.
Life is about making choices.

Life planning isn't about what "should" be.
Life Planning is about stirring up creative possibilities about what COULD be.

Introduction

Part 1: The Big Picture
- Wheel of Life Assessment
- Significant Life Events
- Life Purpose
- Values and Operating Principles
- Five-Year Vision

Part 2: The Year Ahead
- Twelve-Month Action Plan

Part 3: Conditions for Success
- Conditions for Success

Part 4: Monthly Reflection

© *Transformation Systems International 2011*
Contributions by Stephen Hacker,
Tammy Zinsmeister, Stephanie Holmes,
and Sharon Conti
www.tsi4results.com

Introduction

Self-Mastery Exploration

You are about to begin an intentional process designed to help you develop greater awareness of the results you want to produce in your life and your work.

This process combines focused introspection and external coaching to help you get clear about what you want to accomplish, and the strengths, improvement opportunities, and mental mindsets that help you create results for yourself. This process will help you translate insights into effective personal development goals and strategies.

The process will help you get a clear picture of your personal:
- **Desired Future** (where you want to go)
- **Current Reality** (where you are now)
- **Actions** to take that will close the gap between Current Reality and Desired Future.
- **Mental mindsets** necessary to accomplish your intended results.

The purpose of this planning is to help you **live the life you want**—to develop patterns of thinking about intention. It is not something you do once; rather it is an ongoing approach to **living a life with purpose.**

Life Plan

What Is a Life Plan?
- A Life Plan is a living document that connects our daily activities with our deeper understanding of what gives meaning to our lives. Creating a Life Plan helps us define our personal goals and aspirations, and what we want to create of ourselves and in the world around us.

Why Create a Life Plan?
- There is a great deal of power in having and documenting both a personal vision and a clear picture of our current reality. Having this perspective will generate a force within us, which will move us toward our vision and the production of tangible results.

Start Wherever You Are.
- People often hesitate to take the first step in developing a Life Plan. One reason is that many people believe that the document must be perfect and complete. Quite the opposite is intended. The Life Plan is a lifelong working document; you are "working on and revising" the document for the length of your life.
- Make your first version <u>imperfect</u>, knowing that you will enhance it over time. The first step is to start.

Refresh Your Life Plan.
- The Life Plan is intended to be a living document. Plan to revisit your Life Plan once a year, perhaps more frequently in times of personal change. Many people prefer to re-examine their Life Plan near their birthdays.

Part 1: The Big Picture
Wheel of Life

Personal Assessment: Wheel of Life

DESCRIPTION

The sections of the Wheel of Life represent major areas of your life.

See the center as "0" zero SATISFACTION/HAPPINESS, and the outer edge is a 10.

INQUIRY

What is your current level of satisfaction in these areas of your life?

1. **Identify Your Current Reality:** Consider these aspects of your life. Record your current level of satisfaction in each area of your life by making a "dot" on the line. Then connect the dots to draw your current level of satisfaction. Reflect on your Current Reality "circle."

OPTIONAL

2. **Consider Your Desired Future State (Vision).** Draw your wheel as you would like to see in the next five years by making dots indicating the desired future then connect the dots.

3. **Identify Areas of Motivation/interest.** Notice the places where you are eager/interested in change. Use a highlighter to mark these dots.

Example

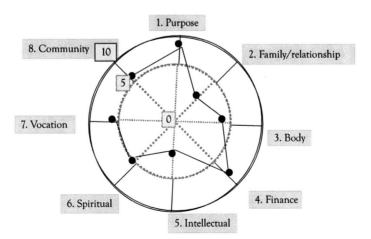

Wheel of Life

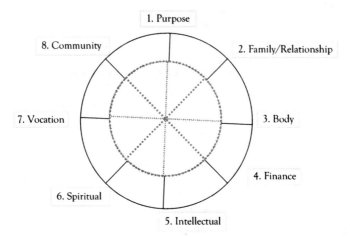

Part 1: The Big Picture
Significant Life Events

What I Have Learned From the Past

DESCRIPTION

A significant life event is a specific happening ... a key episode in your past, set in a particular time and place. It is a specific moment in your life that stands out for you for some reason.

Life has presented us with a variety of situations; each has helped us, taught us things about ourselves, others, and the world. Life's joys and sorrows, challenges and failures contribute to growth. Our past experiences have helped to form who we are today and the quality of our relating to people, events, experiences, and the world.

INQUIRY

Describe events in your life that had the greatest impact; think about those events that have most shaped who you have become as a person and how you see your life. Look back at the Wheel of Life.

Consider the areas from the Wheel of Life and others you think are important.

- Spiritual ▪ Family/Relationship ▪ Body ▪ Financial ▪ Intellectual
- Vocation ▪ Community

"You have to know the past to understand the present."
Dr. Carl Sagan

"I think we all wish we could erase some dark times in our lives. But all of life's experiences, bad and good, make you who you are. Erasing any of life's experiences would be a great mistake." Luis Miguel

"Forgiveness does not change the past, but it does enlarge the future." Paul Boese

"You can clutch the past so tightly to your chest that it leaves your arms too full to embrace the present." Jan Glidewell

"Your imagination is the preview to life's coming attractions."
Albert Einstein

Part 1: The Big Picture
Significant Life Events

Events	Impact(s) of the event on me. Learnings I had, strengths I discovered, decisions I made about the meaning of life
Areas to consider… Look back at the Wheel of Life.	

"What you need to know about the past is that no matter what has happened, it has all worked together to bring you to this very moment. And this is the moment you can choose to make everything new." Unknown

Part 1: The Big Picture
Life Purpose

Life Purpose

DESCRIPTION

Life purpose, like the mission of an organization, is our individual purpose for being on the planet. Life Purpose gives a foundation to your values and vision. Your Purpose and your Values are your guiding stars.

INQUIRY

What is your unique purpose for being on this planet? This is to generate your initial thinking.

- A good place to start is by considering your gifts, the things you love, and the contributions you desire to make. Answer the questions for inquiry.
- Pause and reflect on your responses and scan your responses on prior pages; Significant Life Events. Identify common themes. Consider your strengths and the impact of using your strengths.
- Draft your first version of your Life Purpose.
- Tip: Form a string of three–four words that describe what you bring to the world.

Part 1: The Big Picture
Life Purpose

Reflection
What is your sense of the purpose of your life?
What is your calling, your life's aim?

_____

_____

_____

_____

_____

_____

_____

_____

_____

_____

_____

_____

_____

Your Life Purpose—Version 1.0

_____

_____

_____

_____

_____

_____

_____

_____

_____

_____

_____

You are unique, and if that is not fulfilled, then something has been lost.
There is vitality, a life-force, energy, a quickening that is translated
through you into action and because there is only one of you in
all of time, this expression is unique.
If you block it, it will never exist through any other medium, and be lost.
Martha Graham

Part 1: The Big Picture
Values and Operating Principles

Values and Operating Principles

DESCRIPTION

Values and operating principles guide our life's decisions—big and small. They are the foundation of personal integrity.

- **Core values are** defined by you for you; they need no rational or external justification. Core values are not likely to sway with trends and fads of the day.
- **Operating Principles** are the observable practices and behavioral manifestations of your values—in other words, how you and others will know if you are living your values.

INQUIRY

- List some of your key core values (three to five) and their corresponding operating principles.
- Consider also the source of those values. What does practice of the values create?

Example

Core Value	Operating Principles
Integrity	• *I tell the truth* • *I honor commitments I make* • *I walk the talk* • *I practice my values in all aspects of life*

Part 1: The Big Picture
Values and Operating Principles

Core Value	Operating Principles
1	
2	
3	
4	
5	

You have the brains in your head and feet in your shoes.
You can steer yourself in any direction you choose.
You're on your own and you know what you know.
And you are the one who'll decide where to go.
Dr Seuss

Part 1: The Big Picture
Vision for Life—Your Future

Vision—Five-Year

DESCRIPTION

A Vision gives you a picture of yourself that you "live into" or your desired future. It includes all the aspects of your life—work, health, family, finances, relationships, community, hobby, learning etc.

INQUIRY

1. Five years from now—Imagine yourself. How old are you? How are you engaged in life?

   Imagine a perfect day your life five years from now (you are five years older). Look at the details, where are you living, who are you seeing, talking to? Write this down on the same page.

Tip: If you are struggling with this exercise, try this technique. Close your eyes and get into a relaxed state. Now daydream, for a few minutes you imagine yourself in the future, awakening into a new day. Observe your room, all the details about it. Continue these observations with as much detail as possible. Who is in your family? How do you travel to work? How do you accomplish your work? With whom do you interact? What happens at the end of the day? Continue to imagine this day until you are back in your bed falling asleep.

Part 1: The Big Picture
Vision for Life—your future

Five-Year Vision
What is your vision for what you will create in the next five years?

_____

_____

_____

_____

_____

_____

_____

_____

_____

_____

_____

_____

_____

_____

_____

_____

_____

_____

_____

_____

_____

_____

_____

_____

_____

Part 2: The Year Ahead
One Year

Create an action plan that enables your Vision

DESCRIPTION

In this section, you will envision just one year forward for each area of your life. Consider how your mini-vision (or "point of arrival") for each area of your life is a contribution to achieving the totality of your five-year vision. After clarifying the one-year mini-vision for each area of life, write down the most critical milestones along the way. Next, develop your specific action plan; that is, the list of 'to do' items that are associated with achieving your major milestones. Like any plan your steps may change as life presents different circumstances and opportunities.

Areas of Life

1. Family/Relationship
2. Body
3. Finance
4. Intellectual
5. Spiritual
6. Vocation
7. Community

The point of the plan is to be moving in the right direction toward the vision.

Action Plan: Family/Relationship

PRESENT "POINT OF DEPARTURE" Current Results IN THIS AREA	DESIRED FUTURE "POINT OF ARRIVAL" The results you will create in the next year

CRITICAL
MILESTONES

ACTIONS (DO)

Action Plan: Body

PRESENT "POINT OF DEPARTURE" Current Results IN THIS AREA	DESIRED FUTURE "POINT OF ARRIVAL" The results you will create in the next year

CRITICAL
MILESTONES

ACTIONS (DO)

Action Plan: Finance

PRESENT "POINT OF DEPARTURE" Current Results IN THIS AREA	DESIRED FUTURE "POINT OF ARRIVAL" The results you will create in the next year

CRITICAL MILESTONES

ACTIONS (DO)

Action Plan: Intellectual

PRESENT "POINT OF DEPARTURE" Current Results IN THIS AREA	DESIRED FUTURE "POINT OF ARRIVAL" The results you will create in the next year

CRITICAL
MILESTONES

ACTIONS (DO)

Action Plan: Spiritual

PRESENT "POINT OF DEPARTURE" Current Results IN THIS AREA	DESIRED FUTURE "POINT OF ARRIVAL" The results you will create in the next year

CRITICAL MILESTONES

ACTIONS (DO)

Action Plan: Vocation

PRESENT "POINT OF DEPARTURE" Current Results IN THIS AREA	DESIRED FUTURE "POINT OF ARRIVAL" The results you will create in the next year

CRITICAL MILESTONES

ACTIONS (DO)

Action Plan: Community

PRESENT "POINT OF DEPARTURE" Current Results IN THIS AREA	DESIRED FUTURE "POINT OF ARRIVAL" The results you will create in the next year

CRITICAL MILESTONES	

ACTIONS (DO)	

Part 3: Conditions for Success
Honest Reflection

Setting Conditions for Success

DESCRIPTION

Many good ideas drift into obscurity, never to be completed, because there was no plan to create it into reality. In order to achieve your vision, you will need to marshal internal and external resources.

Your efforts to create your life happen in the midst of your current life. Your current life produces the current results. Your current life is perfectly positioned to produce the current results.

Thoughtful consideration of your current life to see what needs to be cleared or adjusted is a significant contribution to creating Conditions for Success. This is like thoughtful preparing of the soil to plant flowers. A gardener who throws a packet of seeds on the ground still in the packet is less likely to produce flowers than the gardener who cultivates the soil.

INQUIRY

1. Spend some time to honestly identify what will facilitate your success. Record your reflections.
2. Identify any actions you need to take to clear the path before you launch your action plans.
3. Tell at least one person in your life about each of the areas. Telling more people will fortify your commitment to stay in action and generate support for you.

Part 3: Conditions for Success
Honest Reflection

- The mindsets I'm holding are ...
- I'm motivated because ....
- My level of commitment is....
- Support I need...
- What risks will I take?

_____

_____

_____

_____

_____

_____

_____

_____

_____

_____

_____

_____

_____

_____

_____

_____

_____

_____

_____

_____

_____

_____

_____

_____

_____

Part 4: Monthly Reflection
Post Program

To reinforce the personal work that you have done so far, we recommend that you schedule self-reflection time once a month (a half hour to an hour). To follow are a series of exercises that you can complete over the course of the coming year at whatever pace feels appropriate.

"Real education consists of drawing the best out of yourself."

Mahatma Gandhi

MONTH 1:

What is the legacy you would like to have in your organization or in the world? In other words, what would you like to be known for?

_____

_____

_____

_____

_____

_____

_____

_____

_____

_____

MONTH 2:

Write down or reflect upon an example of when you were on purpose this month. What did it feel like? Write down or reflect upon an example of when you were off-purpose. What did it feel like? What did you do or not do to get yourself back on track?

_____

_____

_____

_____

_____

_____

_____

_____

MONTH 3:

Write about or reflect upon an experience this month that gave you joy. What was it? Who was involved? What about it was joyful for you? What does that tell you about yourself?

_____

_____

_____

_____

_____

_____

_____

_____

_____

_____

_____

MONTH 4:

Reflect on your leadership assessment. What progress, if any, have you made with respect to your opportunities for improvement? Why or why not?

What risks will you take in the coming weeks and months to increase your personal effectiveness?

_____

_____

_____

_____

_____

_____

_____

MONTH 5:

Think about someone you know or have observed that you admire and that you consider a great leader (formal or informal). What attributes do they possess and why are they admirable? Consider sharing with them what you admire and the impact they have had on you.

_____

_____

_____

_____

_____

_____

_____

_____

_____

_____

MONTH 6:

Review your life plan and the results you indicated you intend to produce in key aspects of your life. Where are you on track? Where are you off-track? What mid-course adjustments, if any, will you make?

_____

_____

_____

_____

_____

_____

_____

MONTH 7:

Write about or reflect upon an example this month of when you played or felt playful. What impact, if any, did it have on your level of energy and effectiveness?

If you haven't played or felt playful this past month, put down this document right now and figure out how to build PLAY into your day. Use your imagination!

_____

_____

_____

_____

_____

_____

_____

_____

_____

_____

MONTH 8:

Write down or reflect upon an example of when you were on purpose this month or these past few months. What did it feel like? Write down or reflect upon an example of when you were off-purpose. What did it feel like? What did you do or not do to get yourself back on track?

_____

_____

_____

_____

_____

_____

MONTH 9:

Write about or reflect upon your connection to your organization's change efforts. What results are you producing? Why or why not?

_____

_____

_____

_____

_____

_____

_____

_____

_____

_____

_____

_____

MONTH 10:

Reflect on a time in the last month or so when you felt energized. What happened? Who was involved? Why was the experience energizing? What does that tell you about yourself?

_____

_____

_____

_____

_____

_____

_____

MONTH 11:

Reflect on your leadership assessment. What progress, if any, have you made with respect to your opportunities for improvement? Why or why not?

What risks will you take in the coming weeks and months to increase your personal effectiveness?

_____

_____

_____

_____

_____

_____

_____

_____

_____

_____

_____

MONTH 12:

Sit down with your life plan and review the results you have created over the course of the last year. What did you accomplish? Why did you produce the results you did? Why did you not produce the results you didn't? Update your life plan for the coming year.

_____

_____

_____

_____

_____

_____

CHAPTER 5

Coaching Teams: Alignment and Attunement for High Performance

In the early hours of September 11, 2001, I was on a red-eye flight from Portland, Oregon, to Orlando, Florida. The plane landed, I rented a car, and drove east toward the coast where I was to facilitate the annual strategic planning session for NASA's Kennedy Space Center. This year we were conducting the session at an offsite located in Vero Beach. Once I turned on the car's radio, I began to hear emerging reports of a plane colliding with one of the World Trade Center towers. I remember thinking, "How could this happen?" believing a small plane had ventured off course into downtown Manhattan. But something much more tragic was in motion and it wasn't accidental. I arrived at the offsite and went to the conference room reserved for the meeting, where the Center's director and senior staff were already gathered, focused on a television screen. We watched together as the horrific events unfolded that morning—the first tower on fire, the second plane hitting the other tower, the eventual collapse of both, the Pentagon burning, and news about the plane crash in Pennsylvania.

I had arrived at the meeting with a mental plan of the steps I would go through to conduct this planning session to serve NASA. But as I saw the TV images my consciousness quickly shifted from my role in the day's planning session to the agony of the people in the three buildings and on the planes, the unbearable grief or uncertainty their families must be experiencing as they watched these same images, the heroic struggle of the first responders to save lives at the risk of their own. I reflected that I too had been on a plane flight just a few hours earlier and was safely on the ground—I needed to call my wife immediately and let her know

I was okay. She would have just awakened on the West Coast with no idea of what was happening, and I wanted to spare her any worry. I felt an overwhelming need to connect with her and my two children, the tragedy bringing into focus what was most important in my life. I stepped out of the conference room and phoned her, assured her that everything was fine with me, and asked her to give my love to my two children once they awoke. It was difficult being apart from my family at this time of national emergency—I wanted to be with them.

Others in the conference room excused themselves for a few minutes, feeling the same need to connect with loved ones even though they might be only 30 minutes or an hour away. When we had all returned to the room, I sensed the emotions of the group flowing, our hearts going out to the victims. It was a cathartic moment for the group when it became clear, without anyone saying so, that our collective purpose for convening that day, was no longer germane. It belonged to another day, but not this one. The collective consciousness of the group had shifted, and with that the collective will redirected our focus to what were the real priorities now, what needed to be done in light of the new reality we saw on the screen. We suspended the planning session, which had not yet begun, and the director correctly instructed all of us to return to KSC, just a few miles away. But before we adjourned, the director paused and then led us in a prayer for our country and for the victims of these acts of terrorism. This was a demonstrated act of leadership, leadership of our collective spirit. The new team ethos continued through the day. Emergency response plans were initiated even as we traveled to the central administration building on the base. Without knowing if we'd yet seen the full scope of the attacks that day, it dawned on us that the Center itself could be targeted. The director and staff shifted into action to empty the Center of all but crucial personnel.

During the next couple of days, in the midst of suspended daily work and execution of prudent emergency response measures, we struggled to cast the future and scope out critical initiatives required as a planning team. Among the many things I remember was the new meaning these days took on in our individual and collective lives—time that we sometimes just let drift away. Current actions and future plans were seen through the sharp prism of purpose, and purposeful behaviors became the norm for this period. Yes, our brains were engaged as before, individually and as a team, but spirit was noticeably present, the spirit of meaning manifesting itself in a determination to make a difference in the time we have on this earth.

From other experiences coaching or being a part of a team, I know that it doesn't require a cataclysmic event for a team to discover its collective consciousness and exercise its collective will to address unfamiliar challenges and achieve ambitious goals that would not otherwise have been within their "repertoire" of action. In fact, this apparent dualism of individual will and collective will, when aligned toward a vision that resonates with personal purpose as well as team/organizational mission, is the hallmark of highly effective teams and organizations. As earlier chapters discussed, personal purpose is the profound motivating force of spirit, the meaning of an individual's life that directs energy toward creating a desired reality (vision). The more conscious the individual, the greater his or her ability to focus spirit toward action, which we'll call *individual will*. Conscious persons who willingly come together for a common purpose that is aligned with their individual purpose give birth to a collective consciousness—the "we"—which possesses a *collective will* capable of mobilizing even greater reserves of creative energy into productive action.

Individuals awakened to their purpose are a necessary but not fully sufficient condition for a high-performing team. They must freely give their energy, through a process we call alignment and attunement (discussed later), to a compelling collective purpose before a collective consciousness and collective will emerge, which are the bedrock of truly responsive and creative teams essential to organizational transformation. (One can also argue, as I will in chapter 7, that teams in the form of small informal groups are essential to societal transformation). In the domain of teams, these dual dimensions of the individual and the collective inform the work and goals of the transformational coach.

The Coaching Scope

We cast a wide net here and define the domain of team as a group of people with a specific mission. The team might be existing or new, large or small, standing or ad hoc, physical or virtual, with high or low meeting frequency. But whatever its nature, we can say with certainty that a team *is not* a homogeneous whole, nor is there an "average" or typical member. To think otherwise is to overlook the individual spirits sitting on the team and miss the opportunity to awaken each and every person; to act otherwise is to create an environment where individuals can hide amongst the many—the direct opposite of awakening. Often the role of the individual is seen as subordinate to the team: Just consider the well-known saying, "There is no 'I' in "team." The premise of transformational coaching is that "I" does exist in "high performance teams." The dynamics and flow of energy occurring within and across the group are considerable, while the major leverage for transformation always remains within the individual.

The transformational journey of a team and its members follows an arc similar to the wisdom journey for self and individuals, but with some notable differences:

- Discover alignment of individual purpose with collective mission/purpose to discover the strength of the collective will.
- Cast (create) a compelling collective vision.
- Determine attunement of purpose and vision with others to create supportive relationships beyond the team's vision.
- Build a performance culture (mindsets).
- Act (perform), review results, and internalize learnings.

As coach, you will guide the team through this journey toward high performance/effectiveness by employing the 3Es Transformational Coaching model, adapted to the particular nature of teams as a collection of individuals pursuing a common goal. You are concerned with the mission, vision, composition, culture, and performance of the team you are working with. The maturity of the team will also be a factor in how you approach the coaching. A team might be focused on a single initiative within a limited time frame. Or it might be the organization's/unit's leadership team that deals continuously with both the strategic and tactical aspects of leading and managing a great many others, including other teams with narrower scopes and missions. Newly forming teams bring the opportunity for the leader to choose the most suitable members and lay the groundwork early on for culture and dynamics that support high performance. Mature, long-standing teams, well rooted in existing dynamics and relationships, may need to unlearn nonproductive thinking and reframe the relationship between members' objectives and those of the team, and their leader may need to revise her or his notion of what it means to lead a team.

In addition, effective team coaching also requires that you understand some key concepts about (1) the initial development process that sets up a team to become highly effective; (2) the alignment and attunement process for engaging the power of the individual members in the pursuit of collective purpose and vision; and (3) the characteristics and traits that high-performing teams manifest. All these will be discussed early in this chapter.

The key challenge when coaching teams is to be aware of the dynamics taking place within the group as well as with the individual members, and to stay conscious during the process to your own thoughts and reactions so that you are not drawn into personal agendas or team dynamics. Thus, to succeed at coaching a team through transformative change, you need the capacity and skill to coach in three domains simultaneously: yourself, individual team members on a one-to-one basis, and the collective.

The teams that you will coach do not operate independent of the organizations in which they exist. Team coaching, especially with leadership teams, is nearly always part of the larger goal of organizational transformation. If teams are viewed as the fundamental work collective—leader and team members—that together comprise the larger collective of the organization, it is hard to fathom how the larger collective could transform itself to produce breakthrough results without having teams—and the individuals on them—that are able to perform at that level.

For example, the initial coaching focus might be the senior leadership team, which soon discovers that transformation efforts need to encompass the organization as a whole, the subject of the next chapter. With the continuing help of the coach, the senior leadership focuses on strengthening its own capabilities to lead transformation as well as developing an overarching transformation plan for the organization as a whole. Transformation initiatives are cascaded further into the organizational units, whose leadership teams now focus on escalating their effectiveness in leading their part of the organization to breakthrough performance. One or more transformational initiatives may require the formation of new teams with this as its mission; they can be coached about how to come together and work from the start in ways that lead to high performance. Within each team, individual members work to expand their consciousness and undertake the journey toward greater personal effectiveness. Team leaders or members might also embark on becoming transformational coaches in order to leverage transformation at every organizational level. Transformation at this scale is a tapestry with individual threads aligned and segments interwoven into a harmonious whole.

In this book I've chosen to focus first on teams as a separate domain for transformational coaching, even though they commonly occur as a component of a broader coaching effort for the organization as a whole. Team transformation has its own set of considerations and tools and represents a different "discipline" for the coach. But as you read this chapter, do keep in mind that organizational transformation very often will be the backdrop or context for many team-coaching engagements, and team effectiveness is in support of organizational vision and breakthrough results.

The first half of this chapter focuses on coach/team alignment, the initial team development process, the alignment and attunement of individual energies toward collective goals, and understanding the characteristics and traits of high performance teams. The second half discusses the application of the 3Es transformational coaching model to a senior leadership team to illustrate the revitalization and renewal of an existing team in an organizational setting.

What will not be covered in this chapter are the numerous team building and facilitation tools available. These teaming techniques are useful, to be sure. But this text is focused upon reaching beyond the surface into the enormous force of purposeful, conscious individuals voluntarily aligned as a collective will directed toward a shared purpose and vision. When this depth of awareness is present, many of the team tools fade in importance, although some can further fruitful discovery.

Alignment of Coach with Team

As a transformational coach, you may have come to this opportunity with this team via a number of different avenues. You might be the team's leader, or a team member, and thus be very intimately connected with the team already. Alternatively, perhaps you're a coach from another part of the organization or a resource brought in from the outside. Your relationship to the team will shape how you approach the role of coaching it to higher performance. Whatever your relationship, your first step as coach is to get clarity about your own reasons for taking on a coaching role with this team. In other words, as your first act of business, check your own alignment to determine if you have a "vector of energy" attuned to the team's mission/purpose and vision.

What does this mean, a vector of energy? Assuming you have coached yourself through a journey of self-transformation, you have discovered your purpose, your reason for being on the planet, and you have cast a vision, how that purpose will play out in terms of what you want to create in the world. Your spirit, your personal creative energy, is directed toward expressing that purpose and achieving that vision. The team you are engaging also has an expressed mission and a vision for what it hopes to achieve. Is there any common ground between your purpose/vision and that of the team's? In the example depicted in Figure 5.1, something in the team's mission/vision speaks strongly to the person; the individual has discovered a significant vector of personal energy oriented toward the

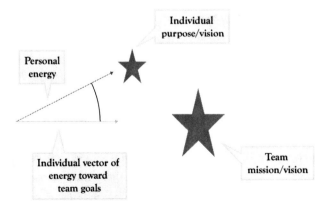

Figure 5.1. Individual alignment.

team's mission and vision. In this case, the potential is high for individual alignment and commitment—the choice ultimately and always resting with the individual.

If you are a member of the team or its leader, how much energy do you have for the team's mission? What level of investment are you willing to make in improving the team's performance? How critical is the team's performance to what you intend to create in the world, your purpose, and your vision for fulfilling that purpose? If you discover a strong alignment, then your energy will flow, serving you and the team, the "I" and the "we."

If you see the team's outcomes as being of low significance in terms of your life's work, it is probably a disservice to remain on the team, particularly if you're its leader. If you envision a high cost in vacating membership—curtailment of your career growth, perceptions that you might be unreliable, strong disappointment or even a sense of abandonment on the part of other team members who've come to rely on you, etc.—and are not willing to incur these costs, then clearly understand why you choose to remain and what personal output (level of contribution going forward) will be necessary to avoid the perceived punitive consequences. I do not recommend this strategy; it is an expensive price to pay in terms of wasting life energy, but at least, it is a conscious choice and purposeful in nature. Above all else, avoid the tendency to unconsciously "slip into" mediocre performance as team leader or team member; stay productive within the team or get off the team, that's the choice—your teammates and organization deserve nothing less of you. It goes without saying that you would find it very difficult in these circumstances to muster your personal passion and build credibility with the team as a coach who can guide it to higher performance, so take off the table the option of coaching the team yourself.

If you are not a member of the team but are a coaching resource from inside or outside the organization, the effectiveness of your support will be contingent upon the degree of alignment between your reasons for wanting to support the team and the team's collective consciousness in requesting the support. Take time to compare purpose/vision alignment as well as expectations on both sides. As obvious as this might seem, support efforts are frequently misaligned with the expectations of the team, leading to unpleasant downstream consequences.

Team Composition

Member Selection for New Teams

A smart, conscious leader with transformational coaching skills might make the decision about who will serve on his or her new team. Alternatively, a leader not yet prepared to coach might seek the assistance of a transformational coach for guidance through the important early stages of formation and development in order to construct a solid foundation for high performance.

Forming a brand new team affords the great advantage of being able to select members, perhaps from a cadre of potential candidates, on the basis of performance factors instead of having to rely on the luck of the draw or the old criterion of "representation of units" within the system or hierarchy. First seek members who have a passion for the work at hand, conscious individuals who have already demonstrated a strong will to achieve something within the area of the team's mission. These are individuals who already have a vector of energy aligned with the team's purpose. A spirit-to-sprit interview will reveal a candidate's level of self-awareness. Past performance will indicate the candidate's consistency and true commitment to his or her purpose.

An individual's skills, of course, can be assets for pursuing an individual and collective purpose. However, as leader or coach do not select skill over individual will. Will—understood here as the decision to apply spirit to a specific vision—is the driving force of great accomplishments. Skills can be acquired; will or drive is formed internally, the person's intrinsic motivation, and is of first order regarding team selection criteria. Many team diversity models overlook the role of passion—a big mistake, as the performance potential of diverse perspectives and skill set absent a strong personal drive is not worth an investment. A group of individuals with a high degree of drive roughly aligned with the team's mission has a higher potential to deliver on the mission, even if they lack the advantages of diverse perspectives or skills. If the collective mission has enough drive behind it, the right resources and skill will be found.

Composition of Existing Teams

Existing teams don't afford the opportunity to pick a new team from scratch and is the more common situation in team coaching. The leader/coach works to establish a culture among existing team members that supports strong alignment between individual purpose and team mission. Over time, people gravitate to the situations and cultures they prefer. A team culture and track record of high performance will attract energetic and purposeful people as additions or replacements and repel individuals who are either largely unconscious or consciously not aligned. Poor performers will tend to find the most lackluster teams. Team growth, resizing, and leader succession all offer opportunities to shift team composition toward highly conscious individuals aligned with the team's purpose.

Frankly, the age-old excuse that lackluster results after a period of time are because the leader inherited a bad team is just nonsense, noise used as an excuse for ineffective leadership. Yes, it is an advantage to have a pro team in place. But transformational leaders work inside and outside the system to create teams no matter what the starting point. It comes down to a matter of the leader's will, the force of purpose and commitment to team *revitalization and renewal.* If the team leader's underlying mindset is to avoid upsetting the status quo, recognize that this mindset generates undistinguished results—more of the same—and breakthrough results in team performance are only a remote possibility. If you are the team leader desiring to coach your team to greater effectiveness, it's time to revisit your own self-awareness and explore why you feel wedded to this mindset. If instead you are coaching the team leader, it is critical that you reassert the goal of creating alignment of energies toward a collective vision and help the leader to appreciate the role of his or her will in this.

The Initial Development Phases for High Performing Teams

Teams that move quickly to become highly effective have a natural progression from their initial formation to producing results. These initial development phases differ in significant ways from the common teaming script of *form, storm, norm, and perform,* a now outdated teaming framework that held value for many years but today is actually counterproductive to breakthrough performance.[1] Compared with teams of just two or three decades ago, today's high performing teams must transcend greater challenges, a less predictable environment, and, of course, a much more complex and rapid pace of change in terms of organizational, business, technological, economic, and social tsunamis. Since their organizations are likewise subject to these same forces, teams face higher expectations than their predecessors did. As mentioned earlier, the key to achieving this level of performance is unleashing the enormous power of individual will to form a collective will directed toward a common vision.

The developmental stages for high-performing teams, described below, pivot around embracing and managing conflict as a means for revealing the authentic convictions and agendas of the individuals on the team as a precursor to discovering the common will. In comparison, the form–storm–norm–perform group development model is actually counterproductive to the depth of alignment needed for high performance teams. The discovery and sharing of personal energies is undervalued, and when differences surface, the group moves into a process of minimizing the unique (and potentially valuable) expression in the misled belief that short-term harmony is in the group's best interest. Rather than moving into open, productive conflict about differences, the norming step demands that each individual comply with the accepted norm.

The team leader/transformational coach eases the new team through the Initial Team Development Phases to embed the healthy dynamics and mindsets that underpin high performance. This encompasses the following four stages, which are not necessarily sequential: Getting Together, Getting Down, Getting Real, and Getting Results.

Getting Together. This initial stage of development includes the articulation of the purpose of the team and its expected output, often with input from key stakeholders/beneficiaries of the team's work. Team structure and membership should be the best fit for team's purpose. Often the option of ad hoc teaming is overlooked in favor of established teams. Many options exist and experimenting is permissible. Team launch signals the official start of the team's work together and includes discussion and agreement on ground rules for relating and everyday interactions.

The team commits to a team assessment and renewal at a future date. The leader is largely responsible for setting the social order, most notably building a culture of team reflection and learning within the team, which will be an important foundation for high team effectiveness in later stages of development.

Getting Down. When conflicts appear, the tendency is to retreat to a pseudo-community state, as explored by M. Scott Peck in his book, *The Different Drum*: Rather than facing conflict and chaos, which matures the group as a team, members act as they think teams are expected to behave, rather than revealing their authentic personas.[2] The reminder—usually from the leader—that "we are all on the same team here" sends members into a polite state from which performance breakthrough is highly unlikely because it suppresses individual spirit, honesty, and the exploration of new views that could lead to collective creative breakthroughs. The team may call upon the spirit of Rodney King: "People, I just want to say, can we all just get along? Can we stop making it horrible? We're all stuck here for a while. Let's try to work it out."[3] There is a false belief that a high-performance team must always give the appearance of agreement, convergence, and lack of conflict. But this stance is not productive considering the real work challenges facing teams today.

Getting down to real team performance isn't rushing to compromise. Unearthing and productively managing conflict enables members to gain a deeper understanding of each individual through honest expression of convictions, agendas, and questions. Masking conflict leads to suboptimal performance. Conflict in itself is not inherently bad, rather it is an important part of the human condition.

Getting Real. Getting real requires a deep sense of honesty in terms of personal understanding and team performance. To move past "the theater of teams" into a high performance collective, team members must be present as individuals and at the same time have the consciousness of a team. To work through conflict, team members must expose their true objectives, bringing to consciousness the authentic will of each team member. Coming clean with individual motivations opens the door to the co-discovery of the collective will. Holding two consciousnesses simultaneously is difficult, which is why so many teams fail, but it is a key to highly effective functioning.

Getting Results. The collective will, once ascertained by the group, represents the alignment of individual and collective purposes and becomes the engine of results. Both individual will and team will are in play. Without individual will, team members with blind allegiance to or passive acceptance of a team goal fall short of producing stellar results. The leader must make certain the results being produced meet the chartered intent.

The Alignment and Attunement Model

The "collective will" central to the early development phases of a high-performing team has no counterpart in the form–storm–norm–perform group development model. This model reflects a organizational/team leadership philosophy, which held great sway for several decades, whereby the leader and ensuing peer pressure knock off the corners of squares and hexagonals and other unique "shapes" of individual members until everyone conforms as a round peg—the norm of team behavior. Quite frankly, the people most desired for today's high performing teams would not tolerate the behavior and activities required under this older model.

As illustrated in the left side of Figure 5.2, it is traditionally held that the energy focus of individuals entering a team or organization points in every direction. People show up in disarray, ready (ostensibly) to be pointed in the right direction. And the role of the leader is to command, influence, direct, cajole, or discipline the individual energies toward the single vision held by the leader. The relationship between leader and the members of the collective is one of control–conform (parent–child), the leader's mindset one of setting vision and directing everyone to go there, and the individual's mindset one of compliance and followership. The language used is a giveaway: "Get her in line," "Straighten him out," "Get them back into line."

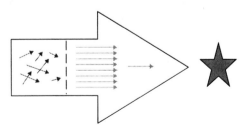

Figure 5.2. Traditional alignment thinking.

A high degree of conformity—all individual energies in Figure 5.2 are now pointing in one direction, toward the vision set by the leader (the star in Figure 5.2)—is largely dependent upon the leader's presence as the external force that manufactures conformity. In the leader's absence, the previous structure—arrows pointing in every direction—quickly returns as the conformity breaks down. In this model, there is neither a collective will nor a collective purpose and vision, just the leader's will and vision. Collective performance is largely dependent upon the leader, who is out in front, leading by example and keeping all members focused. It harkens back to the "perfect man" image of leadership.

Transformative change that leads to breakthrough results on a collective level is possible only when the conscious will of the individual, driven by *personal purpose*, overlaps or aligns with the purpose of the collective, as shown in the vector of energy diagram in Figure 5.1. This does not mean personal will bent to a leader's stronger will, or even to the will of a member majority, but rather a natural synergy discovered by the individual that enables him or her to draw from a deeper source of personal motivation for achieving a shared vision that is mutually inspiring because it is linked to personal vision. Conscious individuals voluntarily form a conscious collective and find the collective will that taps and focuses enormous reserves of energy toward a commonly held vision.

We developed the Alignment and Attunement Model for high performing teams as an approach to team coherence and performance that is grounded in both individual and collective consciousness. As suggested earlier, the gold standard for forming a new team is conscious individuals who have a strong drive rooted in a personal purpose with a large "vector of energy" for the team's mission and vision. In existing teams, the starting point for the leader/coach is more likely a group of individuals with varying levels of consciousness, as shown in the left side of Figure 5.3. Some are clear about where they are going in life and how their participation in the team fits within this life purpose—they are the solid arrows in the figure, included with their aligned vector of energy on the right side of the figure.

Other members are simply following instructions (e.g., the dashed arrow), and their participation follows preconceived notions about how teams are "supposed" to function. And some members are in mystery

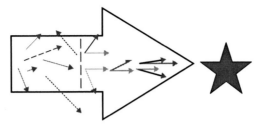

Figure 5.3. Alignment and attunement model.

(the dotted arrows), not sure why they are there and just waiting to see what will happen next. The less conscious the person the more limited the personal energy that member can direct toward team mission and goals, which results in a suboptimal level of collective energy that may or may not be sufficient for generating outstanding results. The role of the transformational leader/coach is to aid the last two categories of team members in developing greater self-mastery, to help them increase individual consciousness and awareness; discover what they want to create in life; and to what degree their life purpose contains a vector of energy aligned to the team's mission/purpose and vision.

Let's say, for example, the organization's mission is to eradicate a particular disease; the particular team's mission is to develop informational programs that will help patients better manage the impact of the disease on their lives and families. An individual on the team, after reflection and deep inquiry, feels called to empower others through communication and teaching—a personal purpose that has a high potential for alignment with the team's mission. However, that isn't always the case. The team member might not find any fit between personal and collective purpose, which must also be honored and the individual encouraged to consider where/how his or her energies might find a more satisfying outlet.

There can also be cases where personal energy is oriented in a direction so different from the team vision that the vector of personal energy, consciously or subconsciously, is actually opposed to the team's—a very bad match indeed, where the individual's continued presence is likely a drain on the team's energy, doing harm in the long run.

The right side of Figure 5.3 represents the goal of alignment of personal and collective energies toward achievement of the collective vision. This doesn't necessarily happen quickly or easily. In this state, however, the leader/coach senses, recognizes, and honors the total expression of the individual within the context of a whole life, and the individual is able to see and enthusiastically contribute to the collective mission/vision within the context of his or her personal purpose/vision.

Dialog and discovery—part of the Explore stage of the 3Es Transformational Coaching model discussed later—reveal individual energy and collective energy. The leader and the evolving consciousness of the group together fine-tune their individual energies toward a collective purpose. This form of alignment results in a conscious enterprise with individuals having high intrinsic motivation directed toward a common goal. Motivation resides within each individual and is not dependent on external controls or influences. The collective impact is a group of individuals with solid understanding of their life's direction, joined together for a collective creation found within the team's goals.

The leader, once clear about his or her alignment with the team's purpose, is responsible for setting the social order and casting the initial team vision. However, the team has input into attuning the vision to more fully reflect the collective purpose and will, which is discussed in more detail in the Enroll Stage of the 3Es coaching model later in the chapter.

Characteristics of High Performance Teams

Based on nearly two decades of experience in coaching teams to high performance, my colleagues and I have noted ten characteristics common to highly effective teams. In conjunction with an assessment of the actual results produced by the team over time, these characteristics serve as useful benchmarks for evaluating to what degree a team manifests the qualities of high performing teams that support their ability to produce breakthrough results:

Robust Leadership: Team leadership is competent and functioning. Leadership varies depending upon the skills needed for the particular situation. Each team member has the opportunity to exercise leadership when the situation warrants.

Quality Decision Making: Decisions are always principle-based and made by the appropriate individual, individuals, or team. Team decision making is of high quality as evidenced by resulting performance.

The team builds its own ways of staying informed and gathering critical information. Sourcing information is a shared responsibility among team members.

Interpersonal Mastery: Relationships are open, honest, and direct. Strong, productive relationships are intentional. A high level of measurable trust is found among individuals, both in dyads and across the team. Risk taking and innovation toward building resilient relationships is rewarded.

Role and Responsibility Clarity: Roles and responsibilities are well defined. All members contribute and understand what is required from them and each other. Individual mastery is apparent in both high- and low-skill tasks. Rewards are based upon the acquisition and productive utilization of skills beneficial to the team.

Pursuit of Results: Team members have a clear understanding of their individual purpose and are driven by personal visions. Solid alignment to organizational purpose and vision exists. Goals are based upon achieving the collective vision. The individual and the team exhibit a high sense of urgency to deliver results for both the short and long term.

Creation Mindset: The team is committed to a vision and aggressively approaches problems as opportunities to achieve that vision. Team members have a mental stance of owning the team results and its processes (no victimization is present). Problem-solving skills are high and effectively used. The team not only solves problems but also innovates in ways that transcend the current problem set.

Resource Strength: All team members are valued by each other, and the team works to maximize the contribution of each member. Individuals take responsibility for their development and the team's growth. Alignment of resources is based upon skill, passion, and demonstrated performance. Unproductive traits or behaviors are readily called out.

Pack Vision: Team members see their individual visions intertwined with the vision and success of the team (and the organization). All team members know each other's individual vectors of energies directed toward the common vision. Strong alignment is born from individual consciousness, not from manipulation.

Engagement with Environment: Interaction with other teams and organizations produces synergy toward objectives. Community is sought with customers, suppliers, up-line leadership, and with other organizational participants.

Team Assessment and Renewal: With the goal of improved results and attainment of team vision, team assessments and renewals occur on a regular basis. Quick response occurs to improvement opportunities.

This list of characteristics has been modified a number of times in recognition that team performance has continued to advance with ongoing experimentation and in response to ever-increasing demands for result—high performance is not a static concept. Teams that were the standard bearers of a decade or two ago have been surpassed by teams—Google for example—that have devised even more effective methods of teaming approaches and methodologies that lead to stellar results. The most recent revision of the high-performance characteristics incorporates research by Marvin Washington and me, published in our book, *Peak Performance: Lessons from the Wild Dogs of Africa.*[4] We discovered four team traits or qualities that we likened to the behavior of wild dogs behaving as a very effective collective (pack). We used the analogy of the wild dogs of Africa to portray these traits as their behavior captured the spirit of organizations like Google. The four pack traits described below have been integrated into the preceding list of ten characteristics of high performing teams:

Pack Vision: The best teams of today do not simply hire highly skilled individuals and then move them to a collective vision. Instead, they seek individuals with an existing fervor for a vision similar to that of the team's and demonstrated performance signifying a devotion to that vision. Being a great accountant alone will not get you a position with Nike; the company seeks candidates who not only bring needed skills such as accounting but also have a burning desire to be part of a team enabling the deep spirit of sport.

Pack Leadership: Building upon the high performance team characteristics, pack leadership is a bias toward leadership by *every* member of the team. Yes, it's situational leadership but goes further in that leadership skills are expected and the team's interactions and work depend upon effective leadership by each member. Teams with this trait find the role of the team leader takes on a unique pattern of facilitation of self-generative, vision-directed leaders toward a collective creation.

Individual Skill: Individual contribution by each member is paramount and critical to building team performance. There are teams in which high-performance individuals do not bring the potential for a high-performance team, but there is little evidence of high-performance teams composed of low-performance individuals. The individual can be seen in self-generating skill development based upon their personal vision and the collective pack vision. The individual takes risks and relentlessly pursues increased personal contribution to the team.

Tenacity: The team displays an unyielding vision quest. The effort needed to accomplish the vision may be more than anticipated, the time required might be longer than expected, but in the end the team stays with the vision until it becomes a reality. The struggle itself is not the focus, nor are the barriers emerging along the way; focus plainly resides upon the end goal. And since the drive is internal, as described in pack vision, the team does not rely upon being inspired externally; outside encouragement may be welcomed but not required.

The Team Effectiveness Assessment tool, in Appendix 5.1, is built around the characteristics of a high-performance team and applied in numerous situations, most commonly as the entry point for the revitalization and renewal of an existing team, one that has a track record together but wishes to greatly improve its effectiveness. In capturing relevant aspects of the team's current state, it supports the 3Es Transformational Coaching work. The assessment also gives the coach, team leader, and team members actionable information about where improvement efforts are likely to be very fruitful.

The best method for conducting the assessment depends on team dynamics. If members are secure and the team has developed a sufficient level of trust, I recommend having the individuals complete the assessment form first, and then convene as a team to discuss the results. Where there is ample agreement about the team's current position vis-à-vis a particular characteristic, discussion is usually brief; if individuals' assessments vary more widely, the discussion centers on what the reasons might be for such differing perceptions—the opportunity here being discovery, that is, exploration and insight. In cases where trust is low and team members lack strong individual voices, it is best to have team members collectively assess the team on each characteristic, facilitated by the transformational coach, who works to have all members engaged in the evaluation, not just the leader or a single assertive individual.

The transformational coach/leader seeks to move teams to higher levels of performance through their mastery of the high-performance characteristics and the pack traits. Other frameworks that reflect the essence of these team qualities exist, so the coach has some choices. It is best, however, if a single, common framework is utilized across the organization. Applying different frameworks for different teams makes it necessary to change assessment method, orientation, language, and mental models—not easy for the coach, and confusing for the organization. Unless there is a conceptual leap in team technology, shifting frameworks to match the latest management guru book will only create waste. Pick one archetype, a framework, and stay with it; get the maximum yield from consistency of approach.

Creating Collective Muscle

The flow of moving a team to a much higher performance state follows the path of the 3Es Transformation Coaching Model, shown in Figure 5.4,

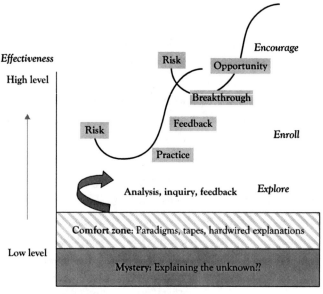

Figure 5.4. Effectiveness coaching model.

combined with the concepts and models already covered in this chapter. The coaching model is the same framework you used for self-coaching (chapter 3) and coaching other individuals (chapter 4). A key difference, however, in its application to teams is that each of the three stages, Explore, Enroll, and Encourage, has five different dimensions or levers for improving collective effectiveness/performance.

For this discussion, we'll focus on an existing senior leadership team that has sought the assistance of a coach outside the team, you, to help it with renewal and revitalization. The team is charged with leading the organization forward through increasingly challenging times. As such, the team purpose, vision, and results will have a high degree of overlap with the organization's mission, vision, and results. The team leader and perhaps some of the team members recognize the requirement that the team itself develops new leadership capabilities and works far more creatively and productively together if the team hopes to lead organizational transformation, which will include leadership teams at other levels of the organization. As you'll see in the next chapter, leadership team revitalization and renewal is, in fact, a part of the planning phase of the 12–18 month Transformation Cycle for organizations. The team members have already completed the team assessment form, so you already have some idea as to what areas will need work.

Explore

In the team setting, the Explore stage of the coaching model includes the five dimensions shown in Figure 5.5. Note that the five dimensions are not necessarily worked in a strict linear sequence. Rather, through

Figure 5.5. Explore dimensions for coaching.

inquiry you navigate among them in a natural flow of discussion, extracting from the conversation what you need to know, bringing to the team's consciousness areas for reflection.

Explore Consciousness

As we have learned in prior chapters, exploring the existing level of consciousness is a critical early element of transformational coaching. In the case of a team, this includes the consciousness of the collective as well as its individual members. The period prior to the start of a meeting or gathering presents a prime opportunity for you, the coach, to connect with the team members individually. Although this period is usually marked by small talk, your goal is to engage on a spirit-to-spirit basis to ascertain individual consciousness levels.

At the beginning of a meeting take the necessary time to connect with the individuals you haven't been able to meet previously. Team members also need to connect with each other. A good strategy is to engage the team in meaningful exercises that lead to deep processing, bringing out honest spirit and expression. Avoid superficial exercises, which if seen as pointless will drag down energy. Many organizational development exercises are shallow and thus promote shallow relationships.

As you begin to uncover the spirit inside members, exploring members' consciousnesses and how they see the work at hand, ask individuals to express the reason for their involvement in the team or issue. Here you are beginning to explore the degree of alignment that currently exists between individual purpose and collective purpose.

Similarly you explore group consciousness through questions and observations. Is the team present or mentally disengaged, focused on other issues? Check to see if the team is preoccupied with a current crisis or hot issue. If this is a case, consider rescheduling or redirecting focus.

Explore Mindsets

Discover where the individual and collective mindsets reside. Of the five primary performance mindsets introduced in chapter 3, where do individuals and the collective team fall? Are there conversations that tend to spiral downward into a scarcity mindset? Does the team realize the power available when collective intentional or willful focus is applied? Is there evidence of oneness thinking, of being one with the staff, one with the customer?

This assessment of the prevailing mindsets provides you with a direction to support or challenge the team and individual members. You guide them toward the more productive mindsets, gently at first, but there may come a time when direct intervention is needed. Tibetan Buddhism has a concept of "wrong thinking." If the team is immersed in wrong thinking, no amount of right guidance will get the job done. Call to consciousness the nonperformance mindsets and set the interactions and thinking on a more productive course. Left unchallenged, unproductive mindsets can wreak havoc in the short term and require greater effort to correct in the future.

Explore Capability

As the coach, you are seeking to understand the aptitude for transformation at both the individual and collective levels of this senior leadership team. Where are the strengths of the individual team members as leaders of transformation? Use the transformational leadership framework, outlined in Figure 5.6, to determine each person's managerial and leadership capabilities.[5] Move beyond simple declarations of strengths and seek performance-based analysis. Conversations about past successes and failures can provide the necessary insights. In what situations have individuals performed visioning, empowering, community building, bold creativity?

Move on to the collective: How has the team performed in the past? Has the team displayed any of the high performance teams characteristics and pack traits discussed earlier in this chapter—pack visioning, creative mindset, pursuit of results, etc.?

Explore Vision Path Integrity

Vision path integrity exists when there is a high degree of alignment among a team's mission, vision, values, strategies, and goals. Team artifacts, including a written overview of these elements, can help in initially

SELF-MASTERY Awareness of one's environment and one's own existence, emotions, sensations, and thoughts is a prerequisite to becoming a transformational leader in any organization. Self-mastery includes clarity of purpose, vision, planning one's direction in life, meditation, reflection, and feedback—all of which are imperative for deliberate and productive growth. Effective transformational leaders have developed self-mastery and are clear about the connection of their personal vision with the vision of the organization. However, self-mastery also extends beyond self to a commitment that others walk a path to self-awareness. Transformational leaders are engaged in the lives of the people in their organizations, encouraging personal growth, feedback, continuous learning, and mentoring.

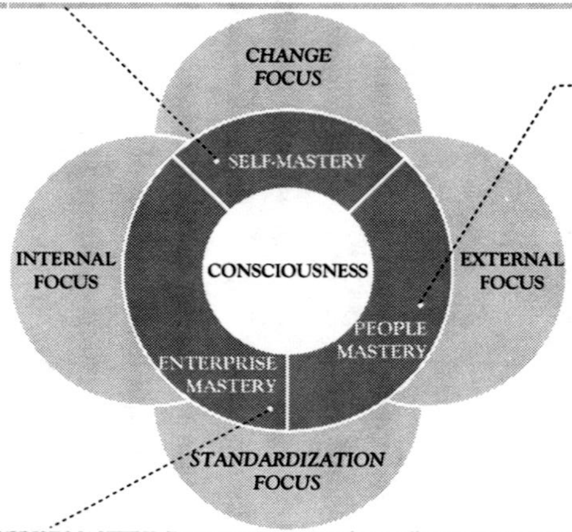

PEOPLE MASTERY Interpersonal or people mastery requires both personal consciousness and collective consciousness—an understanding of the attitudes, behaviors, beliefs, and assumptions of the team/organization. It also involves developing skills in group dynamics, building trust with others, effective communication skills, relationship management, and management of agreements. Gaining awareness and better skills in how one interacts with others is a lifelong journey and commitment to personal growth.

ENTERPRISE MASTERY Enterprise mastery speaks to collective consciousness of the people working within the organization and among its broader stakeholders, a consciousness of shifting value exchanges to which the organization is a party. Understanding the reason for the organization's existence and its "license to operate" are key components. This calls upon the organization's leaders to develop the skills and capacity to be chief architects and engineers for business as executed through strategic planning and design. It also requires competencies in the areas of benchmarking, organizational culture, process improvement, motivation systems, evaluation, and performance measurement.

INTERNAL The internal view points to understanding and appreciation for how the change is experienced within the organization.

EXTERNAL The external view is understanding how the change impacts persons and systems outside the organization.

CONTINUUM OF CHANGE Breakthrough efforts are intended to accomplish radical, step-function performance changes.

Continuous improvement efforts are aimed at achieving gradual, positive changes in performance.

Standardization allows the organization to build upon a strong foundation of successful procedures while removing the non-value-added variations in performing daily work.

Figure 5.6. Transformational leadership.

understanding the vision path, and comparison among the elements can surface discrepancies, misalignment, or even conceptual weakness that would put achievement in doubt even if execution were infallible.

The team's internalization of the way forward may differ from the written vision path. Probe to check individual understanding of the vision path elements and their alignment. Can members tell the story of why the team exists, where it is going, how they as members plan to achieve the vision, the few values that will guide the team's journey? If the team and its members can't tell the simple vision path story, team members' direct reports and bosses, as well as other related teams, are most probably in mystery about the team's purpose and efforts.

Exploring Current Results

What results has the team created recently? Ideally a holistic measurement system is in place, one that combines conceptual depth of performance measurement with simplicity of display. What key measures and reporting methodologies does the team use to monitor results? Does it employ a straightforward measurement panel or scorecard that displays performance in a readily comprehensible format? Does it have relationship charts that show what drives performance, or statistical process control charts?

The review process is just as critical. Are results reviewed on a consistent basis and form the heart of performance reviews? Is there a burning desire to discover cause-and-effect relationships or is the primary objective of reviews to assign or distribute blame? Ascertain the health of the review process.

Enroll

Figure 5.7 shows the five dimensions of the Enroll stage of the 3Es Transformation Coaching model as applied to teams.

Enroll in Vision Casting

Casting a breakthrough vision can be challenging. Given the evolution of teams in using members' collective problem-solving power, employing

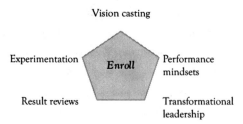

Figure 5.7. Enroll dimensions for coaching.

reason is by now an established response, and many teams work hard to think their way into transformation. Good problem-solving techniques yield results, but transformation is about breaking old patterns to find creative alternatives that will achieve step-function change. Creative thinking is very different from problem solving, and the pattern of solely problem solving the way forward inhibits transformational change.

Rather than simply extrapolating incremental improvement curves, the process of creation involves being open to undisclosed energies and insights, being present as a receptor of these energies and ideas in a process called revelation. Rather than pushing through a conventional multi-step vision process, teams are increasingly using revelation to discover vision, leading to bold ideas and goals.

Teams normally operate at the "elevation" of immediate operational issues, where daily pressures and immediate challenges obstruct a broader, longer-term view of the organization and its environment. Having the "what if" conversation is difficult. Vision revelation is a process for moving the team to a "higher elevation," changing its perspective so that it can see what is needed in the longer term, to spot new possibilities as well as strategic challenges for the team's—and by extension the organization's—future.

When Rotary International declared its vision to rid the planet of polio, it was in spite of the crippling virus's pervasiveness throughout the world. In a way, it made no sense to have such a vision. But through years of struggle and devotion to this vision, polio has been nearly eradicated. More than two billion children have received immunizations, and the number of polio cases has declined by 99% since the launch of the PolioPlus program. That is transformation. The gutsy vision of eradicating polio galvanized the world community, including the World Health

Organization (WHO), to join energies in a focused manner. What was thought to be impossible is now within grasp. Gaining elevation to discover what was needed to change the grave state of affairs produced inspiration—spirit on the move. There are a growing number of examples of spectacular accomplishments in the world that stem from such audacious visions.

Epiphanies, eye-opening revelations, occur in transformative organizations. Leadership teams are learning their way into vision revelation, attracting and sourcing voices of wisdom rather than asserting narrow solutions to a problem. Accessing revelation may take courage, because it seems out of place with structured managerial science. Slowing down and listening to the consciousness of self, group, organization, and the divine are the points of entry.

You guide a leadership team toward vision revelation by enrolling members to do the following:

- Cease *thinking* about the future for a moment and be open to what may be revealed. Ask members to take time away from their normal thinking environment and move into the state of quietness. Where is each being called upon to go? Have them capture in writing what message they receive as to their personal vision.
- Ask the leadership team to cease *thinking* a way forward through persistent barriers. Dedicate time to envision the future of the organization using reflective meditation and other nontraditional methods. Capture in writing the host of possibilities that arise once the mind is put on hold.
- In forming a vision, ask what the world needs of the organization, instead of its current delivery capability. What would make a real difference?

Enroll in Performance Mindsets

The same five performance mindsets outlined for individual effectiveness apply to team members and the collective. Enroll the team into considering its causality—collective accountability for the results it has produced—is necessary to bring forth the team's power of intentionality. The other performance mindsets—abundance, authenticity, oneness, and power beyond measure—are also mental stances that, when adopted by the team, position it for much greater effectiveness and breakthrough results.

Similar to individuals, teams can be stuck in their old stories, can spiral downward in conversation and move to hopelessness punctuated with inaction. Attune your listening to the mindsets reflected in the team's conversations and other interactions. If you hear one of the five nonperformance mindsets arise—that is, the team is in the midst of making a wrong turn in selecting spirit-informed mindsets—step in and offer the team an alternative way to view the situation. Shift the conversation into the opposite, empowering mindset. Given that feeling miserable and disavowing any responsibility for the current situation are default positions for many people, team members might not embrace your suggestion. As they crawfish back from facing the current problem set, you steer them toward a productive course, gently or more persuasively—action(s) that will most certainly need to be repeated in order to build the team's mental muscle memory.

Enroll in Transformative Leadership

Leadership teams can carry the false expectation that managing the current environment will be enough to prosper. Indeed, management of the existing systems and optimizing the present assets are important duties. But leading an organization forward in the tumult of accelerating complex change requires transformational leadership. Enroll the team in the framework of the transformational leadership model (Figure 5.6), wherein each member stretches out in professional growth to develop the competencies needed to guide their own teams as well as the organization as a whole toward radical improvement in performance.

Learning the creative, empowerment, visioning, and community building aspects of transformational leadership are especially important for team members. Use crafted team exercises to shift the individuals out of a managerial focus. Resources such as *The Change Handbook*[6] provide a wealth of methods to bring out leadership qualities and address the whole system. Whatever tools you choose to move the team forward, keep in mind the framework and the resulting behaviors of transformational leadership. Your role is to help the team mature into a group of transformational leaders; don't let an array of clever tools distract your coaching focus or the team's efforts.

Enroll in Experimentation

And now the crunch arrives: taking risks. Excitement can build as the team plays with concepts of team psychology and transformational leadership, but the time soon comes for action, the team's leap into the unknown.

From my experience of leading teams into risk taking, I can attest to the relationship between generation of the "big idea" and post-consideration. When a team has moved to see an exciting world of opportunity and senses power to enact positive change, bold ideas can flow. These ideas must be molded into practical next steps or prototypes developed. Be careful not to allow the molding process and movement to step-by-step action take the life out of the bold idea, to become a time sink during which the great idea seems to erode into a foolish notion. Move briskly toward cementing the audacious idea into action.

At our mid-size manufacturing (400 personnel) and distribution site, the time had come for the leadership team to become more nimble with imposing change and more aggressive in uncovering our latent contribution. Although we had a rich history, an underperforming, unionized-employment system coupled with entrenched technical management threatened our future. My leadership team spent considerable time in laying out a vision path that held promise. A key strategy was to recondition our managers to essentially adopt the characteristics outlined in the transformational leadership model (Figure 5.6). When the time came to develop leadership training, a part of this strategy, ideas flowed. Nontraditional, daylong engagements at such places as an art museum, production theater, university athletic department, and indoor soccer field were proposed as the backdrops to intense learning. Having the entire management team immersed in a new learning environment would create the jolt desired. And I clearly remember the hesitation after our leadership team realized the totality of the six-month plan to which we were about to commit ourselves. It was time to move to action. Yes, we had constructed a bold, unconventional, creative plan, but were we really serious? What if it didn't go as expected? Was this a wasteful engagement? And what support would come from headquarters when the scope of these engagements became clear? What liabilities were we exposing?

Well, something in our leadership team caused us to move forward quickly. Although unspoken, we knew if we doubled-guessed ourselves and watered down the daring nature of our plan, we would fail. The outings were more than successful, providing the needed changes in leadership behaviors. In retrospect, I guess we were risk takers. But the dark moment of hesitation is what sticks in my memory. Thank goodness we did not falter at that point.

Enroll in Result Reviews

Effective results reviews provide both the scoreboard to view progress and the analysis to paint the picture forward. They allow reflection needed to establish the S-curve of improving effectiveness in Figure 5.4. Without effective tactical and strategic reviews, the team has no way of knowing the usefulness of its work, no scoreboard to denote progress. Transformational coaching involves understanding and implementing a first-class review process, which has as its overall purpose the regular and systematic study of whether the action plans are being executed and are achieving desired results. Implementation effectiveness improves when review sessions occur regularly and follow a standardized format. Regular reviews also increase individual accountability, learning, and urgency for delivering results.

Performance measurement and review are disciplines unto themselves, essential to transformation in every domain You will have no difficulty in finding experts resources to deepen your understanding in these disciplines. The next chapter, on organizational transformation, provides an overview of key considerations and includes recommendations for a robust review process that can be effectively used for teams. I encourage you to refer to that material as you work with teams to develop action plans, monitor/evaluate their implementation, and assess their effectiveness in those key result areas critical to the team's mission and vision.

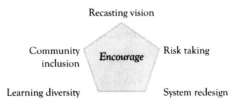

Figure 5.8. Encourage dimensions for coaching.

Encourage

Figure 5.8 shows the five dimensions of the Enroll stage of the 3Es Transformation Coaching model for teams.

Encourage Recasting Vision

Once breakthrough change has been accomplished in a target area, teams as well as individuals have a tendency to celebrate and then fall back into simply managing the new reality. Certainly the leadership team and the organization need to absorb the new reality and work to build systems to better manage it. The coach calls on the team to keep the momentum going by embarking on the next S-curve of increasing effectiveness. This begins with recasting the vision.

Think of it as a vision of a vacation spot. So much time and effort is spent in moving toward the dream, the vision of a great vacation. But what happens after that particular vacation is experienced? What is the next spot on the map, the next vision of a great vacation? So it is with team visioning. There comes a time to recast the vision—an exciting opportunity.

Take time to reflect on the power of the previous visioning journey, which might have been years in coming to full fruition. As a transformational coach this is fertile ground for you to guide the team through deep reflection of consciousness and to further embed performance mindsets in the collective consciousness.

Encourage Risk Taking

If a sufficient number of risk-taking successes can be achieved, the appreciation of bold vision and courageous action become powerful motivations, diminishing the barriers to action that may have plagued the team earlier.

But in the early stages, you play an invaluable role in encouraging the team to move beyond perceived risks. Have the team reflect on the most recent risks and the newly discovered truths about unfounded fears and real accomplishments.

So often, the fears of a team can be magnified by unsubstantiated consequences. The team is more at risk for nonaction than for wrong action. Again, given the movement we are experiencing in world conditions and organizations, teams are more temporal in nature than ever before. The risk is wasting the momentary opening for action, a present chance to make a difference; windows of opportunities do not remain open indefinitely. By reframing the risks at hand, the team can overcome its fears and move forward again.

Encourage System Redesign

As the world changes at an ever-accelerating pace, many of the basic tenets upon which organizational systems and processes have been designed come into question. Even if the mission of the team and organization remains relatively unchanged, to accomplish new visions brings the possibility that simply updating the existing systems that support the team's or organization's work might be inadequate.

For instance, take the reward system in a typical organization. As the vision of spirit-to-spirit interpersonal relationships replaces the unproductive parent-to-child and then the suboptimal adult-to-adult relationship, does the reward system still reek of the old constructs? An hourly pay system rewards simply being present. A skill based pay system rewards gathering up of skill that may or may not be relevant to the new reality, and may or may not be put to use. A new system based on contribution could be in order. This is a far-reaching system redesign. Having orchestrated such a design, it is not for the fainthearted.

To support higher performance in pursuit of a new reality, teams need to evaluate the processes and tools they and their organizations use to get work done. Everything can be questioned. Do the pay system, communication process, and work tasking speak to an outdated parent–child framework or to a suboptimal adult-to-adult relationship? What were the current system's initial design criteria and principles? Are these systems serving us now, or are they an impediment to our future? The next chapter explores the subject of systems in greater detail, and includes a tool for evaluating to what degree each of the major systems (leadership, culture, rewards, communication, etc.) supports the ability to move toward break-through performance. Leadership teams can spread the wealth of deep inquiry by assigning sub-teams to redesign particular systems likely to have the greatest impact on the unit's or organization's ability to achieve the new vision. Ownership and appreciation of new realities can be valuable dividends for such assignments.

Encourage Learning Diversity

With growing consciousness comes the opportunity to learn from an array of different individuals, groups, and organizations. Unique power is provided by learning outside of the team's current mission.

Encourage both members and the team as a whole to explore non-conventional learning opportunities. For example, I provided transformational coaching to a telecommunication service provider that was having trouble providing prompt residential installations to its customers. At the same time, the leadership team was reforming and wanted a team-building experience. Having personally participated in an outdoor-adventure team-building event, I saw the relationship-building benefit of this learning format, although such experiences have limitations, especially when it comes to better appreciation of the value exchange proposition of the team and its organizational mission. So I proposed to combine the inquiry into service issues and team-building by having the leadership go out into the field and literally install service for customers. It was a highly effective learning experience.

Encourage Community Inclusion

As the team gains strength, it is obligated to reach out to share the power of "we" beyond its traditional membership. This is an exciting development. You can guide the team to include more and more individuals and groups in the vision at hand. The team can leverage even greater creative force toward a particular vision.

Similar to one-to-one relationship building, have the team move to inquiry instead of attempting to convert or persuade others to join the effort. Enter into a dialog of meaning with the wider community, seeking to understand where individual passions are aligned. Focus on the common aspect of a future waiting to be created. Initially steer clear of declarations, which divide. Dreams have a way of uniting, while unconscious convictions or positions have a way of separating us.

Widen the circle of influence. Welcome new energy into the work of the team. Seek vision building on a much larger scale. Build a larger, growing movement from the core of team consciousness.

Process View

At times I'll use a process view shown in Figure 5.9 to organize my work for a coaching session with a team, particularly a session in which it has a very defined work objective to achieve, or if one session is all I'll have with a team. The flow of work in the session moves from *Preparation* to *Operation* in the course of the session. A high level of preparation opens the opportunity for the group to attain a new level of performance in the "real" work activities that are the session's objective.

Begin with the end of mind. What are the results to be accomplished from the session? Develop shared understanding with the sponsor on

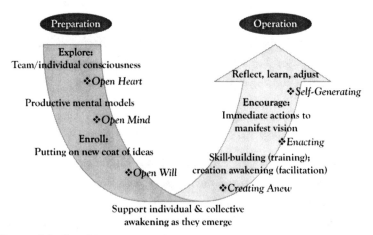

Figure 5.9. Coaching process view.

purpose and objectives or within the team itself prior to the session. Acquire appropriate background and context. Getting the right people in the room produces the most effective session. Prepare a space conducive to learning and dialog that is synergistic with the purpose and objectives. Getting the right room size and room set-up are not afterthoughts but integral to group learning and forward movement.

Plan your coaching along the following path:

1. *Explore the Consciousness* levels of both the team and each member. What spirits inform their thinking? What is currently occupying their attention? Are hearts open to the challenges ahead? To what extent are members awake? To what extent are they simply going through the motions? Prepare in assessing consciousness before the team formally comes together.

2. Identify *Productive Mental Models* that can support a desired shift in individual and group paradigms to match the purpose and objectives of the session. Assess the current mindsets and the shift needed. Use as a guide the five productive mindsets.

3. How will you Enroll individuals in the team to try on a *New Coat of Ideas*, new ways of seeing the world? What personal or organizational stories can you share to illustrate the power and meaning of the chosen mental models?

4. Acknowledge individuals as they begin to awaken. *Support Individual and Collective Awakenings* by calling out the shifts, having members verbalize their change in consciousness. When an individual puts forth old thinking, redirect her to the new shared models. Be aware that in coaching the team, your level of relatedness with any one individual is an investment in the team.

5. In training, move the awakening to *Skill-Building* exercises that allow individuals to practices what they have learned.

6. In facilitation, leverage the awakening toward a *Co-Creation*.

7. Encourage movement of individuals and/or the team to initiate *Immediate Actions* in order to realize the envisioned future. Simply committing to another team meeting or training event as a way to postpone true advancement can be a prescription for failure … a failure in spirit and a loss of the investment by you and the group.

8. *Encourage Reflection*, a key component of setting up the group to self-generate and to own the success of the session. Have the team take the needed time to deeply understand successes and setbacks. Then with the spirit of resiliency, make the needed adjustments and move forward.

During the *Operation* activities, move the team through three areas of evaluation: Did transformation occur? Did individuals/group learn and, ultimately, did the group accomplish the purpose and objectives? Encourage the team to evaluate the results without becoming defensive, but with an eye toward profound learnings offered by the experience.

In the flow from *Preparation* to *Operation*, you are ensuring that emotional movement occurs across the team. From *Open Heart*, to *Open Mind*, and then *Open Will*, the ground is prepared for real transformative change. Then in the *Operational* phase of the session, the energy of *Creating Anew*, to *Enacting* the changes required, and then moving to *Self-Generation* leads the team to real accomplishments and long-term competency. Recognize the emotional travels of the team and individual members. Direct the growing maturity of this immense resource.

Coaching the Team Over Time

The coach's work in the 3Es Transformational Coaching Model is done over many days and many gatherings, and usually in the context of the team's regular meetings to conduct their business together. The team is dealing with consciousness and mindsets and alignment in course of doing its real work. The coach may have the team step back from its work when a particular barrier to team effectiveness emerges, thus working it in real time.

Attain and Maintain Alignment

The coach is co-processing individuals and the collective through all five dimensions of the chevron in each stage of the coaching model. The work with individuals, particularly work at a deep level, is done outside the team setting, in a one-to-one context. Work with different individuals might progress at different rates: One might move rapidly through an S-curve of effectiveness, another might struggle with unwrapping a non-performance mindset or taking the necessary risk to try a new behavior. Full alignment and attunement of individuals with the team will be a work in progress. Changes, new pressures, external circumstances might pull a team member or even the collective back into old dynamics and patterns of behavior. The coach is ever vigilant to bring these occurrences into awareness for the individual/team, helping to glean the insights that support further learning and growth.

Future Focus

As mentioned earlier in the chapter, a leadership team that receives coaching to increase its effectiveness may be simultaneously planning and designing organization-wide transformation efforts that are interwoven with the team's mission, vision, action plans, and results. The end game is organizational transformation. A vision of the organization's future, as developed in the Wall exercise described in the next chapter, is always the desired state from which the team looks back to develop its action plans, rather than standing at the current state and planning incremental improvement, a myopic focus for improvement efforts.

Strategic Versus Tactical Work

The strategic activities of the team, be it re-enlivening the mission, casting the vision, or developing strategic imperatives, require that the individual members and the collective immerse in conceptual "blue-sky" thinking, a creation mindset, and deep reflection about what 'I' and 'we' truly care about. The transformational coaching facilitates (1) the expansion of perspectives, calling upon individuals to diverge from the normal, the everyday, the known, in order to open themselves to the new and uncharted, to risk verbalizing big ideas and concepts, and then (2) moves the team toward convergent thinking, a narrower set of discussions to "try on" and evaluate these ideas/concepts. The cycle is repeated, first divergent thinking, but short of the first round of expansive consideration, and then the convergence process. This pattern allows the team to try on different suits of ideas and concepts without committing prematurely to one.

The process of strategic thinking described above is markedly different than that needed when the team's focus is implementation, problem solving, or something else tactical in nature. In these cases, the coach helps the team move more deliberately toward thinking that converges into action. A multi-step process such as a plan-do-study-act cycle is often the framework for these activities, and may incorporate specialized quality and project management tools to guide actions toward desired results.

From countless team experiences, I've learned that combining these types of work in the same team session leads to disappointment. The open-ended questions and broad considerations of the re-spiriting mission/visioning/strategic design objectives lose every time when coupled with the pragmatic, problem-solving approach needed for execution. The jump into problem solving affords a sense of control and accomplishment, even if the solution takes the organization no closer to its vision. It focuses on eliminating today's organizational "pain," thus preempting and overshadowing the promises of the future state. Allowing the short term to dominate is a common reason why strategic planning sessions often fail; it's a prevailing tendency of teams that the coach or leader will need to manage. Fortunately, the solution to this dilemma is easy: Separate tactical and strategic work into different team sessions. Leadership teams seem to have a strong need to "get after the real business" in the early part of any week. Bring out the lists and the tracking documentation and have a go at it; have the creative power of the team knock down known barriers and work the accountability matrix. Conversely, teams seem more ready to tackle more abstract work in the latter days of a week. Have the team take the nature of its work and the day of the week into account as it schedules its work with you.

That said, even tactical work needs to be done with the vision/future state as the backdrop. Only then can short-term actions consistently propel the organization toward its desired future. The coach's challenge is to keep this perspective ever before the team as it addresses operational plans and issues. The team exists to not only handle problems but also create a future organizational juggernaut. Long-term as well as short-term results are the measure of its effectiveness.

Team Effectiveness Assessment

Level of Team Effectiveness

Characteristic	1	2	3	4
ROBUST LEADERSHIP	Team leader is not competent or functional. Leadership does not vary from situation to situation. Varying team skills are not being utilized in a lead capacity. Members await leader's direction at every turn.	The team's leadership is competent but not functioning. The leader does not vary from situation to situation, but individual skills are beginning to be recognized.	The team's leadership is competent. Different skills are beginning to be utilized. Team members begin to lead when their skills are appropriate, but core leader still reluctant to give up command.	The team's leadership is competent and functioning. Leadership varies depending on the skills needed for the situation. Each team member exercises leadership and takes charge when his/her skills are appropriate to the situation.
QUALITY DECISION MAKING	Decisions made are based on rules, precedents, and current minimum acceptable standards. Often clear decisions are not made; complex situations go unaddressed. Decisions made tend to be operational or technical in nature.	Team begins to make decisions collectively on a case-by-case basis. Teams are willing to struggle through decisions using principles as a base. Decisions begin to address broad organization issues. Decision quality is beginning to increase.	People usually understand intent of principles when making decisions. There is an appreciation of multiple choices and tools available for decision making. Decisions are normally made by team using principle intent.	Decisions are made using principles by the appropriate individual, individuals, or team. Team decision-making processes are defined and result is high-quality decisions that maximize the effectiveness of the organization. Decision reviews are undertaken.
INTERPERSONAL MASTERY	Team members do not relate with one another in an open and honest manner. Informal communication is mostly through the rumor mill. Supervisory communication is not trusted. High level of unproductive, post-meeting	A member sees the need to change the relationship culture of the team. Team begins to develop the ability to deal with conflict through team dialogue. Team begins to discuss issues openly but may drop back to pseudo	Team begins to develop relationship skills to deal even with the more challenging issues. Communication within the team is greatly improved. The efficiencies of reduced waste, redundancy, re-work can be seen. Greater risk is taken	Relationships within the team are open, honest, and direct. Strong, productive relationships are created with intention. A high level of measureable trust is found within the team. Risk taking and innovation toward building resilient relationships

	"water fountain" conversations occurs. Us–them paradigm present within the team.	community when confronted with the largest elephant in the room.	in addressing issues openly and honestly. Trust grows.	is rewarded. There are no elephants in the room.
ROLES AND RESPONSIBILITIES CLARITY	Team roles are rigid and do not change according to varying tasks. Role of leader is unclear. Responsibility of team members is unstated. Narrow skill development. Pay is based on individual performance appraisal.	Team understands how individual contributions support organization objectives. The leader's role is clear. Team accepts a single breakthrough focus while realizing the importance of other goal areas. Rewards are based on individual and team performance appraisals.	Roles and responsibilities begin to become more flexible. Team members begin to understand what they and others need to do to achieve team results. Multiple skills become important. Rewards are based partly on the accomplishment of team tasks.	Individual roles and responsibilities are well defined and accepted based on the team's tasks. All team members contribute and understand what they and others need to do to achieve team results. Team members hold each other accountable for accomplishing tasks and achieving results.
PURSUIT OF RESULTS	People focused on daily routine of their individual job. Goals are fuzzy and oriented toward individual work. Team leader provides results status to team.	Individuals growing in awareness of what it takes to be high performing. Individuals set solid goals. Focus on results begins to drive team's actions. The leader's role in achieving results is beginning to become clear. Sense of urgency to meet short-term goals.	There is a sense of urgency on the part of all team members to sustain team results over time. Team begins to feel ownership for results being created. Team has a thorough understanding of strategies needed to obtain vision. Individuals and team participate in goal setting.	There is a high sense of urgency to obtain team goals in order to make vision a reality. Environmental changes seen as potential advantages. Individual goals are known by team. Goal alignment exists with team and individual. Robust measurement system in place and valued.

(Continued)

Level of Team Effectiveness—(Continued)

Characteristic	1	2	3	4
CREATION MINDSET	Goals set by leader and accepted by team. Key leaders lead short-term problem solving efforts. People issues usually resolved by leader or left unresolved. Problems seen as barriers to achieving vision. Team uses peer resources. Hesitant to use broad resources to solve problems.	Team sets its improvement goals toward achievement of organizational objectives. Urgency to meet goals drives team to participate in problem solving. Team begins to deal with people issues. Team begins to use outside resources to solve longer-term problems.	Team begins to see themselves as creating the future. Problem solving focus to include department/module. Team sets team goals that stretch beyond goals directed by organization. Standardization of the problem solving methodology is in place.	Creative spirit is strong in team and members. Team is committed to vision and aggressively approaches problems as opportunities to create that vision. Members own team results and its processes. Victim mindsets not present. Problem solving skills are high and effectively used; team innovates in ways that transcend current problem set.
RESOURCE STRENGTH	The core team members don't feel valued by each other. Participation levels are low. Some career plans being formed. There is a strong core of skilled individuals who respect each other. Others feel left out. Undefined domain of responsibility for individuals and team. Members await development.	Most team members feel valued by each other. Team members work to maximize capability of everyone. Differences are recognized and accepted and sometimes utilized. Diversity is defined largely by physical nature. Most people have working career plans. Developing team members is leader's role.	All team members are valued by each other and the team works together to maximize the capability of all its members. Differences are valued and utilized. Conversations occur concerning balance between team and individual growth & development. The leader is seen as essential to the decision making process.	All team members are valued by each other. Inner spirit and skill differences are understood and brought to bear on vision attainment. The team works together to maximize the capability of all its members; individuals pursue development with appreciation of team's needs.
PACK VISION	Organizational vision and objectives are understood. Fit between organization	Team understands and aligns with organization vision and objectives. Individuals	Individuals satisfy many of their higher needs within the team. Individuals derive	Team members see their individual visions intertwined with the vision and success

and individual needs unclear. Individuals believe it is the responsibility of the organization to meet personal needs even at the expense of organizational needs. Vision is largely "sold" to members.	recognize long-term benefits of aligning organizational and personal needs. Teams occasionally struggle with changing organizational needs, which require team flexibility.	intrinsic satisfaction from seeing organization succeed. Teams are able to respond positively to changing needs. There is an internalization of principles and organizational direction.	of team and the organization. Individual vectors of energies toward common vision are known by all team members. Strong alignment is born from individual consciousness, not from manipulation.
ENGAGEMENT WITH ENVIRONMENT			
There is little to no interaction with other teams in the organization. Team focus is on its needs and strong boundary prevents interaction with larger community.	Begin to form relationship with key stakeholders. Little is known about other teams and cooperation with these teams is minimal. Certain engagement requirements are understood and acted upon.	Interaction begins with other teams in the organization. Relationship with stakeholders increases. The multitude of existing and potential value exchanges becoming apparent.	Interactions with other teams are productive and lead to increased organizational effectiveness. The team recognizes strengths, diversity, and needs of larger community. Overlapping community visions noted and leveraged.
TEAM ASSESSMENT AND RENEWAL			
Does not happen. New member orientation does not occur.	Self-assessment/renewal await crisis. Team begins look inward for some solutions and sees value of self-assessment.	Team fully realizes that all the power to excel lies within the team. Team uses a team assessment and renewal as the core of its improvement planning process.	The team regularly refines the team assessment and renewal process. A continuous improvement mindset exists. Assessments focus on improving vision attainment. The team is able to quickly respond to changing requirements.

ORGANIZATION:_____   TEAM:_____

ASSESSOR:_____   DATE:_____

CHARATERISTIC	LOW	LEVEL OF EFFECTIVENESS		HIGH
ROBUST LEADERSHIP	1	2	3	4
QUALITY DECISION MAKING	1	2	3	4
INTERPERSONAL MASTERY	1	2	3	4
ROLES AND RESPONSABILITIES	1	2	3	4
PURSUIT OF RESULTS	1	2	3	4
CREATION MINDSET	1	2	3	4
RESOURCE STRENGTH	1	2	3	4
PACK VISION	1	2	3	4
ENGAGEMENT WITH ENVIRONMENT	1	2	3	4
TEAM ASSESSMENT AND RENEWAL	1	2	3	4

CHAPTER 6

Coaching the Whole: Organizational Transformation

Coaching the organization as a whole toward transformation entails a new level of complexity. In this domain, we see increased focus on the greater, collective consciousness of the organization, including how discrete and often disparate units fit into that whole. The coach assists with the integration of new ideas while working to build shared meaning of the organization's purpose, vision, and strategies. Through increased clarity about the organization's creation journey and its mission, departments, units, teams, and employees are better able to link their group and individual efforts into the greater whole in order to co-create the future they desire.

Whether they are for-profit, not-for-profit, NGOs, governmental, or quasi-governmental, organizations employ fundamental systems that allow the total collective and its subgroups to operate as a coherent whole. From a systems perspective, most organizations have formal or informal systems for leadership, planning, people, motivation, measurement, IT, education and training, to name a few—the DNA of these organizations is essentially the same. For example, although mission statements vary dramatically across different types of organizations, the function of the mission statement is consistent across *all* organizations: to answer the fundamental question, "Why do we exist?" Some may resonate more strongly with employees, or be more meaningful in terms of inspiring vision and action, but at least theoretically an organization's reason for being, as reflected in its mission statement, will mobilize organizational spirit (creative energy) toward actions that enable the organization to fulfill its highest purpose.

So don't be drafted into an argument that transformation is more difficult for one kind of organization than another—this is a waste of time. Having led and coached in corporate, small business, governmental, and not-for-profit environments, I can attest that all organizations have significant challenges. In order to attain and sustain a high level of performance, all organizations experience barriers as well as assists to their efforts. They each have strengths they can deploy, baggage they need to leave behind, mental stances that hinder—or facilitate—any effort at transformational change. Some organizations may be in growth markets, which is still no guarantee of long-term success if the vision of what they want to achieve isn't clear or isn't shared by employees, who thus are not self-motivated to pursue it with passion and persistence. Other organizations may be in declining markets or face substantial competitive threats, which need not be a death sentence if the organization is honest about its current reality and can conceive a compelling new vision of its future. Comparing the perceived height of your particular mountain within the Himalayas with another climber's mountain is unproductive. Go climb your mountain.

In this age of an increasingly sophisticated arsenal of methodologies and tools for incremental (continuous) improvement, a real challenge for organizations—even those not adept at using these approaches—is the tendency to seek ways to "fix" even their most serious problems. After all, this is what managers are trained to do. Problem solving and standardization activities are important for organizational excellence, but they alone cannot generate breakthrough results. Responses to chronic performance shortfalls, to major shifts in the business, regulatory, or political landscape, require digging much deeper than finding a process to fix or a leader to replace or a knee-jerk contraction in service or product offerings. Unless the organization stands back periodically and considers a metamorphosis, the current problem drives the action, and the organization responds with a "push" approach that might reflect a myopic vision, a "lock" on the current problem set, or, most certainly, resorting to actions because they have worked in the past—actions derived from embedded nonproductive mindsets that perpetuate the undesirable outcomes.

In contrast, transformation is a "pull" approach that throws the spotlight on the future that the organization and its employees strongly desire to create. In its broadest sense, this creation journey, shown in Figure 6.1, is similar to the wisdom journey for individuals discussed in chapter 2.

Rather than a 10% improvement in this or a 15% reduction in that, transformation takes the deep view—Who are we as individuals and why have we come together as a group?—as well as the long view—What is it that we collectively aspire to create, the impact that we desire to have in the world? The driver of action planning and implementation during each transformation cycle—of which there will be many—is identification of what actions will be most effective in closing the gap between the present (current state) and the future state, and what other actions might be needed to support and sustain the desired changes.

Core to this approach is the principle that current reality/outcomes for the organization and the teams that comprise it are an *accurate reflection* of their current beliefs and desires—despite the fact that these might conflict or even contradict their stated (espoused) beliefs and values.

This perspective not only puts the problems of today in a much different context but also encourages the organization to explore both its past and its current state from a place of greater consciousness, to become aware of the mindsets in operation and, where necessary, to embrace more productive ways of thinking and acting—thereby opening the door to true transformation. This in no way diminishes the severity or implications of the problems the organization currently experiences. Rather you, the transformational coach, create a safe environment in which leaders and employees can acknowledge the problems openly and honestly. You then give them permission to move beyond blaming or defensiveness to

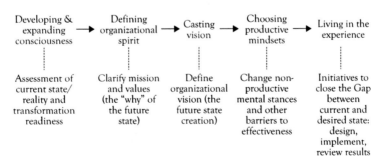

Figure 6.1. Top-level view of organizational transformation—the creation journey.

focus on the opportunity for creation, within the context of the organization's mission and current landscape. This is a higher-level mental stance that energizes, unites, and propels a group toward more positive and profound outcomes—toward breakthrough results. As a result of new beliefs and modes of thinking, the new organization acts and makes decisions differently, creating new outcomes more in line with what it desires. Existing problem sets can resolve, or may be rendered irrelevant in the context of the organization's new direction. The journey may give birth to new problem sets, but leaders and staff have growing awareness and more tools available for exploring the reasons behind them.

The Value-Addition of the Transformational Coach

The Three Es Transformational Coaching Model, introduced in chapter 3 and further developed in chapters 5 and 6, provides the coach with a framework for engaging the organization's leaders, teams, and individuals in the important conversations that can lead to profound shifts in awareness, thinking, and learnings that characterize collective and individual transformation. We can overlay the coaching model on the organization's creation journey, as shown in Figure 6.2, to convey a very broad frame of the coach's primary focus over the key stages of the journey:

- *Explore*: Explore the current state and most importantly, the underlying mindsets and beliefs.

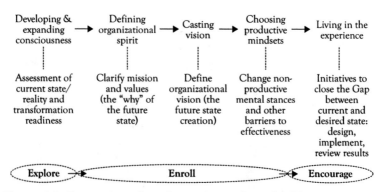

Figure 6.2. *Primary coaching focus, drawn from the Three Es Transformational Coaching model.*

- *Enroll*: Enroll leaders, teams, and individuals to self-dedicate to a higher shared goal; to shift toward more beneficial patterns of thinking; to adopt transformational methodologies/ practices.
- *Encourage*: Encourage the organization and its leaders to make new thinking an ongoing practice; to learn from outcomes of new actions; and to bring increased consciousness to the next transformation cycle.

Coaching Versus Consulting

How does the transformational coach's focus and value-addition differ from that of a consultant, who leaders and HR executives might be more accustomed to seeing as the organization's advisor on a major change initiative?

Consulting infers the providing of expert solutions. We are fortunate to have experts in many walks of life who have built wisdom from experience and deep study. Individual and collective effectiveness can be greatly enhanced by digesting their knowledge and then sensibly applying it to our lives, relationships, and places of work.

Consulting comes from many sources. I have contracted many top-level consultants for advice in my organizational leadership capacity. Overall, the benefits received were worth the effort and monies. Knowing how and when to contract such help is a learned skill, a facet of procurement expertise (for which you can also acquire consulting help). I have also contracted consultants when seeking personal assistance in several aspects of life, from financial to legal. Expert solutions, however, are not limited to a contracted consultant—they can be found in books, multimedia presentations, and in abundance on the Internet. What a blessing: quick and easy access to numerous wisdom perspectives on unlimited subjects!

But transformational coaching differs from consulting. Looking underneath the knowledge into individual and collective thinking is the coach's extended purview. As we've seen in chapter 4, the coach helps individuals engage in deep reflection and adopt more productive mindsets. Far from a linear process, the coach gets close and upfront with individuals to guide a cathartic shift. In particular, the transformation coach is contributing to "aha" insights by supporting, prodding, reflecting, and promoting the individual's growth as a partner.

With a team, consulting is advising on the current best methods of teaming. As chapter 5 illustrated, coaching is determining why a team operates at a less-than-optimum performance level by posing insightful questions that lead to collective reflection and specific alternatives for relating to each other.

At an organizational level, to consult is to bring to the table expertise about macro-level issues or systems, for example, *what* best practices to employ. By way of contrast, to coach is to help the organization discover, for example, *why* best practices are *not* being employed, despite the leadership team's stated intentions to do so. Informing someone of how to do something differs considerably from sitting next to the person, fully invested in their growth, and guiding them through a discovery and change process.

Although the distinction between consulting and coaching is frequently overlooked, understanding it is essential for the coach to be effective and to carefully manage the organization's expectations of the coach's role in its creation journey. Coaching is an extended and more deep-rooted relationship than consulting. Both are valuable. There are times when straightforward consulting is just what the organization needs, and times when additional investments in knowledge will not produce dramatically different results—then a coach's skills are needed to guide the organization and its leaders into new territory.

Let me give you an example of the difference in focus and impact between consulting and coaching, one I have encountered more than once. When I am asked to help with an organization's strategic planning, I undertake a review of results and previous strategic plans. The idea is simply to see how leadership has pursued planning in the past, the methodology used, actions taken, and the impact of the effort. Commonly, I discover the implementation of previous plans to be incomplete. Sometimes leadership's decision to pull back from full implementation has been made with complete consciousness, for example, in response to a significant change in an internal or external factor on which the plan was predicated—a strategic plan, after all, must be a living document. But I've also found cases where the strategic plan has scarcely been implemented, even though the leadership team, supported by external consultants' research and insights, continues to point to the plan as the best way forward. The strategic direction still makes sense to everyone, even though little action has been taken to execute it.

From a purely consulting perspective, the plan appears to be on the mark, the industry expertise and strategic planning methodology correctly applied. The consulting advice continues to be *implement the plan*. However, from a coaching perspective, the better answer lies in getting behind the real intentions of individual leaders and their collective will. It is time to step into the inner workings and explore the internal causes of avoiding implementation. A good coach acknowledges the external conditions that leaders predictably offer as the reasons for inaction, and then presses on to help leaders discover the internal consciousness and demonstrated will underneath the "undesired" results. Coaching involves discovering *why* the leaders created the present state of affairs.

Working with a Dynamic Living System

Who hasn't been through this? You've experienced a problem with your automobile—let's say the engine—and so you take the car in for a checkup to get it resolved. The mechanic inspects the engine, runs some tests in the shop, and does not experience the problem you outlined. Soon after you leave the mechanic's shop, the problem reoccurs. Why did this happen?

The engine is not divorced from the total automobile. It is part of a much more complicated system and, when in motion out on the road, interacts with other subsystems under a wide range of operating and environmental conditions far different from sitting stationary in the shop. The host of other factors that can affect the engine's operation never come into play in this setting. The shop tests and inspection can't possibly replicate how the engine behaves when the car is in a dynamic mode, be it climbing a steep grade, speeding along at 65 mph on the Interstate, or crawling along in rush hour traffic. Even design faults or manufacturing defects may manifest only under a specific set of operating conditions. At a minimum, the mechanic needs to (1) evaluate the engine's performance on the road—in a dynamic state; (2) assess performance problems in the context of all the systems with which the engine interacts—viewing the issue from a holistic rather than fragmented perspective; and (3) once modifications are made, evaluate the impact of the modifications on the auto's performance (another test of performance on the road, under dynamic conditions) to determine the effectiveness of the modifications—assess the outcomes.

Like automobiles, organizations do their work in a dynamic mode. Conditions that exist at one point in time don't remain static. Customers' needs may change, on an individual and collective basis, over the short and the long term. The cost or availability of material, supplies, components, or services may fluctuate in accordance with pressures beyond the organization's control. Technological developments may improve workforce productivity or service quality; they may greatly alter customer expectations or render a current product line obsolete. Economic cycles rain down manna or wreak havoc with strategic and operating plans and performance. As chapter 1 pointed out, nothing stays the same anymore.

An organization is a living system that grows, shrinks, and changes form as time unfolds. Assessing the current state of an organization, and particularly the dynamics that not only contributed to past results but will also influence future outcomes, can't be done through a single-point-in-time assessment. A snapshot alone says very little about how the organization really operates, of the mental stances and beliefs that drive its responses, which in turn produce its future outcomes.

Here the coach plays an invaluable role in observing the dynamics of a leadership team under a variety of conditions: listening closely to explanations of what actions have been taken in the past and the reasons ascribed for their success of failure; detecting patterns of beliefs or behavior; discerning the stories that ascribe meaning to past organizational experiences and color the interpretation of current experiences. Leaders and others within the organization are participants in these dynamics; with coaching they can gain the awareness and objectivity needed to assess the real drivers behind their team's, group's, or their own behavior.

Likewise, the coach continues to be present over time and in a variety of circumstances that enable him or her to enroll a group or individual in new ways of seeing things, to encourage learning and reinforce new behaviors. This can't be done in a limited engagement—coaching is both the coach's and the organization's long-term commitment to its growth.

Given the vibrant, pulsating entity known as the organization, the challenge is to operate from an organizational paradigm that transcends a "building block mindset." We may like the idea of a straightforward path or a list of ten secrets that lead to a better organization. If the organization would give way to simple, linear coaching, then a software package would do the trick. Your skills and past experiences as a transformational coach are of value, but even so each transformational "project" is its own unique story. You are engaged in living system creation, where your opportunity to add greatest value lies not in any cookie-cutter approach but in engaging as an innovative, inspired, artistic, and purpose-centered being.

Transformation Cornerstones

As coaches, my colleagues and I use a holistic strategy for seeding transformational change in organizations, the four Transformation Cornerstones, shown in Figure 6.3. Based on more than twenty years of research and experience, the synergistic cornerstones of self-mastery, interpersonal mastery, value exchange, and change methodology form a foundation for comprehensive long-term strategy and alignment for breakthrough improvement, one that avoids the fragmented results of a single-purpose approach.[1] Throughout the organizational transformational journey, the coach remains alert to all four cornerstones, as they are interactive in nature. The coach helps leaders and others develop new transformational skills, aids in relationship breakthroughs, brings forth the awareness of shifting value

Figure 6.3. Transformation cornerstones.

exchanges in the entire system and, when needed, offers the appropriate change tools or approaches to move the organization forward in its transformation efforts.

Self-Mastery

Through self-mastery, individuals strengthen their connection with the organization by gaining clarity about their personal purpose, values, and direction; and understanding the relationship between their personal vision and the organization's vision. With a focus on improving effectiveness at the individual level, the coach works to raise consciousness about deeply held ways of thinking that often hold back or slow down breakthrough change.

Interpersonal Mastery

Our experience has taught us that poor interpersonal relationships within organizations are a primary driver of problems in performance. The coach's strategy for strengthening the connection between the individual and others in the organization is to nurture individual capacities and skills for intentionally and effectively building productive interpersonal relationships. Too often this foundation cornerstone is limited to diversity training and watered-down emotional intelligence application. Interpersonal mastery has at its heart the ability to connect spirit-to-spirit, which by nature goes beyond the popular approach of shifting from parent–child to adult–adult relationships. Building deep understanding and appreciation of others provides a platform to quickly develop profound trust, effectively provide support, and to bring a new level of performance to agreement making.

Value Exchange

The third block for building the capacity for organizational transformation is to strengthen the connection between the organization and the outside world through a deepened understanding of the organization's value exchange with customers, suppliers, staff, and stakeholders and how that value exchange shifts over time—an especially important consideration given the tsunamis of complex, converging changes on key fronts that can quickly impact an organization's value proposition.

Integrated into transformation activities are opportunities for the leaders to develop and share knowledge about the critical factors that contribute to an organization's survival and success. We have found that dialog is enhanced significantly when representatives of the extended system— customers, suppliers, other key stakeholders—participate in these discussions. Sharing knowledge and information about the business tends to improve everyone's sense of ownership of and commitment to the organization.

One of the most dramatic examples of shifting value exchanges I've encountered emerged from a session I conducted with a senior team of FBI leaders. Historically, as one leader exclaimed, they were primarily judged on catching the criminal. Then almost immediately following September 11, 2001, public and political leaders altered their expectations for the agency: Catch the terrorist *before* the act of terrorism and coordinate information/investigations with other federal agencies (e.g., CIA). In exchange, the public and political leaders would supply additional support and access to intelligence. The game had shifted.

Change Methodology

The coach provides the organization with field-proven technologies for leading transformational change, such as those discussed throughout this chapter—the transformation cycle, the transformation strategy map (the Wall), transformational leadership characteristics, value stream mapping—and other tools to aid innovation and the generative creation process. Transformational methodologies, approaches, and toolboxes are part of a growing body of knowledge in the transformational sciences. Some will stand the test of time, while others may simply supply learnings for developing better methodologies in the future.

I must emphasize that to offer an organization the change methodologies alone will not lead to transformation and only sets up the organization for failure in its efforts. Coaching it in the deep work of the other three transformation cornerstones of self-mastery, interpersonal mastery, and value exchange, is absolutely essential for embedding the capacities to generate breakthrough performance.

Overview of the Transformation Cycle

The Transformation Cycle, based on a plan-do-study-act (PDSA) framework and shown in Figure 6.4, provides a disciplined methodology and tools for planning, achieving, and monitoring breakthrough improvement in the major systems that underpin the organization's ability to perform.[2] It includes many of the traditional components of strategic planning, such as assessing and diagnosing the organization, defining a mission and vision, and identifying improvement objectives to support the vision. The uniqueness of the Transformation Cycle lies in the attention paid to activities important for supporting the large-scale transformation, including the following:

- Cast an organizational vision from the perspective of purpose rather than extrapolating current reality to depict the future.
- Identify the few initiatives that will go furthest to move the organization toward its vision and test individual commitment to the transformation plan.
- Implement the plan as a creation process, not solely as a project to be managed.
- Develop a balanced performance measurement system to track progress and review results from a "causal" stance.
- Systematically improve knowledge and skills and nurture the capabilities, behaviors, and organizational dynamics needed to achieve the organization's vision.
- Seek conscious alignment of the plan and individuals' purpose/vision.

Importantly, woven into the planning stage of the Transformation Cycle are a number of group and individual activities—the CAMP sessions—that focus conversations about self-mastery, interpersonal mastery, and value exchange—the first three of the transformation cornerstones—and help to create conscious commitment and alignment across the organization. Sequential transformation cycles bring the organization ever closer to its vision as it renews and executes against strategic goals in response to internal and external changes.

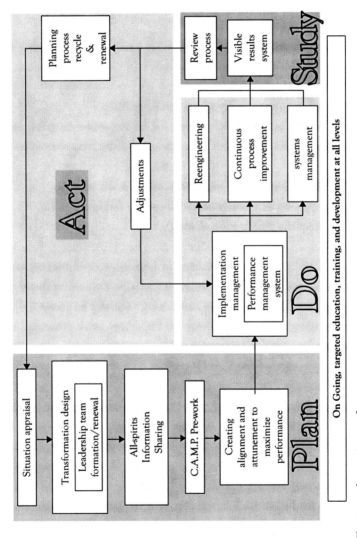

Figure 6.4. The transformation cycle.

Each transformation cycle is typically 12–18 months long and is designed to flow into the next cycle, successively closing the gap between the organization's vision and the actual outcomes it achieves. While the front end of the process is essentially for planning the actions to be taken, the majority of the time will be spent in implementation of actions and careful monitoring of results—the "Living the Experience" stage of the creation journey (Figure 6.1).

The coach and the leadership team lay a solid foundation early in the cycle:

- Define current reality (Situation Appraisal).
- Develop an initial architecture for the improvement effort and identify its leaders and their accountabilities (transformation design).
- Share information about the transformation with all employees in a timely and high-quality fashion (all-spirits information sharing).

A CAMP (Creating Alignment to Maximize Performance) session, the centerpiece of the Transformation Cycle, is a three- to five-day off-site that provides the structure and setting necessary to create a detailed transformation plan and perform the important work grounded in the four transformation cornerstones.

In the course of the CAMP session, participants will have defined the organization's purpose and long-term vision, one to three transformation initiatives, objectives for each initiative, and measures to assess performance. In addition, they develop plans to address key organizational sub-systems that support each initiative. As importantly, a typical CAMP session also includes intensive work at the individual and group levels in which participants are called upon to examine attitudes and behaviors that have held them back in the past, and are invited to explore the consequences of failure to change. Barriers between individuals are surfaced and resolved, and a stronger community is created.

The conclusion of the CAMP session marks the beginning of the Implementation Management phase of the Transformation Cycle.

This phase includes deployment to the broader organization, and in the case of large organizations, additional Transformation Cycles could be employed with subunits or significant divisions. As the transformation initiatives are enacted throughout the organization, the implications for various parts of the organization will differ. Some departments/processes will be at the heart of the transformation initiatives and will experience radical design change (breakthrough change), while others will require continuous performance improvement (incremental change) or systems management (documenting and stabilizing core work processes). Implementation teams work on their assigned objectives, and progress and performance are tracked and reported through a comprehensive measurement system and assessed in monthly and quarterly review sessions (review processes) to determine the effectiveness of the transformation effort.

The planning process recycle and renewal marks the conclusion of one Transformation Cycle and the beginning of another. During the recycle session the transformation plan is modified, if necessary, based on lessons learned. At this point the organization enters back into the Situation Appraisal phase and the cycle is repeated.

The Transformation Cycle is underpinned with ongoing education, training, and development at all levels in the organization. Equipping those in the organizational system with knowledge and skills necessary to improve performance is a key condition for long-term success.

Rather than proceeding with an in-depth examination of all parts of the Transformation Cycle, our focus for the rest of this chapter will be on those aspects of the Transformation Cycle where the coach makes his or her greatest contribution to the creation journey of the organization and its members: *exploring* the current state and the underlying mindsets and beliefs; *enrolling* leaders, teams, and individuals to self-dedicate to a higher shared goal and shift toward more productive mindsets; and *encouraging* the organization and its leaders to make new thinking an ongoing practice and leverage key learnings in order to bring the organization ever closer to the shared vision of the future. Those seeking more detail about the Transformation Cycle are encouraged to read the book, *Transformation Desktop Guide.*[3]

Situation Appraisal

The organization and its leaders most probably have been hard at work to achieve lofty goals, but despite past and ongoing efforts, the organization remains a long way from its desired state. Or because of significant changes in its internal and/or external environment, it finds its current position precarious and unsustainable, but with no clear of view of what its future might be. As coach, you begin at the *Explore* stage of the 3Es Transformational Coaching model to uncover the thinking behind the current state of affairs. How did the organization and its leadership arrive at the existing position? What mindsets contributed to the conditions being experienced? You approach this from an evaluative stance, not a judgment stance. You are simply working to understand—and to help the organization understand—the drivers behind its positive and negative outcomes.

The Situation Appraisal, as the first major activity in the Transformation Cycle, promotes this exploration as well as a number of other important objectives:

- Build/strengthen your (the coach's) knowledge of the organization, its current state, and its dynamics, and provide insights into the collective (and individual) mental stances and mindsets in operation.
- Engage leaders and other participants in dialog about and reflection on an array of factors that, viewed holistically, present a picture of the organization's health, thus raising participants' awareness (consciousness) about the organization's current state and the possibility of a significantly better future.
- Aid relationship development and trust building between you and members of the organization, particularly as an opportunity for you to demonstrate deep listening and your commitment to help the organization move forward.
- Examine the current state from a causal mindset, where actual outcomes provide the clearest indicators of true organizational purpose, and identify any conflicts with the organization's stated purpose/mission, vision, and values.

- Evaluate the readiness of the leaders and the organization to undertake and execute the transformation.
- Assess the health and balance of key organizational systems important for supporting transformational efforts.

It is natural that the coach leads and participates in the assessment. Depending on the size and complexity of the organization, other coaches and/or facilitators might assist in one or more of the assessment activities.

Depending on the size and complexity of the organization, material/data for the assessment is typically obtained through one-on-one interviews with members of the leadership team; small focus groups of managers and staff; online Situation Appraisal forms; review of organizational artifacts; and results of any past assessments done in the organization (e.g., surveys of employee opinion/engagement and customer satisfaction, special studies, etc.).

Past Assessments

Past assessments, particularly if they include any longitudinal data, can reveal much about the organization, including its approach to perceived problems and its success in making changes to improve its effectiveness. The organization may have structured these analyses to reflect one or more preferred orientations for understanding how the organization functions—most commonly by function, activity location, reporting structure, product or service delivery, or major systems (see Figure 6.5). Each view has value as an assessment orientation, as each drives distinctive inputs, outputs, and internal processes. In today's organization, even a single individual might hold roles that span multiple views: An area sales representative, for example, in addition to her functional and geographic focus, might also serve on a new product development team and a companywide customer service task force.

As coach, understand and take advantage of the assessment orientations already in existence within the organization. Listen to both leaders and staff to learn what assessments have been conducted in the past, the actions taken as a result, and the impact on the organization. Listen without judgment, and listen deeply: What is being said about these past

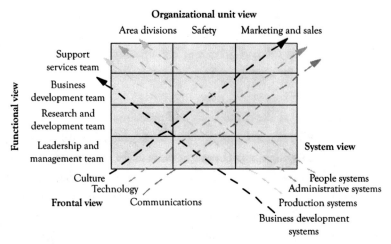

Figure 6.5. Assessment orientations.

efforts, the manner in which they were conducted, and the communication process before, during, and after the assessments?

Situation Appraisal Tool

In addition to a review of past assessments, my colleagues and I use a tool, Situation Appraisal (SA), to gauge the current state of key organizational "fronts" and the organization's transformational readiness, both of which have significant implications for the success of transformation efforts.

Part 1. Organizational Fronts

An assessment of organizational fronts presents a broad view of the following nine mega-systems that, when healthy and in balance with one other and aligned with the organization's mission, vision, and strategic goals, support the organization's ability to operate consistently, efficiently, and effectively across all units and levels now and into the future:

- *Planning*—All strategic planning systems: strategic,
  performance improvement, business, marketing, operations,
  human resources, and daily planning—the entire plan-
  do-study-act cycle.

- *Measurement*—The system for gauging and then communicating multiple levels of performance, including systematic identification of information that supports performance improvement.
- *Culture*—The organization's shared values, beliefs, norms, and system to create the desired culture.
- *Education, training, and development*—The system of teaching knowledge and skills to everyone in the organization so they can personally and professionally improve.
- *Infrastructure*—The system or internal structure by which the organization conducts business, including organizational charts, position descriptions, functional responsibilities, and informal relationships.
- *Technology*—The system for managing "how we accomplish things," including methods, procedures, protocol, hardware and software, and tools.
- *Motivation*—The system of both extrinsic rewards (inducements, recognition, compensation schemes) and intrinsic rewards (found in self-mastery).
- *Politics (community building)*—The informal aspects of performance management including the proactive management of key stakeholders' needs and expectations; anticipation of criticism, boundary spanning; internal communication; and working power bases.
- *Communication*—The system of sharing information among groups and individuals to facilitate coordination, understanding, and cooperation.

Each system contributes in its own specific way to the organization's ability to perform, and yet they are interdependent and must be managed holistically. A weakness in one system can hamper the health of other systems. Conversely, exceptional strength in one system will not necessarily compensate for weaknesses in other systems, and in fact may be drawing away precious resources that, if allocated to strengthening other lagging systems, might result in a larger improvement in the organization's performance. This sometimes occurs when an organization intuitively knows one front is weak, moves to strengthen it, and sees improved

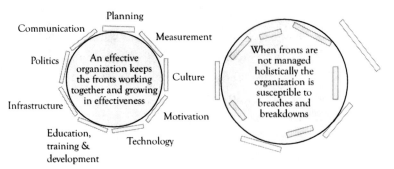

Figure 6.6. Health and balance of organizational fronts.

results follow. However, as it seeks further organizational improvement, it pulls the same lever, producing additional improvement in the same front but with diminishing returns in its impact on organizational performance. The ideal condition is to have all fronts healthy and engaged in supporting breakthrough performance (see Figure 6.6).

The Organizational Fronts Assessment is one of two parts comprising the Situation Appraisal as outlined in Appendix 6.1. This front assessment explores the major components of each of these nine systems—how they are structured, how they work in practice, perceptions of their effectiveness. Through both quantitative assessments and qualitative descriptions, we get a picture of how well the fronts, individually and collectively, can support the transformational effort. The results can also pinpoint systems-focused transformational initiatives that are likely to have a high impact on moving the organization toward its desired future.

Part 2. Transformation Readiness Assessment

We also conduct a transformational readiness assessment to gain insights into what mental models might be at play in the organization, particularly those that stand as potential barriers to the transformation effort. More specifically, the transformational coach seeks answers to the overarching questions in the following four areas:

- *Leadership.* Is leadership conscious, seeing their role in
  creating the organization as it is? Or do leaders with some

time in their positions continue to blame previous leadership
or external circumstances for current results?

- *Burning platform.* Does a burning platform exist to initiate a transformation, or is the threat of change greater than
the present reality? Does the burning platform exist both
within the organizational community psyche and individual
members?

- *Vision.* Are visions alive within the organization as a whole
as well as within individuals? And to what extent do
organizational and individual visions align? Heavy turnover,
for example, could indicate low investment by individuals in
the collective vision, making organizational achievement of
its vision a mere wish. Are the visions clear and compelling? Is
time spent in visioning, or is most of the organization simply
grinding out change with little awareness of shifting requirements that could render these efforts unproductive or even
irrelevant?

- *Past.* What role does the past play in the organization? Are
learnings derived from the past? Does emotional baggage hold
the organization hostage to the past? What kind of records
and artifacts are kept to acknowledge and learn from the past?

The key components of the Transformation Readiness Assessment
have specific questions aimed to discover the current reality. They flag
the presence of any nonproductive mindsets as well as the absence of the
motivation necessary to undertake the difficult journey of collective and
individual transformation. The readiness assessment is included with the
organizational fronts assessment to present a single integrated exercise
to participants, the Situation Appraisal (Appendix 6.1). Together they
enable lucid consideration of what is in store for the transformational
effort.

Conducting the Situation Appraisal

The Situation Appraisal engages a cross-section of individuals in the
organization, the number of whom is highly dependent on the size,

complexity, and transformational acumen of the organization or organizational unit. It may be practical in a very small organization or unit to involve everyone. A medium-sized organization of several hundred employees might seek to include 10% of the workforce, while in a large organization a few percent of all employees might be all that is needed to constitute a representative sample.

The format for gathering input can take multiple forms:

- *Interviews*—The coach meets individually with members of the leadership team and other key leaders in the organization. These discussions include a review of past assessments as well as the topics in the Situation Appraisal tool.
- *Focus Groups*—Small groups of 5–8 participants are particularly useful in exploring the perceptions of front line and support staff. Led by the coach or a facilitator, these sessions allow individuals to build on the reflection of others. The size of the group allows the facilitator to manage the air time to give everyone adequate input and avoid "group think." Based on the group's discussion of each category in the SA tool, the facilitator assigns a rating to the items and captures key comments around the open-ended questions in the SA.
- *Paper or Online Survey*—Depending on organizational size and geographic dispersion, interview and focus group input can also be supplemented with input from individuals who complete hard copy or online electronic SA forms.

The coach and organizational leaders may also decide to probe one or more of the organizational fronts in greater detail—culture, for example—by using an electronic or paper survey specifically designed for the purpose of capturing perceptions and opinions from a representative sample (or, indeed, the entire workforce).

Organizations that are already a couple of cycles into the transformation effort and/or understand the value of broadening input to other stakeholders beyond the organization often choose to involve these stakeholders in the situation appraisal. Participation might be extended to suppliers (upstream), next-in-process customers (downstream), or the governance body (upline) for the organization as a whole (board of directors) or for the organizational unit (the individual or group to whom the unit head reports). As a transformational coach, I can vouch for the value these stakeholders' perspectives bring to the process.

The CAMP Session

A CAMP is the centerpiece of the Transformation Cycle with the following important objectives:

- Create alignment, in terms of (1) the degree to which all are working toward common organizational goals and (2) the degree to which individual intentions are clear and congruent with organizational goals.
- Create attunement, in terms of (1) the degree to which people work collaboratively and (2) the degree to which there is a shared sense of responsibility for the welfare of the entire system,
- Generate awareness of the shifting value exchanges between the organization and all its stakeholders.
- Introduce and use mechanisms to develop a transformation plan (the Wall, discussed in the next section).
- Build community and bring forth collective consciousness and skill development in the area of interpersonal mastery (trust, generative dialog, feedback).
- Provide an environment conducive to personal development and risk-taking opportunities.

CAMP sessions can be structured to accommodate as few as eight and as many as 60 participants. Our bias is to manage participation such that the "extended organizational system" is represented in the room (i.e., a diagonal "slice" of the organization, plus supplier and customer representation).

Pre-Work

Although pre-work for CAMP varies by organization, there is at least one standard assignment for all CAMPs, the Conceptual Image Document (CID).

Prior to CAMP, participants are asked to complete a "Version 1.0" CID, four sets of questions designed to spark focused introspection and self-awareness (see Figure 6.7). The CID considers the "whole person" in that it encompasses both personal and professional dimensions.

The CID provides a means for the participant to reflect on and then broadly articulate his or her vision and goals. During the CAMP off-site session, the individual examines them in the context of the existing vision

CONCEPTUAL IMAGE DOCUMENT		
	How do you see yourself? Who are you?	
	What value do you add?	
1	What are your strengths?	
	What are your weaknesses?	
	What results are you producing, personally and professionally?	
	What is your purpose?	
	What is your vision?	
2	If your life were on tape, and you fast-forwarded the tape so that you are at the end looking back, how do you feel?	
	If you could change the tape, what would you change?	
3	What are your 2–5 year goals and objectives, personally and professionally?	
	What near term (3-6 months) actions will you take to improve yourself, to move toward your goals and objectives, to move toward your vision, and to accomplish your purpose in life?	
	How will you improve the results you are producing?	
4	What risks will you take?	
	What will you read, do, study, experience?	
	What feedback will you seek?	
	What relationships will you mend or improve?	
	How will you build agreements and trust?	

Figure 6.7. Conceptual image document.

and goals of the organization to check for alignment. Some groups have chosen to share their written CIDs with each other as pre-reading for their CAMP session; however, this is not a requirement.

It is important to note that the CID feeds into the Life Plan, described in chapter 3 and contained in the Appendix. Where the CID involves general questions, the Life Plan is specific and calls upon the individual to express in more detail their purpose, vision, values, and initiatives—it's a tool for beginning a personal transformation journey. Often participants receive an evening assignment to complete version 1.0 of their life plan, and the introspective work they've begun with the CID enables them to make good headway in this assignment.

The coach, with input from the leadership team or a transformation design team appointed by leadership, determines what pre-work assignments would best prepare participants for breakthrough thinking as it applies to the organization, relationships, and self. Other CAMP pre-work assignments might include identification of recommended decisions and actions based on the coach's summary of the situation appraisal; identification of key performance indicators; leadership team self-assessment; and/or selected reading assignments.

CAMP Off-Site

Although no two organizations, hence, no two CAMP sessions, are exactly alike, a typical CAMP session includes intensive work at the individual and group levels, designed around the Transformation Cornerstones. Participants are called upon to examine attitudes and behaviors that have held them back in the past and are invited to explore the consequences of failure to change. The Wall exercise, described in detail in the next section, shifts participants' focus to the broader organization and its transformational journey.

Building the transformation plan, focusing on self-mastery, and learning interpersonal skills do not occur in a linear fashion in a CAMP session. Although you as coach preplan an overarching flow, the delivery of CAMP is an art. Sensing the focus and energy of the group, you interweave the themes of personal, interpersonal, and organizational transformation together, moving pieces of each theme forward a bit at a time.

This energizes the group, allows them to see the interdependency of the themes, and promotes deeper learning.

The Wall

As part of the CAMP off-site, we use an exercise called building the Wall, the graphic "storyboard" shown in Figure 6.8, to move the leadership team through the important discussions around casting an organizational vision and defining the journey the organization will take to make this vision a reality. The discussions focus on four elements of the organization's transformational journey:

- *Future*—outlining, or casting, the vision for the organization going forward, the desired future state.
- *Past*—probing past experiences for key learnings.
- *Present*—understanding the organization's current state from the Situation Appraisal results.
- *Closing the Gap*—identifying the largest gaps, and crafting a small number of key initiatives focused on those key organizational systems, or fronts, where improvements will have the largest strategic impact in moving the organization from its present performance to the desired future state.

The Wall documents the results of the discussions as a visual "storyline" whose elements are unique to the organization and form the foundation of a compelling story that resonates with the leadership team. Like any great story, there is a gripping storyline with the promise of a better tomorrow, triumphs and failures in the past, and the crystallizing of will to move forward into the better days ahead. The Wall exercise can also be used at the business unit or functional level to cascade the development and alignment of transformation plans and related efforts throughout the organization.

Note that rather using a conventional left-to-right sequence for building the Wall, you will coach the leadership team through the Wall elements in Figure 6.8 using the sequence outlined above, beginning with the future and ending with closing the gap.

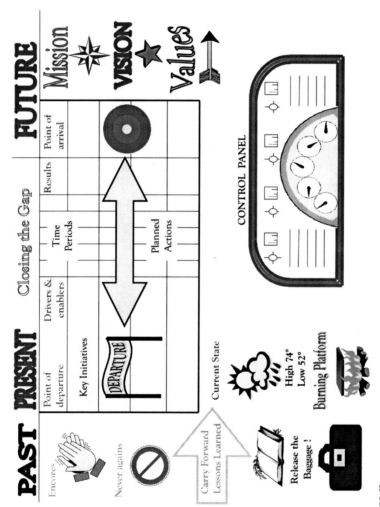

Figure 6.8. The Wall.

Mission → Values

First begin with the essentials of a purpose-driven organization and its future. Have the leadership team examine the mission and values:

- *Purpose or Mission*—The reason for the organization's existence. Always fulfilling when pursued, but never fulfilled, it is the reason for the journey. Represented by the compass rose, it is the true north of the organization.
- *Values*—The three to five key values the organization is not willing to compromise. Operational definitions attached to these few values establish boundaries for the playing field on which the organization and its members pursue the vision.

As discussed in the section on Situation Appraisal, the true (demonstrated) purpose and values of the organization are reflected in current outcomes and actual results. The group takes a deep look to see if the stated mission and values, as evident in organizational artifacts, are indeed a fit with the demonstrated purpose and values. In rediscovering the reason for existing and principles, the process is both personal and corporate.

Allow a significant amount of time to investigate in depth the questions of mission and values. Often this aspect is rushed through. Meaningful conversation and reflection lead to commitment and clarity. As coach, ensure there are sufficient time and an open process that allows the group to articulate the mission and values that best reflect the intentions of the organization. Also allow enough time and space for each participant to compare the organization's mission and values with their individual purpose and values to determine the degree of alignment.

Vision

As an objective, the organizational vision is a destination, usually one to three years out from present. The vision should be alive, appealing to all five senses. It is not simply a description recited from a wallet card.

Rather it is a place with tremendous appeal to individuals throughout the organization. The vision can be experienced in their minds. And the drive to make the vision a reality is a constant force, in large part because each person can visualize his or her dreams within that collective vision. A compelling vision is not just an intellectual concept or, even worse, an empty slogan with the current trend verbiage such as "excellence" and "world class." It brings forth a future state of being, linking all five senses to the picture.

A short, powerful description comes from working a deep, collective meaning. As with personal vision, the organizational vision is cemented when it is alive, clear, and commands high commitment—not arm-twisting or the desire to finish the exercise but one of genuine enthusiasm. The process of crafting a vision will generate excitement and energy in an engaged group.

A great place for the transformational coach to begin is by asking the leadership team open-ended questions to get to the transformative insights as to why the organization exists at all and why the leaders are choosing to be part of the organization. Why are you here? What are you striving for in the future? This is by nature a multilayered inquiry into the personal and collective visions and the relationship between them. Although a leadership team might project a strong sense of knowing, it is still well advised for the coach to ask the "why are we/you here" questions. Even if a high level of consciousness exists, such inquiry brings current awareness to the surface.

Don't succumb to the belief that questions concerning "why" are too sophomoric for a certain organizations and leaders. A friend of mine who unselfishly coaches French priests when they take on a leadership role has shared about the breakthroughs that occurred on several occasions when the priests reflected deeply on the question of "why this path?" I have done work with some churches and groups of faith where I thought the answer to "why" seemed so obvious. But deeper probing revealed an astounding level of unconsciousness among some groups and individuals—not to say the organizations or the people within were disingenuous, but rather they had a less-than-effective understanding of why they were engaged in the pursuits they'd chosen. This is to say that not all people and organizations that project purposeful activities are indeed purposeful. It doesn't make them "bad," but it does reflect a level of consciousness that will not facilitate transformation without deeper work.

In the Wall exercise, leaders might fail, at least initially, in casting a compelling organizational vision—a bold vision that is transformative in nature—and merely propose an extension of the current state instead. An effective coach will stay with it, asking for additional descriptive expressions of what would excite them about a future organization, not steering them toward a particular answer but helping them express a vision that inspires them and generates enthusiasm.

 Control Panel

The vision control panel is a visual depiction of the handful of essential metrics for gauging where the organization is in its journey toward achieving its vision—in short, the key indicators of success. In an airplane these might be altitude, fuel level, speed, direction, and oil pressure; other metrics might be tracked, such as cabin temperature, which may be important to certain facets of the journey, but not as critical over the entire journey as fuel level. Building the vision control panel is often a place to test the vision itself for clarity; if the team can't figure out how to measure "it," the "it" may be too vaguely defined, which will make it very difficult to communicate "it" to the organization in any meaningful way, to determine how to get there, and to know when you've arrived.

The control panel straddles the present and the future. The transformation is a leap forward to a future the organization has most likely never experienced, which often requires a radical change in the organization's approach to measurement. What are the metrics of tomorrow? How do we start to measure that which was not deemed important in the past but will now be important as we build a new future? This will be just the first of many discussions throughout the transformation cycle about measurement. In the latter stages of the transformation cycle in particular, the measurement system will facilitate or hamper monitoring the implementation of action plans and reviewing their results, which are gateways to working on deeper issues about taking accountability for results, learning from mistakes as well as successes, and other aspects of culture and mindsets.

Burning Platform

A burning platform evokes the image of standing in an untenable position, atop a platform on fire. The organizational analogy is the peril of not taking action, of maintaining the current stance. At its core, the burning platform speaks to why the organization must change. What dangers grow as a result of the current state? What menaces the health of the organization?

The burning flames might be fueled by competition, regulation, destructive moral or environmental problems—one or more tsunamis that threaten to overwhelm the organization. The sustainability of the present situation is most certainly in question, at least to those with sufficient foresight. The burning platform supplies substantial initial urgency to overcome organizational inertia and sustain energy toward a vision. Therefore, in the absence of an urgent reason to transform the organization (or the presence of denial that it does exist), odds are the energy required to make such a jump will be harder to muster.

Consider the promise of a great meal. Build a vision in your mind of a top-tier restaurant with your favorite food found in abundance. Imagine with all five of your senses: a welcoming atmosphere, warm lighting, the sounds of laughter and pleasure, the camaraderie of your dining companions, the beautiful presentation, aroma, and flavors of your meal. A compelling vision, yes? Or perhaps it's a vision of fresh corn from the local farmer's field and barbecued chicken on the grill under a bright blue sky, cold beer in hand, and the kids playing in the yard.

The burning platform in either case concerns your appetite. If you are famished, the vision has tremendous power. If you are stuffed from a holiday dinner or three hours of snacking during the broadcast of a football game, the thought of additional food is revolting. The vision hasn't changed; the burning platform simply has no urgency at the moment, supplies no reason, no real power to motivate you to get up off the couch and expend any energy toward making your vision a reality.

The burning platform and the vision work in tandem. The burning platform creates the urgency to move away from a current state that is, quite simply, no longer acceptable to the organization. You are coaching people to realize the price of not moving toward breakthrough. You are not working to drive in fear. Rather, the most powerful burning platform is when individuals simply take a stance that the picture of nonaction is unacceptable, not with boastful exclamations or shaking of dread but a deep conviction that the burning platform image cannot be allowed to happen. In contrast, the vision is the compelling future state, attracting by its nature. A successful transformation hinges upon these two elements generating a powerful push-pull that coalesces commitment and energy around the long, hard work of personal and collective change.

The Situation Appraisal might have revealed that top leadership is acutely aware of a burning platform, but the rest of the organization does not see it. Perhaps the top leaders have not communicated it clearly to the rest of the organization for fear of its implications for attraction, motivation, and retention of key talent, or the impact on perceptions of customers, suppliers, and external stakeholders. Or top leadership might feel it can't reveal a major problem without having a solution already in hand. Perhaps other leaders listened to top management but refused to hear the message, preferring instead to deny a serious problem and avoid having to grapple with what to do about it. The transformational coach asks the necessary questions to get to the heart of the problem, and works with the leaders to address the issue as rapidly as possible in order to lay a strong foundation for the transformational effort.

 *Encores, Never Agains,*
Lessons Learned

To construct the Past portion of the wall, the transformational coach moves back into the "explore" stage of the 3Es coaching model to understand how much baggage the organization carries with it, as revealed through the stories people tell about past events. Do participants see connections between past events and the present? Are they able to extract clear learnings from the past? What are the few key learnings from past successes and failures? Are these learnings shared by participants, or do argumentative, historical revisions ensue?

This part of the Wall engages participants in examining two types of past events that capture the organization at its performance extremes:

- *Encores*—the things accomplished with excellence in the past, whose outcomes indicate high performance; sources of organizational pride.
- *Never Agains*—past occurrences that fell well below the mark, demonstrating poor performance; sources of organizational shame.

The encores and never agains are nearly always embedded in a narrative—stories have been woven around the particulars and eventually become part of the organizational lore. These are valuable experiences that contain the seeds of organizational learning, but if unexamined they also come with both positive and negative baggage. For example, a past success (encore) may make leaders prone to apply the same actions against a new problem, even though the current situation may not be identical to the past. Likening a proposed course of action to a prior failure (never again) can trigger a new round of attributing blame, bring up old hurts, or prevent leaders from taking appropriate risks in changed circumstances. And one person might consider a specific event as a success while another person might see it as a failure, which can lead to time and energy spent unproductively revising history. It is not important that every individual agree whether a situation is an encore or a never again. In fact, the same occurrence may be seen by one person as an encore, by another person as a never again.

The coach's focus is to extract from the experience the essential lessons learned, lessons that are not event dependent and thus are applicable under other circumstances. For example, an organization's investment in a customer service training program for new and recent hires might have been highly rated by participants at the end of training, in large part because it exposed them to a breadth of knowledge about the company, its products and customers, and to many customer service procedures they would use on the job. They left the training feeling well prepared for their jobs. However, within weeks after the initial training sessions, the frontline supervisors began to criticize the program's effectiveness, claiming the new people were unprepared to handle the interpersonal aspects of their interactions with customers, and customer satisfaction with their experience was in fact declining. Supervisors and their bosses wanted the Training & Development director's "head on a plate," while the T&D department railed that the customer service department had failed to convey up front all the important job skills and challenges. Nearly two years after the event, T&D is still trying to regain credibility with its internal customers, and managers are leery of requesting or authorizing any new training programs.

What possible lessons might the organization learn from this experience?

Investment in new employee training is well received by the new hires and creates the conditions for early engagement and loyalty.

The impact of training on new employee performance will fall short of its potential unless training addresses the full range of skills critical to job performance, including behavioral (how to interact appropriately with the customer under various circumstances), and post-training follow-up—to gauge how well trainees are doing in the "real world"—is well planned, executed, and used to improve the training course.

These now stand apart as distilled, useful lessons devoid of the emotional and political baggage that accompanied the actual event and the story it "spawned." Leaders are now free to leverage the lessons learned without becoming embroiled in the nonproductive elements surrounding the history.

You'll need to keep the meeting's focus on the lessons learned as you coach leaders through this portion of the Wall. Otherwise, the strong emotional current linked to the past events is likely to carry the group into negative or unproductive discussions, which keep it anchored to the past in an unhealthy way.

The lessons learned from the encores and never agains free the organization to drop its emotional baggage instead of replaying the battles of the past. In this way, the past really becomes the past. The organization can directly access the lessons learned, now divorced from any political or emotional context, and apply them to future opportunities and challenges.

 *Current State*

The current state is probably the most straightforward element of the Wall exercise. Few leadership teams have any trouble describing it from two perspectives:

- *What's Working*—The organizational assets as they pertain to the journey ahead. What is in the organization's favor today?
- *What's Not Working*—The organizational liabilities. What is holding the organization back today?

Similar to a SWOT analysis (Strengths, Weaknesses, Opportunities, Threats), which is sometimes used to populate this element, what's working and not working is an inventory. Feedback from the Situation Appraisal often sheds light on the current state.

You will have no problem in generating material for this wall element. The caution, however, is to prevent the discussion from getting bogged down in the "organizational liabilities." Even though the Wall is ultimately a creation session with a breakthrough focus, if the coach isn't careful it can devolve into a problem-solving exercise—the energy shifts and the window for creative thinking closes. At times, one or more participants might use this tactic consciously or unconsciously to skirt the more difficult (and perhaps more threatening) aspects of the radical change inherent in moving to the future state. Problem solving, by comparison, falls within the comfort zone of most leaders still close to their managerial roots.

Perhaps the greatest challenge you face at this point is to move the group into a causal mindset to explore the current state—to avoid seeing results as "bad" or "good" but rather as those intended by the leaders, the manifestation of what they truly desire. The coach helps participants to look deeply into the organization's accomplishments and failures as the conscious or unconscious collective will at work. Yes, a different set of goals/outcomes may have been the focus of planning and communications, with very visible endorsement from leaders, but the current reality speaks more loudly. It is always strange to hear an organization's leaders taking credit for accomplishments while attributing disappointing results to external factors.

To reject seeing all results—negative as well as positive—in terms of intentional creation is to remain rooted in a victim mindset where choices are severely limited and authentic learning cannot occur. The existing system and results are what were intended. The organization can take credit for great products, services, and relationships; likewise, it must also be willing to take ownership of poor product or service delivery/performance, shareholders and a public disenchanted with its response to a quality crisis, declining employee engagement, customer desertions, or other undesirable outcomes that dog its current state. Be aware that until the members of the leadership team are willing to accept ownership of all results, your attempts to enroll them in alternative thinking about anything else will encounter the same victim mindset.

⟺ Closing the Gap

The journey from the current state to the vision, with all its implications of radical change, is not likely to be accomplished in the course of one transformation cycle. Selecting the actions needed to close the gap will be a matter of choosing those one to three initiatives likely to have the greatest impact in moving the organization forward, and then building on this progress with additional initiatives in subsequent cycles. If an organization is in its first transformation cycle, initiatives might address major issues around transformation readiness surfaced in the Situation Appraisal—for example, raising cross-organizational awareness about a burning platform, or building the top team's competencies for transformational leadership—or implementing/strengthening a measurement system and mentality, an essential cornerstone to any transformation effort. These create a solid foundation for later cycles and initiatives.

The group's tendency, especially in early cycles, may be to focus on fixing current problems. While many of these may be the source of much "organizational heartburn," and solving one or more of them might appear at first to be a potential "quick win" for the transformation effort, they are more likely to generate incremental improvement than break-through performance. Furthermore, old mindsets are still in play, along with insufficient understanding of the interdependencies with other systems. This is why so many strategic planning sessions lapse into problem solving sessions that are not transformative in nature.

The transformational coach encourages participants to take pause, stand back from the Present represented on the Wall, and shift their orientation to the Future, to imagine that they have accomplished the vision and can now look back to discover the critical contributing initiatives that paved the way for the successful journey. What changes enabled real breakthrough to follow? A truly compelling vision will ground them in that desired future state, a powerful shift in orientation where the future becomes the present, real, taking both mind and spirit to a new place with new possibilities, opening it to a wisdom that is much harder to tap when we are trapped in the current state of disappointment, pressure, longing, and fear. When the participants place themselves in that desired future, the current state becomes, momentarily, the past, and they see themselves free of the concerns and fears and constraints that kept them locked into the nonproductive thoughts and behaviors and their unfavorable outcomes.

From this perspective of having achieved the organizational vision, sit with leaders in a deep inquiry about what actions and changes ultimately set the organization in the right direction, opened the right doors, cleared away formidable hurdles. Commonly, the situation appraisal has spotlighted critical issues with the ability of one or more organizational fronts to support the transformation effort.

Carefully examine each proposed initiative. In what way does it carry the organization closer to its desired future? Is it a knee-jerk reaction to a current state problem? Is it proposed because it seems politically correct?

The team should be looking at one but no more than three major initiatives that target radical change rather then incremental improvement. An initiative may be multifaceted, in which case it can be broken down into discrete manageable projects later in the planning process. An initiative should not be so general in nature or so broadly defined that any activity could qualify as contributing to moving the initiative forward.

Points of Arrival and Departure

The final elements of the Wall are succinct descriptions, in both quantitative and qualitative terms, of the beginning and ending points for each transformation initiative:

- *Point of Departure*—the current state or character of the system, competency, or physical condition that constitutes the focus of the initiative. For instance, if a transformation initiatives call for building a superb sales force, characterize the state of the current sales force—the number of reps, their skill set, current performance level, etc.
- *Point of Arrival*—the short-term (6–18 month) goal set (more or less a mini-vision) that signals the completion of the initiative; a solid, measurable destination. What does the end game look like? Be specific. In the example of the desired sales force, how many sales people will be required? What skills must they have? What volume of sales would individuals be expected to produce? Where would they be located? What infrastructure would be required to support them?

Together the points of departure and arrival of an initiative represent the gap between the present and the future in this one important area of the transformational effort. For instance, we'd know the sales force gap in terms of headcount, skill sets, role structure, performance expectations, etc.

Each initiative necessarily requires a detailed implementation plan, including a timeline, suggested by the gridlines on the Wall graphic. The actual details of planning and implementation are developed and documented later, perhaps using a formal project management approach and software application, with full provisions for tracking progress and results to determine the impact of this work on the vision as a whole.

An Integrated View of Assessment Findings

Your stance as coach is not to draw conclusions, that is, to make judgments, about what the Situation Appraisal reveals but rather to surface and present a summary of your findings and discoveries as launch points for further discussion with the leadership team about the implications for the transformation effort.

A key finding, for example, may be that leaders or certain parts of the organization might not perceive a substantial burning platform for change, despite top leadership's belief that one exists. Without a strong motivation for undertaking significant change over a long period of time, it may be difficult to bring all parts of the organization along in a synchronized effort: A leadership team not unified on the need for transformation is likely to doom the effort. Therefore, the highest priorities for the transformational effort could include doing some foundational work in raising awareness around the real threats facing the organization.

The Achilles' heel of so many organizations is the lack of a whole-system view, especially within the context of purposeful work and vision revelation, that is, consciousness about what the system is aimed at creating. Part of the work of the coach is to take past assessments, for example, about employee engagement or turnover and view them relative to other sources of input—other past assessments as well as new areas probed in the situation appraisal—and then integrate it all into a more comprehensive assessment of the organizational front of *motivation*. Past assessments often have a rather narrow focus, where they were done and evaluated without consideration of other fronts or systems with which they share interdependencies. Given this, past assessments could actually conflict with one another, or resulting initiatives could impact other efforts in unanticipated ways. A coach's holistic view of the interplay among these factors can bring leaders new organizational insights and understandings, as well as reveal patterns of thinking that stand in the way of a whole-system approach to transformation.

Revealing the True Purpose of the Organization

One of the most telling revelations of a Situation Appraisal is a gap or even conflict between the stated purpose, vision, and values of the organization and its "demonstrated" purpose as seen in people's daily actions and the actual results and outcomes being produced. There is a tendency to conclude that the organization's systems actually create the organization's results—some organizations perpetuate the story that the "system" is the barrier to accomplishment. While this has some validity—thus our assessment focuses on the nine organizational fronts—but it is also important to recognize that the systems did not arise on their own; they are actually manifestations of the conscious and unconscious purpose(s) pursued by leaders and other members of the organization.

The organizational artifacts of purpose paint a picture. Be it the mission and vision statement on the wall, the website, the posting of key values on a bulletin board, or the latest leader address on video, these pronouncements tell one story. These expressions are usually well intentioned, but when you as coach look objectively at the results created, you see a mismatch. In short, that which is articulated is not being lived. To understand the true purpose of the organization, look closely at the actual results being created.

Take, for instance, the ability of an organization to connect with its customers. What if surveys or other feedback indicate low customer satisfaction, or, even more critical, a lack of customer delight, despite the lunchroom wall poster that exclaims the importance of the customer? To explain this, one might be tempted to dive into customer feedback mechanisms, or directly investigate the systems that interface with customers. Plenty of customer-sensing tools exist, many of them exceptional. But instead, the transformational coach probes at a deeper level to understand what the disposition of the organization is toward customers in general that such poor performance could result.

The coach views the situation from the lens of an intentional mindset, one of creation orientation: The organization is causal with respect to these poor results. The organization has created poor customer service *for a purpose*, either conscious or unconscious. To address the customer-focused systems without first understanding why the organization chooses to have poor customer relations will be a forced correction at best, and at worst a failed intervention that does not produce measurable improvement. Start by revealing the true organizational purpose that is mirrored in organization and business outcomes and might be at odds with the stated purpose, for it is here that the reasons for poor customer satisfaction and loyalty may well be rooted.

For example, a coach might find that poor customer service by a state agency is linked to a fundamental lack of recognition of its various stakeholders. Possibly the agency sees service to the government hierarchy as paramount, rather than to the public at large. The members of the public who directly interface with the service unit are not even considered to be customers. A common mechanical fix to the issue is to re-label the public as "customers" and governmental offices as "customer service centers," as if semantics alone will lead to the radical shift in awareness required to change thinking and subsequent behavior. But such actions are premature and bound to fail without an examination of the deep-seated beliefs about the value of service and honoring customers. A good transformation coach will begin working with the beliefs and mental stances of leaders and employees toward the public they serve. She initiates an open dialog around meaning and attraction to customer service as an essential purpose for groups and individuals working in this arena. What does it mean to serve the public? Why does the organization currently choose not to be excellent in this regard? What is the organization choosing instead of superior customer service? To what extent do members of the agency desire to live in service to others, and to the public in particular?

The organization may be indignant when asked to engage in such self-examination; offended by any questioning of their altruistic motives. Many may want to move to action without inquiry. Some individuals might point to the written statements about valuing the customer as proof of the organization's commitment to customer service. However, the results clearly demonstrate that this value is not being lived.

It is obvious that the nature of the coach's questions can quickly transport the group into a "big conversation," one that calls upon all members of the organization to delve deeply into their psyche, which requires courage and a safe environment. It would be less threatening for the individuals to simply focus on the customer service mechanisms and seek or supply an expert solution. But because the genesis of the problem often lies within the collective mental stance toward service in general, to focus initially on skill building or process improvements is to put the cart before the horse.

The Situation Appraisal can surface such fundamental problems as this, and the coach will need to determine the best way to explore with the leaders the internal drivers of the unsatisfactory outcomes. Most importantly the coach needs to construct a safe haven for such an inquiry.

A simple exercise is to have the leaders write down the demonstrated mission, vision, and values as they are revealed in current actions and results—with no judgment intended—and then have them compare these to the organization's stated mission, vision, and values. Real insights can arise from this discussion. The Wall exercise, part of the CAMP session and described later in this chapter, is often the forum for exploring such difficult issues within the less-threatening context of painting a path to the future rather than laying blame for the past.

As the coach, you will guide many teams in the organization, beginning with the top leadership, through this exploratory work. You'll help individuals and teams stand back from the organization and disengage from the emotions generated by seeing their results as "good" or "bad." Not until they can study individual and collective performance from a primarily objective viewpoint can real headway be made. These conversations are critical for beginning to instill a causal mindset where it does not currently exist, to coach leaders, teams, and individuals toward accepting that they "own the results," and that blaming or defensiveness or denial only lock them in an unproductive pattern of behavior that produces the same outcomes as in the past.

Bringing the Transformational Story to Life

The organization's transformation story will be one of the most powerful tools the organization can use to engage the entire workforce, and extended partners, in the necessity for and promise of the journey ahead. A truly effective story, filled with meaning and truth, has the potential to touch people at their core and unleash genuine enthusiasm and desire to be involved. An ineffective story, one that is superficial, that fails to resonate with meaning that speaks to the listeners, or that comes across as half-hearted or smacks in the slightest of manipulation, will leave the listener unconvinced, on the fence, or worse, generate cynicism that leads to resistance.

An effective communication strategy throughout each transformation cycle will have at its core members of the leadership team telling the story of the journey, past, present and future. It is essential that the organization's leaders convey the story, not only throughout the organization but also to its the extended community. Your skills as a coach will be tested in the area of helping leaders perform this sacred undertaking.

Honing the Story

The details developed in the Wall exercise during the CAMP session outline each element of the transformation story: the vision being created, how this vision fits the purpose of the organization, the imperative nature of pursuing the vision, and the few transformational initiatives that will facilitate the leap toward the vision. But this is just an outline. It must be crafted into a complete but concise narrative, one that is above all compelling. The coach plays an important role in this. Can you tell the story of the transformational journey that lay ahead for the organization? Do you sense the compelling nature and down-to-earth quality of the story? Play back the description of the future vision to leadership. Practice the story with people outside leadership, outside even the organization. Listen and sense their initial responses. See if the story is digestible to them. Do they get the picture? Does it stir their energy?

Put simply, if the story is confusing and uninspiring to you, odds are it will play the same for the organization. And if it takes a lot of explanation to convince others of its energy, the story is weak. The storyline needs work. Lay out the elements of the story using the Wall, rework the narrative based on the feedback you've received and your intuitive sense of what will resonate with the organization. There are many worthwhile resources on the art of storytelling, and investing time in learning the art can be fun. One text I recommend is *Improving Your Storytelling: Beyond the Basics for All Who Tell Stories in Work and Play* (August House, 1999) by Doug Lipman, who speaks directly of the transformational potential of stories.

Coaching the Storytellers

The creation journey will not transpire if it exists only in the hearts of a few leaders. Leaders are called to share the vision and *inspire* others to join the journey. Inspire, from the Latin word *inspirare*, means to breathe, as in to breathe spirit. Leaders are asked to breathe spirit into the transformational story. In hearing the story, employees and other stake-holders should see the glow of the future state, a vivid picture of what can be created. Unlike manipulation or casting a cult-like trance, which is to exert control or take away free choice, to inspire others in the organization is to welcome them to connect with the spirit of the transformational story—to sense a resonance with their personal purpose and vision—and willingly unleash their own spirits toward the collective vision.

In coaching the storytellers, practice makes perfect. Leaders tend to include too much detail; they fail to connect with the listener and instead flood them with information. For the listener, it's akin to drinking from a fire hydrant—more drenching than thirst quenching. Patiently coach such leaders to slow down and focus on the vital aspects of the message rather than deluging the listeners with a flood of tangential elements. Leaders have been immersed in a long, deep dialog that eventually gave birth to the transformational story; however, the intention in sharing the transformational story now is not to chronicle that conversation in all its detail. The leaders, with the aid of the coach, must distill the salient results into a powerful and efficient narrative, building in detail if and when requested.

Different media channels require different messaging. The coach works with the organization to think through the best manner in which to both present the story and create dialog around the journey. Keeping the creation journey central to the organization requires telling the story more than once. As time and the journey move forward, the story expands in historical depth and richness, and people see the progress already made and the barriers overcome.

Help leaders keep the story alive. Coach them not just to tell, but recognize that the story thrives when others can see themselves within the narrative. In a sense, the story is but one chapter in a much larger novel being co-created by everyone in the organization. When leaders inquire of others what role they will play in the living transformational tale, others begin to move toward the vision, becoming co-creators and not just dutiful followers. Engaged leaders welcome insights and contributions from others, blending their energies into the transformation narrative. Through conversation, leaders can elicit excitement and commitment in others. And ultimately, the transformation story is a personal story told by each individual, expressed in terms of their accomplishments to create something remarkable. Part of your role is to coach leaders in how to breathe spirit into the story, and in the many ways of engaging others about the journey. Encourage leaders to get in touch with their excitement about creating a new future, and with their leadership calling to coach others to do the same.

Performance Measurement and Review

Implementation is the phase where many an initiative loses—or never gains—traction, where efforts waver and their connection to the larger goal becomes vague. To enact successful implementation of the transformation plan, an organization must have a solid measurement system for capturing and tracking results. And to be an effective transformation coach, you must have strength in measurement. Your measurement acumen, or the lack thereof, will be made evident throughout the entire spectrum of coaching domains: From self to individual, teams, and especially organizations, skill in building and nurturing measurement systems is absolutely necessary for assuring a reliable method for providing legitimate performance feedback. As I've stressed in other chapters, such feedback is essential for gauging the impact of transformation efforts on the key areas where radical change is desired. Many organizations already understand that key corporate measures are not only an important management tool but also a visible means of keeping the story of the transformation journey vibrant and relevant for everyone.

Measurement is a discipline in its own right. Being a former operations leader with an engineering background and strong focus on process and product quality, designing and working with measurement systems has long been part of my skill set. However, it might be a challenge for coaches centered upon interpersonal might and the mystic aspects of leadership. For these, I strongly recommend study of the subject, as it is not the intention of this book to cover this in any depth.

A Few Key Points about the Measurement System

Weaknesses in the measurement system—one of the nine organizational fronts mentioned earlier in this chapter—often surfaces early in the

Situation Appraisal and the Wall exercise, and improving the system will sooner or later become an imperative for leaders. I have frequently found the need to press the issue, particularly when mindsets and cultural factors present formidable invisible barriers to putting a good system in place. Until these are brought to light and worked through, even a well-designed measurement system will be difficult to embed. For example, some organizations have an aversion to performance measures as they fear the contextual nature of the entire performance is not being considered—a set of measures is never a perfect reflection of the whole—and thus building and sharing a complete measurement system is a low priority for them. Perhaps because of a bad prior experience with performance data, leadership might feel it best to produce a set of measures for each need rather than devising a comprehensive set of measures that can be tailored on occasion if needed. If the organization does not already have one, emphasize that leaders need to develop version 1.0 of a comprehensive measurement system. It won't be perfect, but flying blindly is no substitute.

The coach will often need to raise awareness about why a measurement system is essential to the transformation and what the characteristics of a good system are. Below are a few points I've found important to highlight in these conversations with organizational leaders:

- The system should depict the cascading nature of work. The individual contributor must be able to see the connection between his/her efforts and achieving the desired organizational outcomes that bring the organization closer to its vision. (See Figure 6.9.)

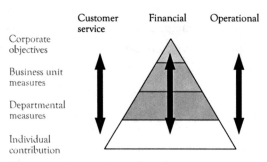

Figure 6.9. The cascading nature of work.

- Measures should reflect and thereby raise awareness of any cross-functional/disciplinary interdependencies, thereby highlighting the need for cooperation, support, and possible integration of work between potential silos.
- Above all, the measurement system must be easily understood if it is to play a role in focusing efforts and guiding decisions. Having all performance data in a standard format is a must. Individuals should not have to work to interpret the format for each measure but rather focus on the information emanating from the data. The units of measurement—for example, Internet sales volume, new product delivery cycle time, equipment capability ratios, etc.—should be carefully selected.

Drivers and Enablers

Knowing the connection between outcome results and drivers of these results provides context and meaning to the daily work. What are the few key contributors that when improved will drive or influence the desired outcome to become a reality? These causal contributors are known as *drivers* and *enablers*. Drivers contribute directly to the outcome; enablers influence the system to make obtaining the outcome easier.

A way to see the difference is envisioning a flow of water through a pipe. The driver in this case is pressure, for without pressure at one end of the pipe, water will not flow. But the amount of pressure required is determined in large part by the pipe's internal dimension. If the size of the pipe were to increase, then the water would be enabled to flow more easily. Increasing the size of the pipe by itself will not have water move, but enough pressure in the current pipe size will accomplish the task, however costly to the system. Likewise, drivers alone will do the job but at a high cost. Best to combine with some enablers. Cost cutting in a business setting might be a driver toward increased profits, whereas training in lean systems will not directly increase profits or even cut costs, but it could enable staff to make wise system improvements that will.

Comprehensive analysis can reveal eye-opening relationships between desired outcomes and their primary drivers and enablers. Thus these are well worth mapping with system mapping and value stream mapping techniques. Use the learnings from these and other analyses as input which measures to choose and which nesting relationship to depict. When it comes to portraying or representing the measurement system, however, simplify for clarity (see Figure 6.10).

Individual Performance Management

The measurement system for aggregate performance should ultimately be linked with a solid performance management system for individual basis that encompasses a plan-do-study-act cycle (see Figure 6.11). The individual's performance plan incorporates a career plan (long-term) and a work plan (near-term), both aligned with the organization's transformational plan. Again, the objective here is not to cover this aspect of performance management in detail—many excellent resources are available to help build a comprehensive contribution system. However, the

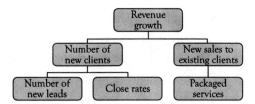

Figure 6.10. Example of primary drivers and enablers.

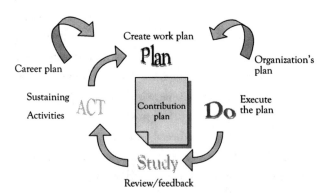

Figure 6.11. PDSA cycle for individual performance management system.

transformational coach must examine the organization's individual performance management process to ensure it is robust in nature. If it is not, this could be a priority for transformational coaching.

Review Process

A solid organizational performance management system has at its heart a productive review process for transformational initiatives and supporting action. In three decades of transformational change implementation, a key learning for us has been the importance of performance reviews. We believe in the holistic approach of the transformation, but if one single element had to be chosen as most important, the performance review element would be the priority. Establishing a method to regularly review performance improvement status is vital. Without this element, plans and actions are without a rudder. The performance reviews mandate accountability, force the measurement of performance, deliver course correction, and drive vision clarity. An organization not committed to performance reviews will find it difficult at best to attain transformational results.

The detailed transformation plans that emerge from the CAMP session address the organization's key one to three transformation initiatives as well as transformation initiatives and improvement plans in each part of the organization. These action plans are launched and managed as projects with teams, timelines, objectives, and metrics for gauging progress and outcomes. The review process has as its overall purpose the regular and systematic study of whether the action plans are being executed and are achieving desired results. However, as we'll see, this is far from a mechanistic exercise and offers the transformation coach very fertile opportunities for embedding productive mindsets and practices seeding a culture oriented toward breakthrough performance—all of which are drivers of transformation success.

Progress reviews most positively impact implementation effectiveness when they follow a standardized format and occur on a regular basis, thus instilling personal and organizational discipline around an activity that may initially be greeted as a waste of time, or, when results are disappointing, as downright painful. They also bring a transparency to the entire implementation stage of the Transformation Cycle by making results and the reasons for them visible beyond the team working the particular project. The sessions establish that the work is important and create a recurring forum for senior leadership and the implementation team or individual to communicate with each other. Regular reviews also increase individual accountability and urgency for delivering results.

For the organization this is the mechanism for keeping the transformation effort on track: assuring that actions are not only occurring as intended but also producing the performance improvements that take the organization closer to its desired future. For the individuals and teams, these are the opportunities to discover personal and collective patterns of thinking (and the ensuing behaviors) that are obstructing greater effectiveness, and to learn more productive mindsets that pave the way for co-creating the desired results. These two aspects are, of course, interdependent. The transformational coach plays a pivotal role in reinforcing the need for progress reviews, participating from a place of deep inquiry and listening, and leveraging the learning opportunities that present themselves.

There are two types of reviews: monthly and quarterly. The monthly review focuses on the execution of the action plans and achievement of their objectives in relationship to each transformational initiative. The action plans represent tasks that, when executed, will enable the transformation initiatives to move forward toward their Points of Arrival. The focus of the quarterly review is whether the results achieved by each transformation initiative are having the desired impact on the key performance areas, the handful of metrics in the control panel developed as part of the Wall exercise.

Monthly Progress Review

The intent of the monthly review session is to allow the accountable persons and/or teams to share with leadership what is working and what is not, relative to the initiatives. Participants include the individuals responsible for execution, the leadership team, and the transformation coach. Ideally, the first reviews occur within one month of chartering the initiatives.

Monthly Review Questions. The individuals should be prepared to answer the following questions during the monthly review:

Did we execute the action plan for the objective as planned?

If not, why not? And what do we need to do to get back on track?

If we have executed the action plan as planned, is the result as expected?

What are the one or two key learnings at this point in the execution process?

Gap Analysis Questions. When the action plan was not executed as planned, the individuals are expected to complete a gap analysis prior to the review meeting. This prepares them to answer the monthly review questions listed above when they do meet with the leadership team and the coach. The gap analysis is a systematic method of attempting to get to the root cause of why the action plan did not get executed as expected. The questions the individuals ask themselves when completing a gap analysis are similar to the monthly review questions:

1. Did we execute the action plan for the objective as planned? If not, why not?
2. Why did this situation or event occur?
3. What do we need to do to get back on track with this action plan and achieve the objective?

With the assistance of the coach, both sets of questions provide a framework for reviews and course corrections in which individuals and groups can learn from their actions (the Encourage phase of the 3Es Transformational Coaching Model). These questions and the insights they generate enable the coach to continue to reinforce the adoption of productive mindsets, opening the door to conscious creation. As coach, you strive within these meetings to nurture an environment conducive to learning by asking questions that draw out knowledge without creating defensiveness. You watch out for judgment statements that might shut down learning. The review process serves to provide insights, and insights require open dialog. You encourage high performance standards and provide feedback, but if personal performance issues need to be addressed, these should be dealt with outside the context of the review meeting.

The process goes beyond generating an organizational report card. Reports on the actions taken and current results should have already been distributed and studied before the review. Too often conversations center on the accuracy of the data presented or the portrayal of results. Getting these issues resolved prior to the review is important. The power of the review rests in the reinforcement of new thinking and consideration of the deeper reasons underpinning performance as it relates to the individual, team, and organization. These are big conversations to hold. The defense mechanism is to overly analyze the measurement system. Obviously, the measurement system, including the data gathering and information portrayal, is important. But the measurement system is a living vehicle for insight to performance. And stalling out at the gate with measurement system discussions hinders the ability to have the deeper conversation.

So have an accountable agent for the measurement system who works on its quality and effectiveness. Distribute updates and results prior to result reviews, and work as many issues as possible prior to the gatherings. From experience, I can say this is something you as transformational coach will probably need to help move ahead. But once you have, then the reviews can dive deeply into learnings about the collective and individual reasons for whatever levels of performance are being experienced.

It is only with new insights to self and the collective that the future can be different. You encourage the participants to consider "Why did we do or not do what we set out to accomplish? What happened inside me/ us along the way?"

When the unproductive focus on the outside influences rears its head, as it inevitably will, you can point to a system that despite outside demands and internal complexity performed. Think of the payroll system. With all the complications and challenges people got paid. Why? Because it was high on the list of importance as far as the individual was concerned and the organization vision was aligned to this priority. So, given that the organization can get the things done it really cares about, what happened in the nonperformance areas?

When participants rationalize disappointing progress or outcomes are through nonproductive mindsets, they are severely limiting the range of options available for addressing the issues and getting initiatives back on track. You help the group think more deeply about shifting to more productive ways of thinking: adopting intentionality versus resorting to victimhood, seeing abundance rather than scarcity, the power rather than limits, oneness instead of detachment, and authenticity versus image making—these are the true and most deeply valuable learnings of the progress reviews.

The coach facilitates each review meeting with a goal of quicker access to the profound and shorter duration of unconscious actions. I have seen these review sessions be the highlight of the month with breakthrough after breakthrough. And I have experienced the pain in having these reviews struggle to move beyond an undesirable chore.

Quarterly Progress Review

In a quarterly review, leaders step back from the action plans. The leadership team has as its ultimate goal the achievement of key performance areas, the measures of having attained the vision, as depicted in the Control Panel portion of the Wall. The transformational initiatives were thought to be the levers best pulled to produce the breakthrough vision. Now that the initiatives are being executed, are they indeed the right levers? In the quarterly review, the leaders assess what kind of impact the progress toward or attainment of the transformational initiative objectives is having in the key performance areas—or more broadly, whether the implementation of the transformation plan is effectively bringing the organization closer to the vision and breakthrough performance. Is the expected cause and effect relationship between the transformational initiatives and achievement of the vision correct?

Typical questions during a quarterly review include the following:

1. Are these particular transformational initiatives improving key performance areas? How?
2. Are all initiatives impacting the key performance areas, and how are they interacting with each other?
3. Is there anything that needs to be done to improve the performance trend we are experiencing in the key performance areas?
4. How can leadership better support each transformational initiative team's work?

You are listening to the quality of the discussions and evaluating the leadership team's "honesty" with regards to the assessment. Sometimes, leadership teams live in hope when breakthrough performance fails to materialize. It is true that there could be a delay function inherent in the whole system: The transformational initiatives are the right levers but performance has an unexpected lagging characteristic. But if the leadership has moved to a dream world of waiting "just a few more months" when it is evident that the breakthrough isn't going to arrive, you need to prompt a different conversation. Bring the team back to the compelling vision, the ever-hotter burning platform, and their conscious wills to actually produce a transformation. If one or more transformational initiatives is not being accomplished as desired or is ineffective in its performance impact, it is time for the team to roll up its sleeves and alter the plan.

The COLA Case Study

The case study of COLA presents an excellent example of how transformational coaching in the four domains of self, individuals, teams, and organization were integrated with methodologies and tools in an organizationwide multiyear initiative to successfully create breakthrough performance.

In 1988, as the U.S. Congress was poised to enact a series of requirements for medical labs, known as the Clinical Laboratory Improvement Amendments (CLIA 88), four medical organizations took the initiative to create a private alternative for ensuring compliance with the new federal standards. The American Medical Association (AMA), the College of American Pathologists (CAP), the American Society of Internal Medicine (ASIM),[4] and the American Academy of Family Physicians (AAFP) funded the creation of COLA, a not-for-profit organization focused on improving the quality of laboratory testing in physician office laboratories through peer review and education. The strength of COLA's leadership team—along with the collective vision, commitment, conviction, and financial investment of the founding organizations—led to COLA's unprecedented rise to become the largest laboratory accreditation program in the United States.

During its first decade, COLA worked to maximize its operational efficiency so that it could continue to offer physicians a low-cost accreditation alternative to government inspection of their office lab. COLA quickly built a reputation as an industry leader for its excellent operations and high customer value.

By the mid-1990s, however, changing market forces—mainly a shrinking number of physician office laboratories—compelled COLA's board of directors to explore options for ensuring COLA's financial health, resulting in the first call for diversification in 1995. COLA launched research and development efforts to study the feasibility of extending its accreditation services to all types of medical testing sites, including large hospitals, home healthcare agencies, mobile testing sites, and nursing homes. Over the next several years, COLA invested reserves in new product development and made technology the centerpiece of its accreditation program operation, realizing significant efficiencies as a result.

But as the manufacturers of test instruments and kits simplified testing technology, physicians began to switch from more intensely regulated testing to the category of "waived" testing, which is exempt from routine on-site inspection. In addition, many physicians were closing their office laboratories and turning instead to the growing number of reference laboratories for testing services. Fewer testing sites led to a steady decline in the number of new laboratories that contracted for COLA's education and accreditation services and the number of existing clients renewing their contracts with COLA (see Figure 6.12). Revenues began a precipitous decline. Because the success of its low-cost operations model was tied

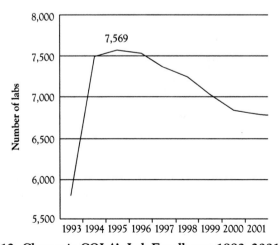

Figure 6.12. Change in COLA's Lab Enrollment 1993–2001.

to the volume of laboratories to be surveyed within a geographic area, the decreasing client base made it increasingly difficult for COLA to realize the economies of scale built into operations, and operating margins also shrank. Even the flagship laboratory accreditation product was no longer supporting itself.

In the meantime, COLA launched several new products, but these met with only marginal success rather than the hoped-for boost in revenue growth. In order to close the gap created by declining operating revenues, COLA soon found itself having to draw on earnings from the investments it had built up through years of operation.

A Burning Platform

In 2001, COLA's founding chief executive officer, Dr. Stephen Kroger, a visionary and leader committed to quality in laboratory medicine, retired. With COLA's markets continuing to contract and lab enrollments still in free fall, the board appointed then COO Doug Beigel (coauthor of this article) as CEO. Doug sensed that if the organization didn't radically rethink the way it did business, COLA's current business model would fail within five years—a bleak end to COLA's success as a force in the accreditation industry, and a threat to its very survival. But he found little conviction at any level of the organization about such a burning platform; no "outside the box" thinking about possible solutions beyond such incremental improvements as scale-backs in product offerings and further cost-reduction strategies; and only wishful thinking about capturing a larger share of a declining market. While the board of directors had long been supportive and committed to COLA's mission, the sense of urgency to create an expanded value proposition was low.

Limited by a vision of COLA as simply "doing good" as an alternative to government regulation, the organization labored under a collective mindset of "work harder and perhaps we will survive." Cutting costs might prolong survival, but from Doug's perspective, to thrive would require that COLA and its leaders be bold, break the bonds of the past, and redirect resources to new areas—in short, create a new paradigm for the organization. Given the fundamental changes in COLA's markets, the organization had to understand that past success would not guarantee a bright future and, in fact, any attachment to the past would only guarantee failure.

Incremental improvements would not suffice. Future success was possible only through transformational change—a very large leap indeed for an accreditation organization whose core capabilities centered around quality and standardization, and even more to the point, for a cadre of leaders that had grown up with organizational systems designed largely to control and maintain. Transforming the business would have to begin with transforming the organization—its systems *and* its people, and in ways that would lead to breakthrough improvement.

In late 2001, COLA's CEO Doug Beigel partnered with my consulting firm, Transformation Systems International (TSI), to apply transformational sciences, methods, and tools to the challenge of helping COLA leaders guide the organization through one of the most critical periods in its history. Thus began a journey that continues today.

The Individual Domain: Coaching the CEO

COLA's CEO Doug Beigel was open to an in-depth coaching relationship in order to create breakthrough performance at COLA and develop his capability as a transformational leader. Initially, we embarked upon exploring his reasons for committing his energies toward COLA's transformative journey. Moving beyond the surface explanations, we spent considerable time in the *EXPLORE* stage of the 3Es coaching model as applied in the domain of Individuals (Coaching Others, Chapter 4).

In deep inquiry, my questions to Doug included:

What was his burning platform? Why did he feel compelled to do anything different? What if COLA continued to muddle along for a few more years while he worked hard to optimize the current business? He could demonstrate his work ethic, gain experience, and leap to another organization before the ship sank. So what if COLA eventually failed? The board was sharing the driver's seat and didn't seem overly concerned. Doug brought a new consciousness to his internal need to move forward with transforming the organization ... even in the face of difficulties ahead and risks to be encountered. His burning platform complemented the real threats to COLA's longevity. He felt failure of COLA would mean failure of his leadership regardless of what others would say.

What were his purpose, vision, and values? Doug's calling was to generate a leap in healthcare quality through creating an organization which substantially improved laboratory medicine. This drive was discovered in the life planning process, where purpose, vision, and values are made explicit. He became clearer in his vision of an organization having much more impact on patient health. When he took stock of the present COLA, it was lacking in making the contributions found in his vision.

How had his will and accompanying action produced the current state? When asked to consider his will to transform COLA within the context of his life as a whole, a new resolve came forth. Quiet in nature, this resolve was clearly seen by staff as Doug moved in his mind from "managing the store" to leading something of great value to the world.

The transformation coaching approach employed zoomed out toward a life context with Doug. My open-end questions to him focused upon developing his consciousness of meaning ... what was he doing in life? Why had he chosen to lead COLA?

Initially these conversations were stilted given our new relationship. My approach was deep inquiry, listening, and then framing his responses back to him. After a period encompassing several months, trust had grown sufficiently allowing for the most candid and forthright exchanges. The largest lever in building trust was my commitment to help Doug and COLA, manifested often in small but meaningful ways as the engagement progressed: staying fully present and focused on Doug and COLA, not pressing my own agenda or point of view; refraining from seizing the moment to display my own knowledge or experience; allowing Doug the space to discover his own wisdom and personal truth on a matter. A transformational coach learns with experience to avoid the temptation to posture as the wise content consultant, armed with myriad facts and a portfolio of war stories, which from the start undermines credibility and the potential to be of real value to the individual and the organization.

Due to the depth of our conversations and the authenticity required, Doug and I developed a meaningful friendship that continues today. This is not always the case, but we discovered a good deal of alignment in our lives and a friendship grew beyond the COLA work. My experience with coaching is that the work is relationship in nature, not technical advice giving. And if you have engaged in self-mastery work, becoming conscious of your purpose, vision, and values, you have something to offer others in relationship building.

Change Methodology—The Transformation Cycle

In August 2001 Doug and his executive team adopted and then launched COLA's first 18-month Transformation Cycle (2001–2002). Committing to this change methodology challenged the members of COLA's executive team to move away from a "program-of-the-month" mentality and begin to envision themselves as the architects of transformational change, able to develop new pathways for leading COLA into the future.

Situation Appraisal

Given the severity of the current threat that COLA faced, the situation appraisal, the initial step in the first transformation cycle, examined all nine major organizational systems, or fronts, important for achieving performance improvement: planning; measurement; culture; motivation; education, training, and development; infrastructure; technology; politics; and communication. The CEO realized that resources were limited, and that service levels to physician office laboratories—the core business—had to be maintained even as the organization remade itself. The situation appraisal provided data about the current state of the organization that the executive team would draw on in the next step of the cycle to understand which fronts to leverage at which times in order to optimize improvement efforts.

As characteristic with many such efforts, the situation appraisal was the most straightforward element. The process of gathering data presented my coaching partner Tammy Roberts and me the chance to build relationships and demonstrate listening skills to people from many segments and multiple levels of the organization. Our presentation of the appraisal's findings, including encouraging leaders to view them from a holistic and nonjudgmental perspective, added to our credibility as apolitical "partners" committed to honest dialog. Since the situation appraisal included a focus on the health and balance of nine key mega-systems as well as the organization's readiness for transformational change, we were able to help people understand the long-term direction the transformational effort might take to position the organization for breakthrough results.

Strategic Plan for Transformation

With the data from the situation appraisal in hand, the executive team engaged in the Wall exercise in an off-site session process. The Wall proved to be a powerful tool for achieving clarity and alignment around COLA's strategic direction, not only within the executive team but eventually at all levels of the organization. Through its use Doug and his team were able to utilize learnings from the past, develop a new understanding of both the present (the current state/situational analysis) and the future, and then outline a new vision for COLA.

Casting a Vision

COLA's founding vision had been the "preferred compliance vehicle" for laboratories. Indeed, its entire history was closely interwoven with the federal government regulations. As a key outcome in this early stage of the transformation journey, the executive team conceived a new vision for COLA: a larger, more significant role in medicine as the premier clinical laboratory education, consultation, and accreditation organization. This broader vision would enable COLA to offer a greater value exchange with its clients by supporting laboratories' goals for greater safety, efficiency, compliance, quality, and—above all—delivery of the best possible patient care.

Closing the Gap

The executive team proceeded to identify and prioritize the gaps between present performance and the desired vision/future state and then to select key breakthrough initiatives. Although work needed to be done on every organizational front, too many initiatives risked overwhelming the organization and diluting resources beyond the level of effectiveness. The team chose and sequenced the top three priorities according to which changes needed to happen first in order to set the stage and build the capabilities needed to drive subsequent changes on other fronts in the years to come. These three transformation initiatives—to address major gaps on the planning/political, measurement, and leadership development/culture fronts—formed a broad roadmap that would later be communicated to the organization as a whole, and would then guide more detailed transformation planning by mid-level managers and system owners to assure buy-in and alignment of efforts across all parts of the organization.

The Governance Initiative. In the absence of a sense of urgency and a new vision for COLA, especially at the top of the organization, a sort of blind adherence to COLA's current business model and operating style would continue to hamper any movement forward. The governance initiative, led by the CEO, sought to awaken the consciousness of the board of directors to the burning platform COLA faced and to develop board members' commitment to COLA's long-term success.

Doug led the board of directors in a process similar to the Wall exercise done by the executive team to achieve understanding and agreement about lessons from the past, a new vision of the future that was not hamstrung by the past, and the core competencies needed to carry forward. He sought the freedom to experiment in new markets and with new approaches to the core business. At the same time, he engaged the board in a candid discussion about how it and the executive team worked together, laying the foundation at this level for the trust-based relationship essential for leading COLA into a very different future.

The Balanced Scorecard Initiative. Earlier in 2001, Doug had introduced a rudimentary Balanced Scorecard to begin to create a set of reliable metrics for gauging business and organizational performance. As a result of the August 2001 Wall exercise, it became clear to the executive team that the initial attempt at a measurement system was not adequately linked to the emerging vision and strategic direction—in short, it had to be strengthened as an integral part of the transformation design. They also saw the need to engage all the leaders in the organization in measurement, with the goal of embedding a causal mentality and a disciplined practice that linked individual and collective action to measurable organizational and business results.

The team adopted the COLA Strategic Scorecard, a few key performance indicators/metrics visibly displayed in control charts, as the "control panel" for gauging and communicating progress toward successful achievement of the vision and strategic goals. The expectations were that the scorecard would continue to be strengthened and refined over subsequent transformation cycles until COLA had a robust system that made performance results visible to the entire organization. As an important element for assuring follow-through, the executive team also declared its firm commitment to monthly and quarterly reviews to monitor and evaluate the effect of change actions on performance as reflected in the Strategic Scorecard.

The Transformational Leadership Initiative. The goal of the Transformational Leadership initiative (discussed in detail below) was to go well beyond conventional leadership development programs and help COLA leaders build the personal and collective capacity (self-mastery and interpersonal mastery) for leading transformative change. It first engaged the entire executive team in an individual and group process of *personal* and *interpersonal* change, and would eventually encompass all COLA managers and system owners.

The Transformational Leadership Initiative

Traditionally, organizations promote their best managers to leadership positions—including leadership of transformation initiatives—which require different work and thus different skill sets than management roles. Likewise, COLA was relying on its best managers at the executive and middle management levels to lead its transformation because they had a deep understanding of the business itself and were superior performers as managers. Unfortunately, great managers are not necessarily equipped to be great leaders of transformational change.

The transformational leadership initiative, launched in the autumn of 2001 with all members of the executive leadership team, including the CEO, combined a CAMP-like multiday off-site meeting with individual and group transformational coaching over a period of several months.

We initially focused on helping the team understand the differences between management and leadership:

Management. Management is defined here as management of a system/ subsystem, rather than a position or title. Major management tasks can be viewed as planning, budgeting, organizing, staffing, controlling, and problem solving. Great managers organize the current known assets and resources of the organization to deliver upon its present mission. Skillful in the areas of analysis and administration, they are energetic in their work and demonstrate high individual performance. It is said that management is of the mind—combining both intellect and hard work.

Leadership. Key leadership tasks might be described as establishing direction, aligning people, motivating, and inspiring. This is why leadership is often said to be of the spirit. It is well understood theoretically that leaders move organizations to a new place. Driven by a deep personal commitment to the goal at hand, leaders seek to effectively address expected and unexpected barriers.[5] Transformational leaders, in particular, are designers, stewards, and teachers. They are responsible for building organizations in which people continually expand their capabilities for understanding complexity, clarifying vision, and improving mental models.

We then introduced the executive team to the Transformational Leadership Model, shown in Figure 6.13 on the next page, as a framework for thinking about the full spectrum of individual leadership capacities and talents, including those needed to drive transformative change in organizations. Note that the three components of consciousness—self-mastery, people (interpersonal) mastery, and enterprise mastery correspond to three of the four transformation cornerstones discussed in the last chapter.

Each member of COLA's executive team began a transformation journey at the personal and interpersonal level, gaining a deeper understanding of self in terms of life purpose, vision, and values and pursuing his/her own development process, which included an assessment of current level of leadership skills. The process included one-on-one coaching conversations similar to those between Doug and me at the beginning of our involvement in COLA's transformation work. I was joined by other transformation coaches, most notably Tammy Roberts, to work with the executive team. We also conducted group sessions with the team, each designed to bring forth individuals' spirits and deepen their experience of COLA as more than just a job or a place to manage.

Inevitably, there was push back from several people while doing the self-mastery work. For us as transformational coaches these are moments of truth: Are we secure enough in self (our consciousness and ability) to avoid judging the challenger and allowing the conversation to devolve, disastrously, to one of "right or wrong"? Getting hooked into this dynamic can derail a session—it's not a pretty sight. Instead, we used the challenge

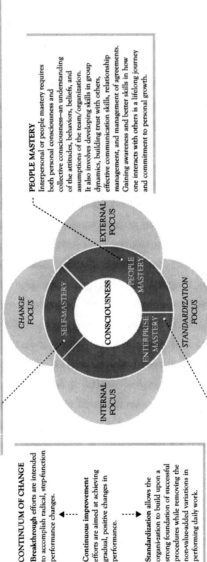

SELF-MASTERY Awareness of one's environment and one's own existence, emotions, sensations, and thoughts is a prerequisite to becoming a transformational leader in any organization. Self-mastery includes clarity of purpose, vision, planning one's direction in life, meditation, reflection, and feedback—all of which are imperative for deliberate and productive growth. Effective transformational leaders have developed self-mastery and are clear about the connection of their personal vision with the vision of the organization. However, self-mastery also extends beyond self to a commitment that others walk a path to self-awareness. Transformational leaders are engaged in the lives of the people in their organizations, encouraging personal growth, feedback, continuous learning, and mentoring.

PEOPLE MASTERY Interpersonal or people mastery requires both personal consciousness and collective consciousness—an understanding of the attitudes, behaviors, beliefs, and assumptions of the team/organization. It also involves developing skills in group dynamics, building trust with others, effective communication skills, relationship management, and management of agreements. Gaining awareness and better skills in how one interacts with others is a lifelong journey and commitment to personal growth.

ENTERPRISE MASTERY Enterprise mastery speaks to collective consciousness of the people working within the organization and among its broader stakeholders, a consciousness of shifting value exchanges to which the organization is a party. Understanding the reason for the organization's existence and its "license to operate" are key components. This calls upon the organization's leaders to develop the skills and capacity to be chief architects and engineers for business as executed through strategic planning and design. It also requires competencies in the areas of benchmarking, organizational culture, process improvement, motivation systems, evaluation, and performance measurement.

INTERNAL The internal view points to understanding and appreciation for how the change is experienced within the organization.

EXTERNAL The external view is understanding how the change impacts persons and systems outside the organization.

CONTINUUM OF CHANGE Breakthrough efforts are intended to accomplish radical, step-function performance changes.

Continuous improvement efforts are aimed at achieving gradual, positive changes in performance.

Standardization allows the organization to build upon a strong foundation of successful procedures while removing the non-value-added variations in performing daily work.

Figure 6.13. Transformational leadership model.

to build trust and accelerate the individual's growth, projecting empathy for the difficult work facing the individual while pressing on with the tough concrete conversation about self-mastery—not in the abstract but as embodied in each participant.

As significantly, the team also began a series of conversations to understand more deeply the mental models (mindsets) that informed COLA's current performance levels. For the most part, these conversations occurred in the context of the business conducted at all regular team meetings, with the transformational coach in attendance to help facilitate the team's reflections and learnings.

Through open-ended conversations and coaching, COLA's top leaders began to understand how the team itself was holding the organization back. They came to realize that in their daily practice, they had each dedicated a large amount of their time to management of the day-to-day issues, operating from a largely management orientation focused on optimizing current systems, with little focus on the future of the organization. They were "stuck" in the story of COLA's past success and in an old CEO-driven command-and-control management style that no longer served the organization. The executives soon saw that COLA's success in the future depended upon the creation of new organizational systems and substantive changes, which they would be equipped to lead only if they—individually and collectively—developed the requisite transformational leadership capacities.

With time of the essence, the executive team asked of itself high commitment to personal and relationship transformation. Members coached one another to unfreeze old paradigms and committed to trying new approaches to leadership. They focused on building trust with each other, moving away from the historical CEO-centered command-and-control to shared leadership, in which they would work together on a series of high impact efforts. A *real* team began to emerge with new characteristics and qualities, including a collective vision; a high level of trust among members (essential for sharing leadership); and high consciousness of personal purpose, vision, and value, including individual strengths that would contribute to the team's overall success. Finally, the team began to effectively generate a mindset that embraced creativity and to demonstrate greater tenacity in seeing things through.

Engaging the Rest of the Organization

The remaining steps in the plan phase of COLA's 2001–2002 Transformation Cycle were designed and executed with the following overarching intentions:

- Energize the rest of COLA's managers and staff around the transformational journey and the transformation design developed by the executive team.
- Align efforts COLA-wide around the transformation initiatives by involving mid-level managers and system owners in the creation of detailed implementation plans in their parts of the organization.
- Begin the process of developing transformational leadership capabilities below the executive team level.

The Transformation Design developed by the executive team was communicated to the entire organization at the first All Spirits Information Sharing session, which prepared people for CAMP, a three-day forum that engaged all employees in the transformation platform and built a common "transformation" vocabulary the organization could utilize going forward.

COLA's managers and system owners would be leaders of transformation in their areas of the organization. The CAMP event used the concept of "alignment and attunement" to invite these individuals to find their own life direction and how that direction "fit" with the new vision of COLA, to discover their personal passion and how they aspire to contribute to the transformation plan. In short, the CAMP event sought to create an "organization of meaning" at COLA, in which purpose informs all parts of the organization to operate with a strong sense of intent and common will to achieve breakthrough results. Participants completed a number of pre-work assignments and then convened in an off-site event, also attended in full by the executive team, that provided the structure and setting necessary for aligning and attuning this broader leadership group to the main task at hand, developing a detailed transformation plan for the current cycle.

In 2001, COLA's first-ever CAMP event expanded to mid-level managers and system owners the process of building a capacity for transformational leadership through the development of self, interpersonal, and enterprise consciousness—the same journey the executive team had begun a few months earlier. As their CAMP pre-work, participants used a life-planning tool, which had also been used by the executive team, to expand their own self-knowledge to foster personal clarity about one's life purpose, vision, and goals. This clarity enabled individuals to powerfully engage in the change underway, to design and declare their new "fit" within the organization and how they wished to contribute.

The CAMP event itself included intensive work at the individual and group levels. The managers and system owners were called upon to examine attitudes and behaviors that have held them—and COLA—back in the past, and were invited to explore the consequences of failure to change. As with the earlier governance initiative with the board of directors, a dawning awareness of COLA's burning platform fueled these discussions with a sense of great urgency and purpose. TSI's CAMP facilitators then introduced the participants to more effective mindsets for achieving performance improvement at COLA.

As we cascaded through the organization, the challenging multiday sessions brought forth tremendous energy. Most people were willing to drop smaller matters and conversations of the past in order to engage in "big conversations" around transformation. It is important to note that if I as transformational coach had entered into smaller conversations centered on technical aspects of change—coming from a teaching mode—the past thinking, in never being examined, would have been reinforced, denying any real transformative change. Conversations could so easily have been theory based and far removed from the individual. Transformation hinges upon engaging people with big concepts and at a personal level, which sometimes demands courage on the part of a transformation coach.

COLA made a considerable investment in changing the mindset of the larger leadership body, and on focusing the managers and system owners on consciousness at the individual and collective levels and action that leads to specific measurable results. As the CAMP participants articulated a clear life plan, a deeper consciousness emerged for many about the "fit" of work life into their total life. With this new clarity of self and life direction, many COLA managers sensed a stronger "call to leadership," while several self-selected out of leadership positions to focus their life energy on their passion. As a later benefit for COLA's transformation journey, individuals who shifted roles within the organization were able to do so with purpose rather than as "victims" of the change effort underway.

Building on this foundation and the top transformation initiatives identified by the executive team, the CAMP participants then created detailed transformation plans to drive change efforts in all the parts of COLA's organization during the transformation cycle, initiatives that leveraged the full continuum of change—transformational, continuous improvement, and standardization—needed to strengthen performance in the core business while making breakthrough change. The plans included targets, objectives, and performance measures to link action to measurable results and nurture the notion of a performance culture at COLA.

Implementation and Review Phases

The end of the CAMP event marked the beginning of the Implementation (Do) phase of the transformation cycle, during which implementation teams carried out the work in the transformation plan. In the Study phase of the cycle, the executive team met monthly with the implementation teams to review progress against their objectives, and quarterly to review the impact of the implementation efforts on the Balanced Scorecard performance metrics, making whatever adjustments were necessary to the implementation plans. In addition, all mid-level managers and system owners, meeting together on a quarterly basis, continued to engage in conversations about the concept of transformational leadership, deepening over time their collective understanding of what would be required to lead the transformation of COLA.

Working with Mindsets

From a coaching perspective, the initial review sessions varied from very effective to discouraging. Despite the considerable groundwork already done to help individuals shift from victim to causal mindsets, people often attributed the reasons for bumps in implementation to outside factors, with little connection to the choices they made along the way. This presented ample coaching openings. Having people approach mindsets in the abstract, or see different mindsets at work in their pasts, is much different than working mindsets in real time, when they are immersed in the moment. My role was not to force or to be right about adopting a more productive pattern of thinking but rather to continually bring to consciousness the underlying mindsets at work and create space for reflection and course correction. This position is best taken not as an outsider refereeing the proceedings but as a team member immersed in the review who has the ability to step above the fray and coach.

As transformational coaches, we actively encouraged individuals during the progress reviews to experiment with new mindsets and adopt new approaches that would open the door greater personal and team effectiveness. COLA's executive team, building their skills as transformational leaders, increasingly reached out to all staff, and an environment of mutual encouragement began to emerge.

As suggested earlier, however, this is not to say that every person chose to engage at a new level. Several leaders and staff separated from the organization, either voluntarily or not … either conscious in their direction or not. There was no exodus. But some people were stuck in the old culture as the organization changed to become more authentic, causal, and appreciative of the abundance available. Leadership and staff were encouraged to consciously choose where they could best give value and find alignment with their life's purpose. For some, this was outside of COLA.

Among those departing were members of the senior leadership team. With each farewell came the opportunity to select new energy aligned with the new COLA vision. Sometimes senior positions were filled internally, sometimes externally. COLA's selection process evolved to explicitly include evaluations along the four transformational cornerstones of self-mastery, interpersonal mastery, moving to new value exchanges, and competence with transformational methods.

Strengthening the Measurement System

Work on the balanced scorecard initiative moved slowly during the first year, and as is the case with many projects, the delay in establishing a comprehensive performance measurement system hindered the transformation initiative. Many processes and results were being measured, but COLA was still striving to develop a control panel of metrics that truly captured the key result areas most relevant to COLA's vision (future state). This hampered the ability to demonstrate cause-and-effect relationships between specific improvement efforts and organizational/business outcomes, and thus senior leadership's ability to make informed decisions.

It had been anticipated that work on the measurement initiative would probably span more than one transformation cycle, and ultimately a comprehensive scorecard was embraced and routinely populated with valuable information. I believe the adherence to the monthly and quarterly review process was the forcing function: It became painful to have yet another discussion about the accuracy or representation of performance data rather than diving into an inquiry about the underlying reasons for current performance that leads to real learning and decisive action. This frustration, shared by the entire senior leadership team, helped to drive the measurement initiative forward, leading to the establishment of a solid measurement system.

Subsequent Transformation Cycles at COLA

COLA's initial 2001–2002 Transformation Cycle and its three transformational initiatives laid a organizational foundation that then enabled COLA to drive in later cycles for breakthrough results in key performance areas. For each ensuing 18-month transformation cycle, the organization again focused on just two to three key transformation initiatives.

The work on cultural transformation begun by COLA's leaders in the 2001–2002 cycle continued, and over time the organization shifted away from a culture focused predominately on "doing good" to a culture focused on performance to achieve the new, compelling shared vision. A new mindset has also emerged, one centered on (1) intentional thinking (a shift from a victim mentality to shaping results); (2) the necessity for breakthrough results; and (3) a shift from scarcity thinking (which feeds competition and protectiveness) to abundance thinking (which engenders collaboration and commitment to mutual goals).

In addition, the second and third cycles gave birth to new transformation initiatives for achieving the following:

- Stronger sales and marketing capabilities.
- An effective research and product development process.
- Transformation of IT systems and capabilities.
- Access to expertise through effective partnerships with vendors.
- Expansion into international markets.

The first three initiatives listed above had particularly significant implications for the organization and, ultimately, for the turnaround of COLA's business.

Sales and Marketing Capabilities

COLA had a ten-year history of fits and starts in attempting to turn around its sales and marketing efforts, to no avail. Better sales techniques alone would not bring about the needed change. To survive and succeed, COLA had to radically transform its approach to sales and marketing, beginning with changing a culture that viewed selling as a "necessary evil" at best. In 2004, COLA partnered with an outside firm, whose owners and unique approach mirrored values shared by COLA, to assist it in understanding how to best equip the organization with new capacity for effective sales and marketing, including nurturing the necessary shift in mindset and acquisition of desired skills.

The initiative helped an organization staffed predominantly with quality improvement educators to eventually see that *everyone* in COLA is part of the sales team—an initially difficult hurdle to overcome, and perhaps the greatest challenge for many people in the organization. Ultimately, the entire organization embraced a deeper meaning for "selling" as a vehicle for client quality improvement and greater fulfillment of COLA's new vision. Why not keep customers informed of "meaningful" products and services from COLA if such offerings could help customers to do their work more effectively and better fulfill their own organization's mission?

COLA staff also reflected much more deeply about their relationship with customers, and with each other, in terms of redefinition of roles and embracing new responsibilities in this area. A key to breakthrough change was the realignment of the role of COLA surveyors, from one of execution, focused solely on providing clients with technical counsel and the routine on-site survey for accreditation, to that of strategic partner, serving as the frontline, face-to-face connection with the customer and actively contributing ideas that will generate greater value for customers and COLA alike. Invited to become full players in achieving COLA's new vision, these members of staff have embraced their expanded role as "COLA ambassadors" and are now an integral part of building the business.

The initiative (1) helped individuals and groups to recognize or develop a passion for selling by finding a deep connection between sales and vision—both personal and organizational—and then (2) equipped them with a sales philosophy, methods, and tools that would help ensure their success.

Also in 2004, COLA implemented a number of tools to support greater sales efforts:

- An IT system that more effectively managed sales leads, with a capacity for handling a 500-fold increase in the number of monthly sales leads
- A custom pricing model that enabled COLA to better compete on price state-by-state with local competitors for laboratory accreditation services

COLA also understood from its own history that sustainable sales success hinged upon customer loyalty and retention—for example, renewal of contracts and purchase of additional products/services—which in turn are influenced by the quality of COLA's customer service. In order to stimulate its own thinking and creativity about how to better serve its customers, in 2004 COLA also began to benchmark organizations that excelled in customer service, which has led to its implementation of a number of new practices to strengthen this important function.

R&D Process

Another major initiative entailed the development of an effective process for vetting new products and services aligned with COLA's new vision and value exchange. This led to the subsequent launch of new accreditation products for transfusion services in 2004 and anatomic pathology services in 2005. The products opened new markets, enabling COLA staff, now equipped with greater sales and marketing capabilities, to attract larger, more complex laboratories across the country as new COLA clients.

IT Transformation

Beginning in 2005, COLA launched a redesign of its legacy IT systems and built a paperless, real-time accreditation program. As a result of these innovations, COLA and its clients now enjoy a portal for accreditation and quality laboratory medicine that is truly state-of-the-art in the industry. The success of these initiatives required not only surmounting technical challenges but also changing entrenched thought patterns and organizational dynamics that stood in the way of success.

In an organization focused primarily on quality, it was difficult at any level of the organization to admit failure, an underlying pattern that surfaced in a robust and adverse way as COLA began to implement the many facets of its IT transformation. The scope and visibility of the work suddenly raised the potential for individual and group failure, and with it potential threats to personal and organizational identities based on a commitment to always delivering excellence. In response, the organization acted out of a need to "paint a good picture" of progress rather than openly acknowledging and addressing any problems encountered, thus obscuring any clear picture of the actual performance of the IT implementation. Eventually the organization became aware of the underlying counterproductive patterns of thought and began to face the hard facts of an implementation in trouble on multiple fronts. With this awareness, COLA staff learned how to best trust one another in terms of communicating failures, and to make quick course adjustments that minimized lost time and resources and got the implementation back on track.

The Turnaround

COLA's CEO understood that transformation was a long-term matter that required patiently laying the all-important organizational groundwork in the early cycles and then tackling major performance gaps with targeted initiatives in later cycles, all guided by the new vision of COLA as the desired future state.

Business Metrics

During the second and third transformation cycles, the organization began to harvest the hoped-for breakthrough results, one of the most impressive being the turnaround in laboratory enrollments. As shown in Figure 6.14, the long-term decline in the number of enrollments, which had begun in 1996, turned the corner during COLA's second transformation cycle, after the launch of the sales and marketing initiative. Further fueled by new product launches in 2004 and 2005, growth in annual enrollments continued to accelerate through 2007. This breakthrough performance has been broad-based, reflecting COLA's improved effectiveness in attracting new clients, retaining existing clients, and increasing revenues per client.

With the widespread economic recession, COLA has once again found itself facing harsh external constraints on it business, as have countless other organizations. But this time COLA has been able to respond from a position of much greater financial and operational strength, thanks to its

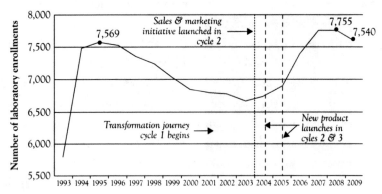

Figure 6.14. Growth in COLA's Laboratory Enrollment, 1993–2009.

work at transformation. Even with the downturn in its markets in 2008 and 2009, COLA has still sustained an overall 11% increase in laboratory enrollments since 2001.

Between 2001 and 2009, the eight years of COLA's transformation journey, COLA also reaped impressive gains in other key business metrics despite the global recession:

- Substantial increases in total revenues (57%), accreditation revenue per lab (40%), and sales of its education product (568%).
- Consecutive net operating surpluses in the last three fiscal years (the first time this has happened in its history, and a further indicator of the robustness of its transformation).
- An ROI of 7.5% on its major investments (2004–2009) in IT initiatives and additional development.

Organizational Metrics

During the same eight-year period, the organization has been able to preserve and further develop its internal capabilities through high retention and internal growth, and to further expand capabilities in key areas though effective external partnerships:

- COLA has experienced 0% turnover in sales, production, and accounting staff.
- Staff size has doubled in sales, production, and accounting, and more than doubled in IT and accreditation, while operating margins have grown.
- As an outgrowth of its partnering initiative and other aspects of its transformation, COLA has tripled the number of industry partners—all quality-driven organizations drawn to COLA's vision of improving laboratory medicine and patient care.

As one more positive measure of transformational change, the role of the transformational coaches in COLA's journey decreased over time as COLA's leaders throughout the organization became more effectual at leading the ongoing process of reinventing self, relationships, and the organization. Whereas in the earlier years of COLA's journey Tammy and I had conducted orientation of new leaders and staff to accelerate their integration into the transformation effort, as the new culture grew in strength, leaders and managers grew more adept at both selecting and bringing on board people with the self, interpersonal, and enterprise mastery and the aptitude for applying transformational technology needed to augment the organization's capacity for achieving breakthrough results.

Reflection on the Journey

With support of the board, the COLA executive team and the entire staff have not only accomplished the targeted breakthrough performance results they sought but also developed a new core competency for navigating future business and economic tsunamis. Today, COLA is a more resilient, energized organization engaged in a greater value exchange with customers, vendors, and, indeed, all its stakeholders, internal and external. Financial stability has replaced the burning platform that threatened its very survival. And even as the organization contemplates even greater changes that loom ahead for the healthcare industry, it does so with a strong sense of purpose and confidence as it continues to strengthen its capabilities for leading and creating transformational change.

Transformation
SYSTEMS INTERNATIONAL

Situation
Appraisal

For Whole System Transformation

_____   _____
Name   Organization

_____
Date

Situation Appraisal

This instrument is designed to aid in the transformation of an organization. As part of the Transformation Cycle, it combines an assessment focused upon the health of major organizational systems (Frontal Assessment) and the organization's fitness to undertake transformational change (Transformation Readiness Assessment).

Frontal Assessment Components	Rating Average
Planning	
Infrastructure	
Measurement	
Education, Training, and Development	
Motivation	
Communication	
Technology	
Politics	
Culture	

Transformation Readiness

Assessment Components	Rating Average
Leadership	
Burning Platform	
Vision	
Past	

The situation appraisal can be completed by individuals and/or be the product of a focus group.

Contributors to the creation and evolution of this tool include Eileen Van Aken, Ray Butler, Stephen Hacker, and Tammy Roberts.

PLANNING

1 = Strongly Disagree   2 = Disagree   3 = Neutral   4 = Agree   5 = Strongly Agree

Clear, comprehensive system for strategic, tactical, operational, and transformation planning exists	1	2	3	4	5
Planning system involves the extended system (Customers, suppliers, hierarchy, staff)	1	2	3	4	5
Planning system focuses on both long- and short-term goals and objectives	1	2	3	4	5
Strategic, tactical, operational, and transformational planning are well integrated	1	2	3	4	5
Systematic review and improvement of the planning system is in place and effective	1	2	3	4	5

Describe your planning system (strategic, tactical, operational, and transformational).

Who is involved in the planning process (customers, stakeholders, suppliers, hierarchy, staff)? How are they involved?

How are your 15-, 10-, 5-year goals incorporated? What is the organization's time frame for planning?

How are strategic, tactical, transformational plans linked? What does the flow of information between the systems look like? Who is involved in each type? Are those responsible for implementing the plans involved in developing the plan?

How effective is your current planning system? How do you know? What is the PDSA cycle associated with planning?

INFRASTRUCTURE

1 = Strongly Disagree   2 = Disagree   3 = Neutral   4 = Agree   5 = Strongly Agree

Organizational structure supports the short- and long-term goals and objectives of the organization	1	2	3	4	5
Visible, clear linkage between organizational objectives, team actions, and individual work plans	1	2	3	4	5
High level of decision making at every level with appropriate information directly available	1	2	3	4	5
Work system recognizes and values the diverse contributions of each individual	1	2	3	4	5
Teams use a structured, documented chartering process and have a clear purpose	1	2	3	4	5

Describe your organizational structure. What is your structure for doing your work? For handling crises? For improvement? How do these structures support the organization's goals?

Describe your work. How does it relate to the organization's goals? How do the teams where you are a member relate to organizational goals?

How do you (your team) make decisions? How much authority do you (your team) have? How are responsibility and accountability assigned and distributed?

Does the organization recognize the individual contribution of its members? If so, how?

What is your process for starting up teams? Are there team charters? What do the charters involve? Team training? Clear purpose?

MEASUREMENT

1 = Strongly Disagree   2 = Disagree   3 = Neutral   4 = Agree   5 = Strongly Agree

Visible measurement system is in place, reflecting both process and results measures	1	2	3	4	5
Systematic and ongoing efforts to improve the measurement system	1	2	3	4	5
Clear line of sight measures exist from the individual to the organization	1	2	3	4	5
Balanced scorecard of measures in place	1	2	3	4	5
Meaningful benchmarking is performed	1	2	3	4	5

Describe your measurement system. Are the measures visible? Examples of process and result measures. How is the information used? To make what types of decisions?

How do you conduct improvement to your measurement system? Who is responsible for improving the measurement system? What improvements are being made to what and how you measure?

How do your measures link to the organization's measures? What impact does improving your area have on the whole organization? How do you know?

Do your measures cover financials? Internal business processes? Employee/staff measures? Customer satisfaction? Innovation? Learning and Development?

Do you benchmark? Within industry? Outside industry? What lessons have you learned through benchmarking within the last 2 years?

EDUCATION, TRAINING, AND DEVELOPMENT (ET&D)

1 = Strongly Disagree   2 = Disagree   3 = Neutral   4 = Agree   5 = Strongly Agree

Clear, communicated ET&D plans in place to support the organization's objectives	1	2	3	4	5
Individuals improving beyond current assignment requirements	1	2	3	4	5
ET&D is driven by a customer focus	1	2	3	4	5
Systematic review and improvement performed on the ET&D system	1	2	3	4	5
Involvement of a cross-section of employees in developing and owning the ET&D plan	1	2	3	4	5

Describe your ET&D system. How does ET&D support organizational objectives? Does everyone in the organization know what the ET&D plan is?

Is your ET&D system providing comprehensive development for individuals, beyond the immediate assignment? Does the ET&D system assist individuals in better understanding complexity, examine their mindsets, and deepen their comprehension of purpose?

How do you determine ET&D needs? How do you determine ET&D expectations? How do you determine the skill level of the workforce?

How do you determine the effectiveness of the ET&D system? How do you develop internal resources to continue the training? Is your training based on skills? Knowledge? Do you have clearly defined outcomes and outputs for training? What are the major mindsets informing the system?

Who develops the ET&D plan? How are employees involved in the development?

MOTIVATION

1 = Strongly Disagree   2 = Disagree   3 = Neutral   4 = Agree   5 = Strongly Agree

Effective performance management system in place and understood by all employees	1	2	3	4	5
Employees experience meaningfulness in their work, life plans in existence	1	2	3	4	5
Clearly defined measures for the motivation system exist	1	2	3	4	5
Employees have a causal mindset in their actions	1	2	3	4	5
Full complement of strategies to initiate, direct, and sustain desired individual and team behaviors	1	2	3	4	5

Describe your performance management system. How is this system communicated to employees? How do you determine if the system is effective?

How do you view your work? What is its purpose? Why do you show up each day? Do you have a life plan, and if so, is there strong alignment with your work?

How do you know if your reward and recognition system is effective? What measures are in place to determine motivation level?

Do you have the knowledge of the results you produce? What is the link between your actions and organizational results? Do you see the cause and subsequent impact of your efforts?

Do you have defined desired individual behaviors? Team behaviors? What different methods do you use to develop those behaviors? What is the role of intrinsic/extrinsic rewards?

COMMUNICATION

1 = Strongly Disagree   2 = Disagree   3 = Neutral   4 = Agree   5 = Strongly Agree

Diversity of effective information sharing approaches	1	2	3	4	5
Communication is open, honest, direct	1	2	3	4	5
Organizational vision, values, and operating principles are known and reinforced by action	1	2	3	4	5
People share their deeper connection with work, who they are beyond current work assignment	1	2	3	4	5
Formal and informal feedback loops between organizational layers are established and used	1	2	3	4	5

Describe your communication system. What methods do you use to communicate? What information is shared using each method? How is effectiveness determined?

What informs your organizational communication? Is communication open, honest, direct? Does communication build trust?

What organizational information is shared with employees? What are the organization's values/operating principles? What is the organization's vision? How are they communicated? Reinforced by action?

Do employees share the purpose and role of work in their life? Is there openness around why people are choosing to devote their lives to their current work?

How do the different layers of the organization communicate? What feedback loops are used? How are managers incorporated into the communication process?

TECHNOLOGY

1 = Strongly Disagree   2 = Disagree   3 = Neutral   4 = Agree   5 = Strongly Agree

Continuous improvement process is standardized and utilized throughout the organization	1	2	3	4	5
Core processes are defined, mapped, and well-documented	1	2	3	4	5
Use of leading edge technology in core work	1	2	3	4	5
Problem solving process is standardized and utilized throughout the organization	1	2	3	4	5
Use of data/information in decision making is pervasive	1	2	3	4	5

Do you use the methods/techniques/tools for continuous process improvement? How? How are learnings from using these tools shared within the organization?

What are your core operational processes? Have they been defined thoroughly? Are they well-documented?

How do you stay on the cutting edge of your core technology? What have been recent improvements in how you do your work?

What processes do you use to solve problems? How are learnings shared? Do you reward innovation and creativity in improvement efforts? How?

How are decisions informed? To what degree are you currently getting the information needed to make wise decisions and what are some of the data streams?

POLITICS

1 = Strongly Disagree   2 = Disagree   3 = Neutral   4 = Agree   5 = Strongly Agree

Commitment for change is fostered effectively with all stakeholders	1	2	3	4	5
All significant stakeholders are known and involved in the change effort	1	2	3	4	5
Key people with informal and formal power are aligned with the organization's direction	1	2	3	4	5
Critical thinkers are involved in the change effort	1	2	3	4	5
Bases of power (both formal and informal) are known and managed	1	2	3	4	5

Who are the key stakeholders in transformational efforts? Internal? External? Hierarchy? Staff? Suppliers? Customers?

How do you keep the key stakeholders involved and seek their commitment to the transformational effort?

What are the key bases of power in the organization? Management? Staff? Informal? Formal? How do you seek their alignment to the organization's direction?

Who are the critical thinkers adding value to the effort? How do you handle critics? How do you incorporate them into the effort?

How do you manage power in the organization? What knowledge is shared about the bases of power?

CULTURE

1 = Strongly Disagree   2 = Disagree   3 = Neutral   4 = Agree   5 = Strongly Agree

Trust level among all within the extended system is high	1	2	3	4	5
Strong alignment of all with espoused values and operating principles	1	2	3 ·	4	5
Decisions are made in the context of values and operating principles	1	2	3	4	5
Employees demonstrate a personal ownership for the organization, seek alignment with their life purpose and direction	1	2	3	4	5
A conscious effort is under way to shape the culture to support transformational change	1	2	3	4	5

What is the level of trust within the organization, suppliers, and customers? How do you know? What steps are being taken to improve the level of trust within the extended system?

How are the organization's values reinforced by action? To what extent do people know and support the values? What evidence speaks to the degree of alignment?

Are organizational values incorporated in the decision making process? Are the organization's vision and goals within the context of the organization's values?

How do employees feel about the organization? How do they demonstrate ownership for the organization? Is there a strong alignment between the organization's mission and individual life purpose?

What is the process for influencing organizational culture? How willing is the organization to seek continuous improvement? How willing is the organization to seek transformational change?

LEADERSHIP

1 = Strongly Disagree   2 = Disagree   3 = Neutral   4 = Agree   5 = Strongly Agree

Autonomy is pervasive and leadership is shared	1	2	3	4	5
Leadership demonstrates openness to different points of view and new ideas	1	2	3	4	5
Leadership holds people accountable for achieving results	1	2	3	4	5
Leadership celebrates success and new learnings, including learning from errors in the past	1	2	3	4	5
Leadership provides organization with the tools and resources needed to achieve objectives	1	2	3	4	5

Describe the leadership of this organization. What type of decisions do you make? Give examples. How much autonomy do you see at your level? How is leadership shared? How does leadership model the organization's values and operating principles?

How does leadership react to alternative points of view? What new ideas have been implemented recently?

Does leadership hold people accountable for results? In what ways? How is this responsibility shared within teams?

What new learnings has the organization had recently? How were these learnings shared? Give an example of celebrating the successes and learnings from mistakes of the past.

How has organizational leadership provided tools to achieve objectives? What interactions do leaders have with individuals and teams concerning results? What is the nature of these interactions?

BURNING PLATFORM

1 = Strongly Disagree   2 = Disagree   3 = Neutral   4 = Agree   5 = Strongly Agree

Clearly defined and communicated need for change	1	2	3	4	5
People recognize the importance of continuous improvement and transformational efforts	1	2	3	4	5
Environment has been scanned and analyzed for the future requirements for work	1	2	3	4	5
Clear understanding of what the "best in class" are doing	1	2	3	4	5
Personal growth, improvement, and transformation are seen as necessary and important	1	2	3	4	5

Describe your organization's mandate for change. Why does your organization need to change? How is this message communicated throughout the organization?

How do individuals react to the message of improvement? How do they react to radical change or transformative change?

What are the environmental factors involved in the change? What are the future requirements of your work?

What does "best in class" mean for your industry? What are the models for the future? In what ways? What examples are informing your transformational effort?

How do individuals view the need to change? In what ways will the individual benefit? Any costs? How must you change within your profession?

CREATION/VISION

1 = Strongly Disagree   2 = Disagree   3 = Neutral   4 = Agree   5 = Strongly Agree

Clearly defined vision of the organization	1	2	3	4	5
Vision is communicated throughout the organization on an ongoing basis	1	2	3	4	5
Consistent demonstration of leadership's personal connection to the vision	1	2	3	4	5
Consistent demonstration of personal vision alignment with organizational vision	1	2	3	4	5
Tactical and operational objectives are in place to support the vision	1	2	3	4	5

What is the organization's vision? How was it developed?

How has the vision been communicated to all employees? What are the plans to communicate the vision?

How does leadership demonstrate its connection to the vision? What behaviors do the leaders demonstrate?

Do individuals share their personal vision? How do they share? How do these align with the organization's vision?

What strategic and tactical objectives do you have? How will these support achieving the vision? What operational objectives are in place? How will these support achieving the vision?

PAST

1 = Strongly Disagree   2 = Disagree   3 = Neutral   4 = Agree   5 = Strongly Agree

Past learnings are captured and utilized	1	2	3	4	5
Consistent record of the past	1	2	3	4	5
Organization does not live in the past	1	2	3	4	5
Past is celebrated	1	2	3	4	5
Past is not a barrier to change	1	2	3	4	5

How are learnings from the past gathered and brought forward to help with today's initiatives? What are some of the learnings from the organization's past? What would the organization repeat? What would the organization not do again?

How is the past recorded? Where is the record of the past kept? Is it consistent over time? Is there a shared storyline concerning how the organization has gotten to this point?

Does the organization live in the past? Are the decisions and directions of today anchored unproductively in the past?

How is the past celebrated? In what ways? Successes and failures?

Is the past a barrier to change? Do individuals carry emotional baggage about past decisions or occurrences? How do you know?

CHAPTER 7

Shepherding Societal Transformation

As we have learned, transformation begins with self. Without a high level of self-mastery you thrash around in a low consciousness state. Not much help to others. With growing consciousness and effectiveness through self-coaching, outreach in coaching others—individuals, teams, and organizations—is possible, thus benefiting increasing numbers of people and groups. However, your impact can be even broader. As chapter 1 described, our society and individual communities are experiencing tsunamis of transformational change of once unimaginable breadth, speed, and intensity. You have the opportunity to bring your transformational knowledge and skill to bear upon society—work that is not inherently more valuable than individual, team, or organizational transformation, but potentially broader in scope.

Society in this context refers to our structured human convergence as defined through our customs, institutions, and traditions. Society is the way we humans choose to come together and commune. Indeed, we speak of a world society and distinct national societies. Yet diverse communities can be found within these larger social structures. A community is a body of individuals bound together by common interests, aims, and/or place within a larger society. We know of commonwealths: people linked together for common purposes. I understand that these two terms, society and community, can be used in the reverse hierarchical sequence. The difference comes about in defining the scope of each. For our learnings, I have chosen to address society in the big "S" form and community as the subset, small "c." As we will discover, communities provide a place of immense leverage in transforming larger societies.

Societal transformations are unlike those in the domains of self, individuals, teams, and organizations. The multi-cause relationships are enormous; the players can rarely be gathered together as a whole; and communication is nonlinear. People come and go in social movements and their contributions are seldom recognized. Instead, we tend to place a single or very few individuals on the stage as the "founders" or "champions" of the transformation. The identities of the actual catalysts of the transformation are often not known. Nevertheless, at the heart of societal transformation are human beings bent upon transforming the present into a different future. And you have the power to be an agent for societal transformation at any time. Knowing how to best use your energies to achieve such a transformation is the focus of this last chapter, which aims to be less instructive in the methodologies for creating societal transformation and, instead, to outline broad arenas for your investigation and experimentation, which taken together convey the essence of a successful approach to societal transformation.

Notice that the title of this chapter intentionally switches from the expression "coaching," which the earlier chapters used extensively, to "shepherding." The latter term better acknowledges the guiding role of a leader in relationship to a social movement. Bringing into existence the concrete shifts in societal consciousness from clouds of ill-defined forces is by its nature more akin to channeling. Instead of a planned coaching relationship in the domains of self, individuals, teams, and organization, your energies in the societal realm will not be applied in a necessarily systematic fashion along a linear timetable. The outcome of your efforts will be less predictable given the volatile nature of societal transformation and the multitude of factors at play. You will probably be coaching individuals and teams, but shepherding societal transformation requires a rich palette of skills to facilitate the many direct forces already in motion—it calls upon deeper sensing of movement, and a stronger hand outside you orchestrating the change.

Society in Motion

As a shepherd of societal transformation, it is important to understand a great many societies are already in motion. The leader's challenge is not so much initiating change as marshaling the available energy into a collective vision and aiding the process of building collective consciousness.

Let's sample some of the types of societal motion in play. Then we can glean insights into how best to shepherd transformation.

Coupled with the exponential increase in world population, the type of governance being employed is creating fertile ground for transformative change. Leaps in democratic initiatives have led to historical breakthroughs in self-governance (today 60% of the world's population lives under a democratic government versus 31% in 1950[1]). Among the reasons for global democratization is an outcrop of the technological revolution in communications. A Rand Corporation study points to a strong correlation between democracy and interconnectivity, interconnectivity being the ability of a population to connect freely and inexpensively across borders.[2] Technology has brought increased freedom and methods for sharing ideas, leading to greater individual political strength. Additionally, this same communication technology has brought the world closer together and changed the very way we view our neighbors. More democratic states in turn result in diminished country-to-country warfare. From massive wars claiming millions of lives in the first half of the 20th century, we are now experiencing the smallest population percentage of war-related deaths in human history. Yes, the world is changing at an accelerated pace.

Within the tsunamis of massive change, these are but a few of the promising signs of positive progress. There is ample evidence of a societal maturation under way. We are transcending or surmounting many of the problem sets of the past, while at the same time our new world brings forth distinctive challenges of its own. By the very nature of transformation, when paradigms shift and new thought patterns emerge, our perspectives of problems are altered.

In his book, *The Empathic Civilization*, Jeremy Rifkin points to the dawning age of a shift toward our understanding of the inherent connection with each other. The biological, cognitive, emotional, and spiritual connections have always been present, but evolutionarily it is only now that we are prepared to embrace that we are fundamentally an empathic species. As he states:

> At the very core of the human story is the paradoxical relationship between empathy and entropy. Throughout history new energy regimes have converged with new communication

revolution, creating ever more complex societies. More technologically advanced civilizations, in turn, have brought diverse people together, heightened empathic sensitivity, and expanded human consciousness. But these increasingly more complicated milieus require more extensive energy use and speed us toward resource depletion.

The irony is that our growing empathic awareness has been made possible by an ever-greater consumption of the Earth's energy and other resources, resulting in a dramatic deterioration of the health of the planet.

We now face the haunting prospect of approaching global empathy in a highly energy-intensive, interconnected world, riding on the back of the escalating entropy bill that now threatens catastrophic climate change and our very existence. Resolving the empathy/entropy paradox will likely be the critical test of our species, the ability to survive and flourish on Earth in the future.[3]

The consciousness of empathy, deep understanding of our connectivity to one another, is rising. But accompanying this revelation is the perilous course of our impact on the planet on which we reside. So, the need for another leap in our society presents itself, a transformation to capable stewards of this planet.

The sustainability movement has formed in response to this need. The concerns about our environment, our economic structure, and social systems have birthed the concept of a "triple bottom line." Organizations such as The Natural Step (TNS) and their Four Sustainability Principles have helped change our collective consciousness and led to increased sustainable practices. TNS has greatly aided the sustainability cause, but it is important not to lose the essence of a movement by substituting a single organization. A shepherd of social transformation faces a real danger in overinvestment within a single organization—let alone in a single charismatic leader. You will need the capacity to stand back and assess the health of the social change as a whole, looking to shift your energies according to the needs of the holistic change sought. Sometimes it might mean advancing a particular organization; in other cases it might mean disengaging from an organization and investing elsewhere. It might mean working with a specific leadership group, or perhaps shifting your focus to help develop leaders outside of the parade.

Despite how critical the ideas and principles underlying a social movement are, individual initiative is also essential for creating societal shifts. Leaders are indispensable as a reservoir of initiative, and leadership development builds the bench strength needed to shepherd societal transformation. When looking back on history, we tend to see a social movement in isolation, possibly attributing the shift to a transformation superstar. With a somewhat deeper look we will find that many leaders were needed to make the breakthrough.

In the 1990s, the Truth and Reconciliation Commission provided a radical shift in our concept of justice. Following the violence and marginalization of human beings during the apartheid era in South Africa, a body was formed with the groundbreaking focus of restoring relationships of the victims and the perpetrators of violence on a societal basis. This effort was divided into three committees: Human Rights Violations, Reparation and Rehabilitation, and Amnesty. Although not perfect, this approach opened a new door to restoring a broken community. Archbishop Desmond Tutu, serving as chair, received the bulk of international recognition for its formation, but many others were transformational shepherds of this innovative creation, such as Mary Burton, Glenda Wildschut, and Dr. Alex Boraine. Each contributed as a transformation advocate. People with many different political opinions reached beyond the squabble of the day and rose up to support, to guide this movement.

Chile, Liberia, Peru, and Sierra Leone are among the countries that have since established their own Truth and Reconciliation committees to deal with the aftermath of dark periods in their history. In each of these cases, transformational shepherds moved to amend the social order. There are lessons from these catalysts of change that can inform you in your particular quest.

Gaining the Wisdom and Skills to Meet the Unique Challenges of Societal Transformation

Working with transformation on a community or societal level is an extension of the mastery developed in working in the domains of self, relationships, teams, and organizations, albeit often without as straightforward metrics for assessing the immediate impact. Leaders who shepherd transformation in communities and society have developed transformational skills in all these domains. It would be a mistake to underestimate the impact of one-to-one transformation in a societal movement, but likewise, it would be erroneous to simply believe that the skill of one-to-one transformational coaching is sufficient for shifting the social order.

Peter Block, in his book *Community: The Structure of Belonging*, makes the point that the wisdom around individual transformation is insufficient for understanding the dynamics of community transformation:

> The essential challenge is to transform the isolation and self-interest within our communities into connectedness and caring for the whole. The key is to identify how this transformation occurs. We begin by shifting our attention from the problems of community to the possibility of community. We also need to acknowledge that our wisdom about individual transformation is not enough when it comes to community transformation.[4]

Similarly insufficient is the wisdom regarding transformation of teams and organizations. Yes, the insights developed by coaching these domains are invaluable, but the fabrics of communities or the expanded society offer distinct challenges not present in the other domains. The organizational components are not to be found in an organizational chart or a team roster. The places and times for coming together are varied, and the reward systems for belonging are copious. Accountability is chosen; engagement is optional. Leadership is more often than not without official anointment or a formal nature.

Therefore, when considering shepherding societal transformation, skill development starts with a deeper wisdom concerning the Transformation Spheres of Being, Knowing, Relating, and Generating. (See chapter 3 for a detailed discussion of these spheres.) Short of a multistep process spelling out a clear methodology, let's take another dive into the wells of the Transformational Spheres, this time with an eye toward societal transformation, to gain an appreciation of the journey and key elements of skill building required in this domain. The discussion below of each sphere explores specific aspects relevant to societal transformation.

Additionally, there is a growing focus on societal transformation supported by increased written material and communities of inquiry. I highly recommend finding others of like interest to discuss and explore methods. Wisdom exists within formal associations and even in informal circles. But beware of the societal transformation "gurus." Understanding that your particular circumstances and the target of your shepherding are unique, do not disconnect your mind or spirit to blindly follow the direction of another.

Being: Your Purpose Is Determining the Course

There is no shortage of good causes—the environment and global warming, poverty, and social justice, to name just a few. The world needs transformation, no doubt. But getting swept up in a good idea, a noble cause, without the vitality to see it through is wasteful and misdirects others. It is less a matter of orchestrating a movement than aligning one's choice of cause with one's life purpose, enabling leaders to leverage the power of individual and collective spirit to create the desired change.

A point of leverage is the degree of drive devoted to the societal transformation. As a shepherd, you may be guiding leaders or be part of a group of leaders committed to a step-function societal change. Assess the connection between the leaders (of which you could be one) and their life purpose. What level of consciousness exists with regard to life purpose speaks to future focus and energy, and congruency between the sought-after change and declared life purpose foretells the degree of success likely to be achieved. Too many times an idea sounds enticing and possibly sensible, but without a deeper link to an individual's life purpose the strains of change will destroy resolve, and what is left will be a failed effort and an ineffective leader. It is important that the leader(s) become that purpose, unleashing spirit to drive the change.

Once you become aware of your purpose in life (see chapter 3), something magical happens. Life responds by giving you ample opportunity to create according to this purpose. Although choosing a life purpose (some would say, discovering your life purpose) is a conscious choice, after accepting this purpose, daily decisions are molded by this calling. No longer is the purpose about you; you become the purpose.

This shift to a purpose-driven life, a phrase Rick Warren made famous, results in taking actions according to understood purpose and lessening the grip of the many influences vying for attention. Being overly concerned about ego, physical wellbeing, or external approval has derailed many a leader. Gandhi's statement, "You must be the change you want to see in the world,"[5] applies fully.

Invariably there are momentary lapses of living the purpose, be it Martin Luther King, Jr. and his marital infidelity, Gandhi's broken relationship with his son, or the apostle Peter denying Christ. However, resiliency is born of a purpose-driven spirit, the unrelenting need to move forward in creation. One is compelled by the need to live a purpose and "get back on the horse that threw you." A shallow grasp of life purpose leaves the leader vulnerable.

Remember the latter part of Viktor Frankl's quote in chapter 3, that a person is bound to move forward in light of purpose as "each man is questioned by life and he can answer to life by answering for his own life, to life he can only respond by being responsible." The leader self-corrects because his response is self-obligated to be in line with his or her discovered purpose.

So, whoever desires to shepherd societal transformation must understand the relationship between the targeted social change and his or her personal life purpose. The Transformational Sphere of Knowing is where you make your inquiries. Questions such as the following can lead to discovery:

1. Why is such a societal change important to you?
2. Why are you called to lead such a change?
3. What is the connection with this desired transformation and your purpose in life?
4. Why this? Why not other more pressing societal changes?
5. How much are you willing to give in order to realize this vision?
6. Do you see any sacrifices to be made?
7. What could derail you?

Answers to these questions will reveal the depth of your purpose consciousness. And the questions may well prompt you or other leaders to assess their involvement in the particular transformation effort.

Al Siebert, a colleague and friend of mine, was a thought leader in the area of resiliency. He passed away recently and his memory conjures up his strong, lifelong devotion to the study of what makes some people bounce back from adversity with increased wisdom while others wilt.[6] Working with Al over many years on many different projects, I witnessed firsthand his ability to provide leaders with insights into their response to hardship. His research, writings, and coaching on the subject of resiliency were unmatched.

I valued his expertise and held an appreciation of resiliency, and we would effectively co-deliver leadership development workshops as a team. So, it seemed quite natural to ask him to help with a wider scope of deliverables to organizations, to join with me on several broader projects. He said no ... several times. Was he not interested in the grand projects, ones that delivered concrete benefits to large numbers of people? Did he not want to expand his relationship with me while developing strategic initiatives and practical improvement skills with organizations? Once I moved away from centering on me, there was an obvious and simple reason. Al so loved the resiliency work and understood it was at the heart of his life's purpose that he did not venture off course to other endeavors. That clarity of purpose delivered his mastery. This is not to say that one must be a single-subject juggernaut but rather that clearly identifying your life focus allows for greater leverage. He was the change he sought and it came through in his work.

Likewise, Mother Teresa was sometimes criticized for not working on the causes of poverty but focusing on the outcome instead, the impoverished spirits considered societal outcasts. She was devoted to showing the face of Christ to the poorest of the poor, as she had been instructed in her second calling (marked as Inspiration Day in the Society of Missionaries). Despite the criticism, she knew her purpose on this earth and would not be moved off target. Yes, she cared about the social ills producing suffering and dehumanization. But she was clear about her purpose in life: to serve the poor as the Divine would.

Knowing: Collective Consciousness and Collective Visioning

In a world obsessed with charismatic leaders, the full force of collective consciousness is often overlooked. Most destructive to breakthrough change is the image of the grand, magnetic leader addressing throngs of followers mesmerized in admiring devotion to the leader's vision.

It is nothing new to gain a devoted following by swaying people through brilliant oratory and invoking unconscious drives. Leaders who claim to enlighten others and then choose to program them into specific mindsets have experienced tremendous success in the past and present. But sustainable societal change comes from the building of individual consciousness, an awakening to something greater, and then helping to form a collective of purpose-driven people committed to creation. Be it civil rights, democratization, or faith identity, lasting transformation comes forth through awakened individuals, not obedience garnered through threat, shame, or undelivered promises. The societal shift, if not achieved through an expansion of individual and collective consciousness, slips back to the status quo. Think of past movements that failed to hold their ground—the abolition movement, re-education camps in China and Cambodia, order imposed by peacekeeping forces. Unless there is a conscious transformation within the individual and society, existing mindsets prevail.

To shepherd transformation on the societal level, it is essential to build collective consciousness to a critical mass, developing champions who hold a purpose-driven energy to establish new behaviors from transformed mindsets. Remember the success of the Keep American Beautiful campaign? A shift in our littering and polluting behaviors were in large part due to the conscious awakening triggered by a public service announcement in 1971, an ad that featured a Native American chief played by Iron Eyes Cody.[7] Without saying a word the chief shed a tear as he overlooked several pollution-filled scenes. In short, the ad stirred a collective consciousness about America's polluting behavior, born from a separation mindset wherein humans saw themselves apart from—and above—the natural environment.

We now have littering laws and bottle return provisions, but the real change in littering behavior came about with a transformation of our collective consciousness. Unfortunately, the expansion and deepening of the movement, now referred to as the environmental movement, lost ground when it failed to adequately leverage the inherent connection each person feels toward the environment. And by "knowing" what was right, the movement spent too much effort demonizing others. The label of environmentalist became a lightning rod, having disenfranchised large groups of nature-loving people. Farmers, ranchers, hunters, fisherman, and outdoors enthusiasts were left on the side and often cast as the opposition of the righteous, shaming leaders of the environmental movement. As people within the movement gradually came to understand that others have a passion for the environment and might want to be part of the policy-making process for move forward, the movement has regained momentum. The collective "knowing" is much broader and powerful than the movement leaders' "knowing."

Similarly, a leader may well need to initiate the vision process, but it is not until the collective vision is created that great headway can be made. A crucial skill for shepherding societal transformation is the ability to aid a team or group in casting a collective vision. (See chapter 5.)

Although planning the steps to achieve progress toward the collective vision is typically an element in the visioning process, expanding our knowing depends in part upon being open to mystery. Staying receptive to help from the universe at large is sometimes difficult for hard-charging leaders. Be open to existing forces moving in the direction sought and listen to energies of others and the world as a whole. You can reject or overlook valuable help if your only sensing mechanisms are your eyes alone.

Relating: Conflict and Opposition

I am astounded each time a leader shares his or her surprise in encountering deep opposition to the proposed social change endorsed by the leader. Society by definition is the collection of mental models held in large by society and the behaviors they produce. Societal transformation is the shifting or reconstitution of these mindsets and behaviors. No wonder opposition arises. Expect it. And then leverage it. Allow the opposing energy to transform itself into increased awareness, which can produce champions where detractors once existed.

Transformational leadership does not move to judgment when conflict or opposition erupts as the result of the declared new societal vision. Take Martin Luther King, Jr. as an example. When Rosa Parks ignited fervor over segregation with her refusal to vacate a bus seat, King and the Southern Christian Leadership Conference could have attempted to quiet the conflict and seek a return to the prevailing social conditions. But wisely King knew the status quo masked the ills of segregation, and the arrest of Parks shed a bright light for expanding consciousness about the issue. Therefore, he opted to use the fire lit by Parks to launch the Montgomery boycott, choosing to spotlight the conflict uncovered by Park's action in order to advance the transformation to a more just society.

The lesson is to leverage conflict and opposition. Having a relationship to conflict and opposition allows you to appreciate the energy contained within others and to develop the wisdom to move from conflict to co-creation.

It is difficult not to negatively judge opposition. However, exploring what triggers your response might reveal many insights into deeper aspects of yourself that generate a counterproductive behavior or blind you to opportunities in your transformation efforts. Why such a reaction by you to opposition? If resistance is expected given the transformative nature of the change you seek, why the tendency to flare when it appears? Understanding how you relate to disagreement and the reasons behind your reactions is indispensable to the expansion of the shepherd's self-awareness.

Generating: Communities of Actions and Small Group Leveraging

In societal movements, as with more defined organizations, small groups hold the key to discovering and building genuine commitment. It is not gathering of all in a convention center and conducting a telling session that produces deep commitment.

Peter Block was on the money when he stated:

The future is created one room at a time, one gathering at a time. Each gathering needs to become an example of the future we want to create. This means the small group is where transformation takes place. Large-scale transformation occurs when enough small group shifts lead to the larger change. Small groups have the most leverage when they meet as part of a larger gathering. At these moments, citizens experience the intimacy of the small circle and are simultaneously aware that they are part of a larger whole that shares their concerns.[8]

Identify leaders from wherever they may be. Bring them together in co-creation and allow the passion to build toward a collective vision. Tap into this united talent by forming small groups where real discussion and learnings can occur.

Many large-group processes now exist to bring people together in generative dialog. An effective one, general in nature, is the World Café process.[9] These discovery discussions address issues of meaning, issues that hold passion for participants. Each participant grows in wisdom by performing a dance of alternating between listening, contributing, honoring, and reflection. The stated position is "the wisdom is in the room," and the purpose of the process is to bring forth this wisdom.

I have used this methodology many times in many situations—for world leaders of laboratory medicine, health reform projects within specific countries, and professionals in customer-supplier relationships, to name a few. Each time we used a tailored process, combining the base approach of the World Café with other elements of such processes as Open Space, Appreciative Inquiry, and Leadership Dojo, and the groups achieved breakthrough in collective consciousness. An excellent resource outlining these and many more methods is *The Change Handbook*.[10]

Shepherding societal transformation calls for being well versed in the practices of building community through small-group processes. It is through small groups that the individual gains wisdom and joins others at a higher level of collective consciousness. The wisdom and energy generated from approaching societal change in this manner provides congruency of life purpose and action, thus delivering the staying power to accomplish the desired transformation.

Effectiveness in Shepherding

Successful shepherding of societal transformation is a huge undertaking. And success is possible by understanding the following:

- Purpose-driven energy is essential.
- Visioning needs to be collective in nature.

- Conflict and opposition are strengthening in nature.
- Building community through small groups expands individual and collective consciousness.

Simply declaring the evident need for societal transformation and your declaration on the way it should be will not bring about the change you want to accomplish. Building deeper wisdom of self, by diving again into the wells of Being, Knowing, Relating, and Generating, and wisdom within a larger community must be at the top of your list, followed by the move to action by a broad base of transformational leaders. This is how large-scale transformation has been and is being accomplished.

Seeing the Whole Spectrum

Our transformational coaching journey has covered the waterfront: learning to coach self, individuals, teams, and organizations, and finally taking a look into shepherding societal change. This book has consistently called for expanding the consciousness of each entity. Why do I/we take such actions? Create such results? What is the purpose of my/our actions? What is the vision? These lines of inquiry drive a self and collective reflection that underpins transformative change. When coupled with continued deepening of wisdom within the spheres of Being, Knowing, Relating, and Generating, the world opens up with transformation possibilities (Figure 7.1).

I give no apologies for the breadth of the approach to coaching for transformation. It is extensive and fails to be reduced to a few steps able to fit on a laminated wallet card. However, the level of complexity, spiritual richness, learning capability, adaptability, and dynamic creativity found

Being: The pure, unchanging, formless ground of existence from which individual and collective creations are manifest; the essence of you.	Knowing: One's knowledge and wisdom as accessed through the full range of human senses and experience, derived from the exploration of life's mysteries.
Relating: The quality or disposition of thoughts, beliefs and emotions that inform the choices of one's connection to self, others and all aspects of life.	Generating: Manifesting from spirit; bringing forth visions, mental models, and actions giving rise to new possibilities and transformation.

Figure 7.1. Being, knowing, relating and generating definitions.

within each of us is simply amazing—God-created. And then the degree of complexity—and possibilities—explodes when we come together as individuals, teams, organizations, and society at large. What a wonderful time to be alive and exercise our engaging spirits!

Developing Insights

1. Think of sustainable, societal transformations you have experienced in the past. How were these accomplished? What lessons can you gather from the leaders?
2. What societal transformation(s) do you have a passion to achieve? What has been your approach to date? How would the tenets outlined in this chapter help you accelerate progress?

Notes

Chapter 1

1. Kurzweil (2001, March 7).
2. Bourne (2009, June).
3. Friedman (2008), p. 49.
4. Kotter (2008), p. xi.
5. Naisbitt (2006), p. 43.
6. Hargrove (1995, revised in 2002), p. 15.
7. Ibid, p. 13.

Chapter 2

1. Hacker, Jouslin de Noray and Johnson (2001).
2. Begley (2004, November 5), B1.
3. Rock and Schwartz.
4. Bohm (1994), p. 5.
5. Ibid., p. 16.
6. Blackmore (2006).
7. McIntosh (2007), pp. 13–14.
8. Ibid., p. 11.
9. Gonzalez-Balado (1996), p. 35.
10. Tolle (1999).
11. Mitroff and Denton (1999), p. xv.
12. Mill (1863), p. 223.

Chapter 3

1. Vreeland (2001), p. 38.
2. Frankl (1992), p. 113.
3. Pink (2005), p. 26.
4. http://www.kff.org/entmedia/entmedia012010nr.cfm.
5. I was to learn later that this feeling is not uncommon among adopting parents.
6. Hoskins (1968).
7. http://www.workingwithoneness.org/about.html.

8. Thomas (2003), p. 84.
9. Jaworski (1996).
10. http://www.brainyquote.com/quotes/quotes/p/petermarsh382640.html.

Chapter 4

1. Flaherty (2005), p. 54.
2. Zander and Zander (2000), p. 125.
3. For a more detailed discussion, see Hacker and Willard (2001).

Chapter 5

1. Tuckman (1965), pp. 384–399.
2. Peck (1987).
3. The Rodney King Beating (LAPD Officers') Trial: In Their Own Words, http://www.law.umkc.edu/faculty/projects/ftrials/lapd/kingownwords.html.
4. Hacker and Washington (2007).
5. For more detail about the transformational leadership model, see Hacker and Roberts (2004).
6. Holman, Devane, and Cady (2007).

Chapter 6

1. Hacker and Wilson (2005); also see Sink and Morris (1995).
2. The Transformation Cycle was developed by the Performance Center as a holistic methodology for leading total organizational change and improvement, developed through fifteen years of research and field-testing. It integrates TPC's knowledge and experience, along with the work of Deming, Juran, Sink, Hacker, Senge, Kilmann, Lawler, Weisbord, Kanter, Peck, Covey, Hammer, and other leaders in the area of organizational change. The Transformation Cycle has been applied successfully in numerous public and private sector organizations. TPC's contributions to the field of performance improvement can best be seen as integration and synthesis of multidisciplinary methods for improving performance.
3. Hacker and Wilson (2005).
4. ASIM is now known as the American College of Physicians.
5. Bruch and Ghoshal (2004).

Chapter 7

1. Rummel.
2. Kedzie.
3. Rifkin (2009), e-book reference 98–104 and 104–111.
4. Block (2008), p. 1.
5. "The Quotations Page," http://www.quotationspage.com/quotes/Mahatma_Gandhi/.
6. See Siebert (2005).
7. http://www.thewall.net/view/547/psa-native-american-1970s/.
8. Block (2008), p. 93.
9. See Brown with David Isaacs (2005).
10. See Holman, Devane, and Cady (2007).

References

Begley, S. (2004, November 5). Scans of monk's brain show meditation alters structure, functioning. *Wall Street Journal*.

Blackmore, S. (2006). *Conversation on consciousness*. New York, NY: Oxford University Press.

Block, P. (2008). *Community: The structure of belonging*. San Francisco, CA: Berrett-Koehler.

Bohm, D. (1994). *Thought as a system*. New York, NY: Routledge.

Bourne, Jr., J. K. (2009, June). The global food crisis: The end of plenty. *National Geographic 215*, http://ngm.nationalgeographic.com/2009/06/cheap-food/bourne-text/2

Brown, J., & Isaacs, D. (2005). *The world café: Shaping our futures through conversations that matter*. San Francisco, CA: Berrett-Koehler.

Bruch, H., & Ghoshal, S. (2004). *A bias for action: How effective managers harness their willpower, achieve results, and stop wasting time*. Boston, MA: Harvard Business School Press.

Flaherty, J. (2005). *Coaching: Evoking excellence in others*. Oxford: Elsevier Butterworth-Heinemann.

Frankl, V. E. (1992). *Man's search for meaning*. Boston, MA: Beacon Press.

Friedman, T. (2008). *Hot, flat and crowded*. New York, NY: Farrar, Straus and Giroux.

Gonzalez-Balado, J. L. (1996). *Mother Teresa: In my own words*. London: Hodder & Stoughton.

Hacker, S., & Roberts, T. (2004). *Transformational leadership: Creating organizations of meaning*. Milwaukee, WI: Quality Press.

Hacker, S., & Willard, M. L. (2001). *The trust imperative: Performance improvement through productive relationships*. Milwaukee, WI: Quality Press.

Hacker, S., Jouslin de Noray, B., & Johnson, C. (2001). Standardization versus improvement: Approaches for changing work process performance. *European Quality*. London: European Quality Publications, Ltd.

Hacker, S. K., & Washington, M. (2007). *Leading peak performance: Lessons from the wild dogs of Africa*. Milwaukee, WI: Quality Press.

Hacker, S. K., & Wilson, M. C., & Schilling, C. S. (2005). *Transformation desktop guide: Work miracles in your organization*. Salem, NH: Goal/QPC.

Hargrove, R. (1995, revised in 2002). *Masterful coaching*. San Francisco, CA: Jossey-Bass/Pfeiffer.

Holman, P., Devane, T., & Cady, S. (2007). *The change handbook*. San Francisco, CA: Berrett-Koehler Publishers.

Hoskins, L. (1968). *"I have a dream": The quotations of Martin Luther King Jr.* New York, NY: Grosset & Dunlap.

Jaworski, J. (1996). *Synchronicity: The inner path of leadership.* San Francisco, CA: Berrett-Koehler.

Kedzie, C. *International implications for global democratization,* http://www.rand.org/pubs/monograph_reports/MR650/mr650.ch6/ch6.html

Kotter, J. P. (2008). *A sense of urgency.* Boston, MA: Harvard Business Press.

Kurzweil, R. (2001, March 7). The law of accelerated returns. *Kurzweil Accelerating Intelligence,* http://www.kurzweilai.net/the-law-of-accelerating-returns

McIntosh, S. (2007). *Integral consciousness and the future of evolution.* St. Paul, MN: Paragon House.

Mill, J. S. (1863, first published in 1859). *On liberty.* London: Longmans, Green, Reader & Dryer.

Mitroff, I. I., & Denton, E. A. (1999). *A spiritual audit of corporate America.* San Francisco, CA: Jossey-Bass.

Naisbitt, J. (2006). *Mind set!* New York, NY: HarperCollins.

Peck, M.S. (1987). *The different drum: Community making and peace.* New York, NY: Simon & Schuster.

Pink, D. H. (2005). *A whole new mind.* New York, NY: Riverhead Books, Penguin Group.

Rifkin, J. (2009). *The empathic civilization: The race to global consciousness in a world of crisis.* New York, NY: Penguin Group.

Rock D., & Schwartz, J. Neuroscience of leadership. *Strategy and Business 43,* http://www.strategy-business.com/article/06207

Rummel, R. J. Democratic peace clock, http://www.hawaii.edu/powerkills/DP.CLOCK.HTM

Siebert, A. (2005). *The resiliency advantage.* San Francisco: Berrett-Koehler.

Sink, D. S., & Morris, W. T., with Johnston, C. S. (1995). *By what method: Leading large-scale quality and productivity improvement efforts.* Norcross, GA: Industrial Engineering and Management Press.

Thomas, E. (2003). *John Paul Jones: Sailor, hero, father of the American Navy.* New York, NY: Simon & Schuster.

Tolle, E. (1999). *The power of now.* Novato, CA: New World Library.

Tuckman, B. (1965). Developmental sequence in small groups. *Psychological Bulletin 63*(6).

Vreeland, N., ed. (2001). *The Dalai Lama.* Boston, MA: Little Brown and Company.

Zander, B., & Zander, B. S. (2000). *The art of possibility.* Boston, MA: Harvard Business School Press.

Index

Announcing the Business Expert Press Digital Library

Concise E-books Business Students Need for Classroom and Research

This book can also be purchased in an e-book collection by your library as

- a one-time purchase,
- that is owned forever,
- allows for simultaneous readers,
- has no restrictions on printing, and
- can be downloaded as PDFs from within the library community.

Our digital library collections are a great solution to beat the rising cost of textbooks. e-books can be loaded into their course management systems or onto student's e-book readers.

The **Business Expert Press** digital libraries are very affordable, with no obligation to buy in future years. For more information, please visit **www.businessexpertpress. com/librarians**. To set up a trial in the United States, please contact **Adam Chesler** at *adam.chesler@businessexpertpress.com* for all other regions, contact **Nicole Lee** at *nicole.lee@igroupnet.com*.

OTHER TITLES IN OUR HUMAN RESOURCE MANAGEMENT AND ORGANIZATIONAL BEHAVIOR COLLECTION

Collection Editors: **Stan Gully and Jean Phillips**, *Rutgers*

- *Career Management* by Vijay Sathe
- *Developing Employee Talent to Perform* by Kim Warren
- *Conducting Performance Appraisals* by Michael Gordon and Vernon Miller
- *Culturally Intelligent Leadership: Leading Through Intercultural Interactions* by Mai Moua
- *Letting People Go: The People-Centered Approach to Firing and Laying Off Employees* by Matt Shlosberg
- *The Five Golden Rules of Negotiation* by Philippe Korda
- *Cross-Cultural Management* by Veronica Velo

CPSIA information can be obtained at www.ICGtesting.com
Printed in the USA
BVOW03s0448151214

379064BV00006B/13/P